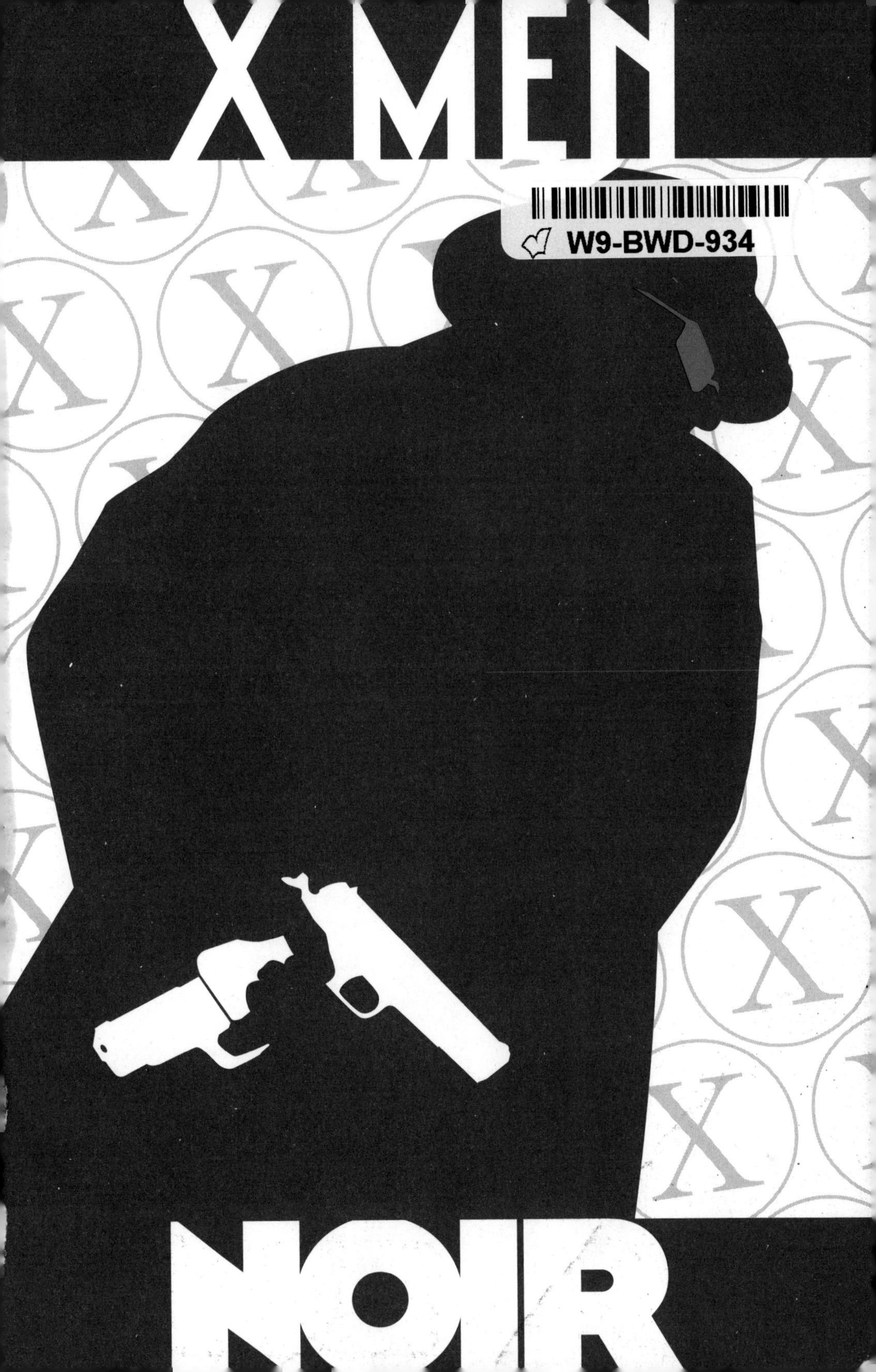
X MEN
NOIR

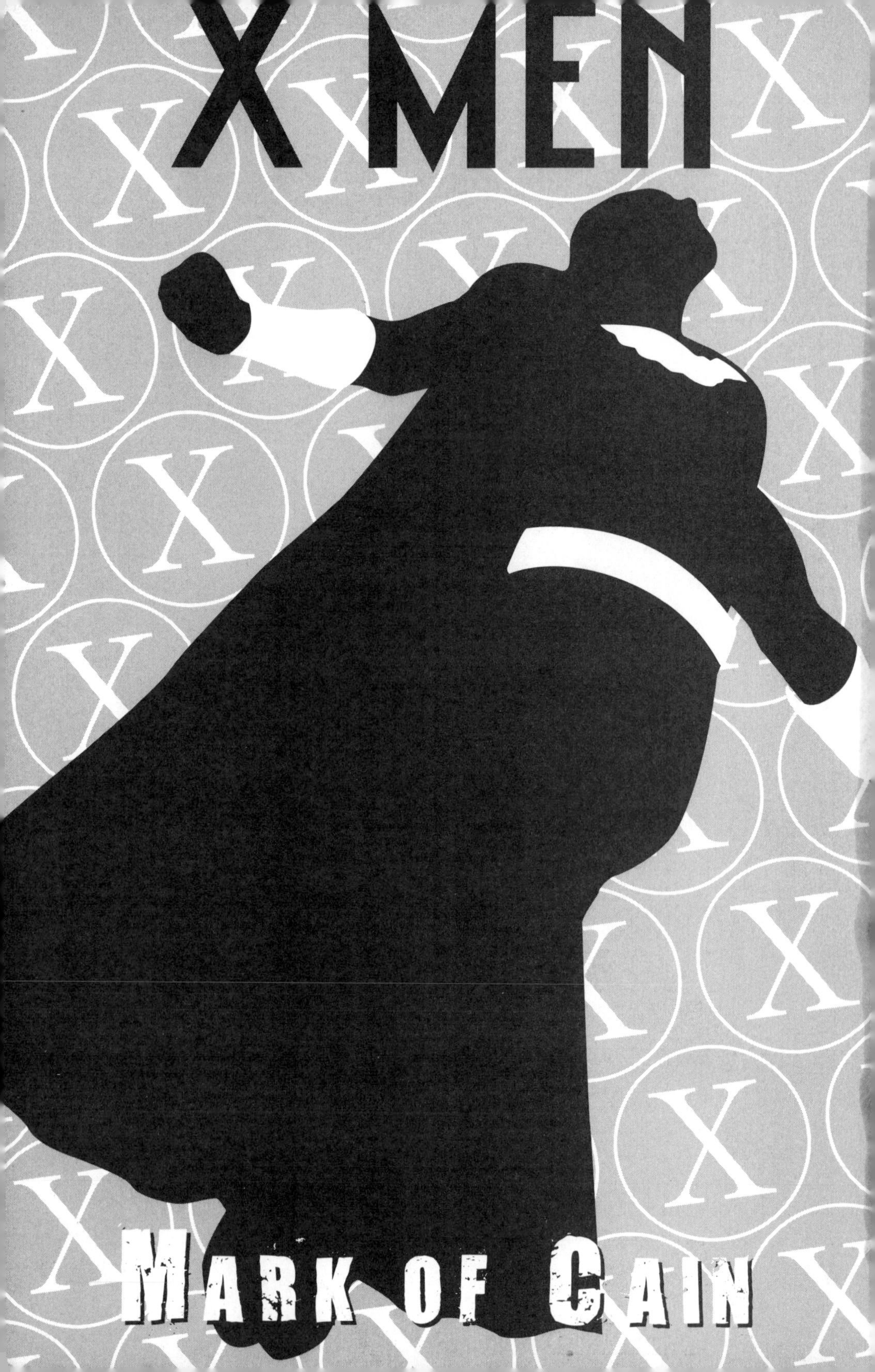
X MEN
MARK OF CAIN

WRITER
FRED VAN LENTE

ART
DENNIS CALERO

LETTERS
VC'S CLAYTON CLOWES

ASSISTANT EDITOR
MICHAEL HORWITZ

EDITOR
NATHAN COSBY

COLLECTION EDITOR
JENNIFER GRÜNWALD

EDITORIAL ASSISTANTS
JAMES EMMETT & JOE HOCHSTEIN

ASSISTANT EDITORS
ALEX STARBUCK & NELSON RIBEIRO

EDITOR, SPECIAL PROJECTS
MARK D. BEAZLEY

SENIOR EDITOR, SPECIAL PROJECTS
JEFF YOUNGQUIST

SENIOR VICE PRESIDENT OF SALES
DAVID GABRIEL

BOOK DESIGN
JEFF POWELL

EDITOR IN CHIEF
JOE QUESADA

PUBLISHER
DAN BUCKLEY

EXECUTIVE PRODUCER
ALAN FINE

X-MEN NOIR: MARK OF CAIN. Contains material originally published in magazine form as X-MEN NOIR: MARK OF CAIN #1-4. First printing 2010. ISBN# 978-0-7851-4437-3. Published by MARVEL WORLDWIDE, INC., a subsidiary of MARVEL ENTERTAINMENT, LLC. OFFICE OF PUBLICATION: 417 5th Avenue, New York, NY 10016. Copyright © 2009 and 2010 Marvel Characters, Inc. All rights reserved. $14.99 per copy in the U.S. and $16.99 in Canada (GST #R127032852); Canadian Agreement #40668537. All characters featured in this issue and the distinctive names and likenesses thereof, and all related indicia are trademarks of Marvel Characters, Inc. No similarity between any of the names, characters, persons, and/or institutions in this magazine with those of any living or dead person or institution is intended, and any such similarity which may exist is purely coincidental. **Printed in the U.S.A.** ALAN FINE, EVP - Office of the President, Marvel Worldwide, Inc. and EVP & CMO Marvel Characters B.V.; DAN BUCKLEY, Chief Executive Officer and Publisher - Print, Animation & Digital Media; JIM SOKOLOWSKI, Chief Operating Officer; DAVID GABRIEL, SVP of Publishing Sales & Circulation; DAVID BOGART, SVP of Business Affairs & Talent Management; MICHAEL PASCIULLO, VP Merchandising & Communications; JIM O'KEEFE, VP of Operations & Logistics; DAN CARR, Executive Director of Publishing Technology; JUSTIN F. GABRIE, Director of Publishing & Editorial Operations; SUSAN CRESPI, Editorial Operations Manager; ALEX MORALES, Publishing Operations Manager; STAN LEE, Chairman Emeritus. For information regarding advertising in Marvel Comics or on Marvel.com, please contact Ron Stern, VP of Business Development, at rstern@marvel.com. For Marvel subscription inquiries, please call 800-217-9158. **Manufactured between 11/19/10 and 12/8/10 by R.R. DONNELLEY, INC. (CRAWFORD), CRAWFORDSVILLE, IN, USA.**

10 9 8 7 6 5 4 3 2 1

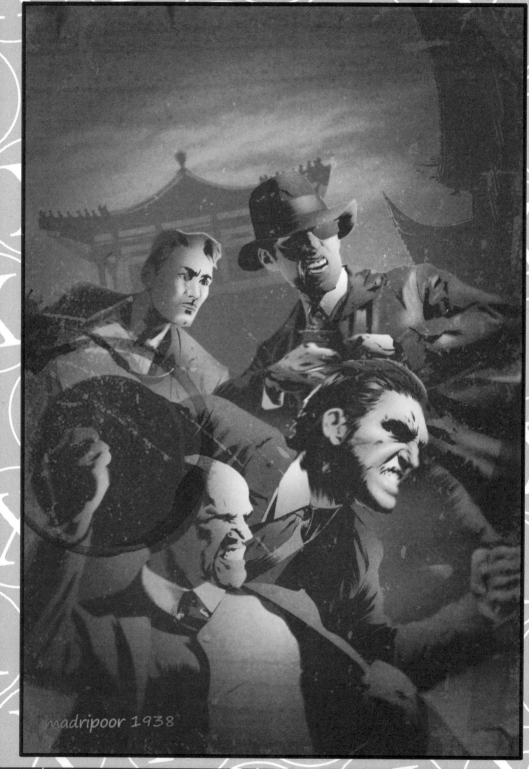

madripoor 1938

ONE

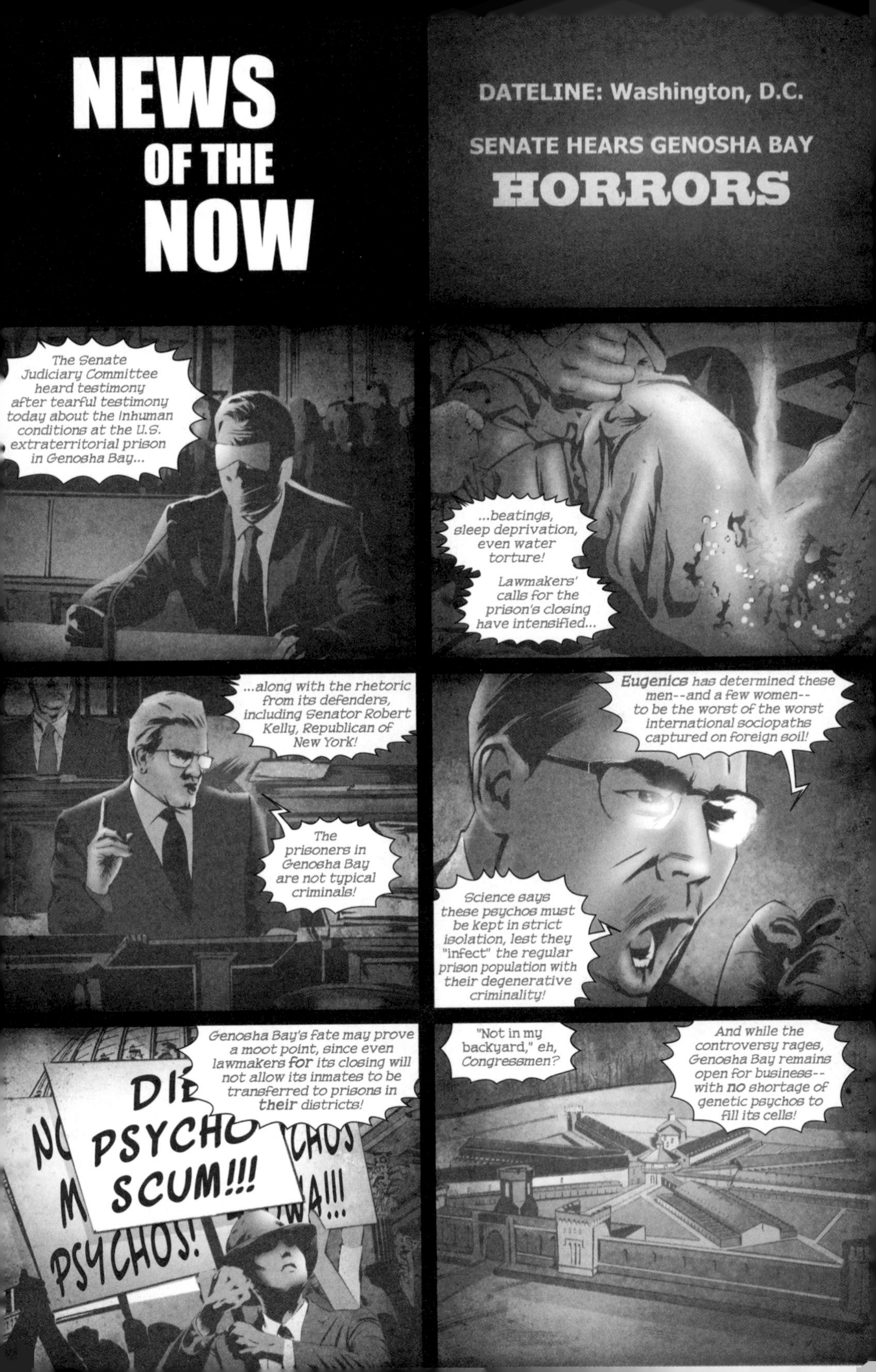
NEWS OF THE NOW
DATELINE: Washington, D.C.
SENATE HEARS GENOSHA BAY HORRORS
The Senate Judiciary Committee heard testimony after tearful testimony today about the inhuman conditions at the U.S. extraterritorial prison in Genosha Bay...
...beatings, sleep deprivation, even water torture!
Lawmakers' calls for the prison's closing have intensified...
...along with the rhetoric from its defenders, including Senator Robert Kelly, Republican of New York!
The prisoners in Genosha Bay are not typical criminals!
Eugenics has determined these men--and a few women--to be the worst of the worst international sociopaths captured on foreign soil!
Science says these psychos must be kept in strict isolation, lest they "infect" the regular prison population with their degenerative criminality!
Genosha Bay's fate may prove a moot point, since even lawmakers for its closing will not allow its inmates to be transferred to prisons in their districts!
DIE PSYCHO SCUM!!!
PSYCHOS!
"Not in my backyard," eh, Congressmen?
And while the controversy rages, Genosha Bay remains open for business--with no shortage of genetic psychos to fill its cells!

DATELINE: New York, NY

"PROFESSOR OF CRIME"
RELEASED

From one prison to another, as renegade psychiatrist Charles Xavier, who ran a reform school that taught kids how to be better criminals instead of reforming them...

...was released today from Riker's Island jail!

The District Attorney was forced to drop all charges against the leader of the so-called "X Men," since anyone who could testify against him was dead!

The People's primary witness, Chief of Detectives Eric Magnus, was slain at the bloody massacre on Welfare Island a few months back!

"The Professor of Crime" has maintained his innocence throughout, however, going so far to swear:

Chief Detective Magnus and I worked on many difficult juvenile cases together, and we became close friends.

And I swear to the public, with his daughter Wanda standing by my side...

...I will not rest until I have brought his killers to justice!

If you're listening to this, you so-called "Angel," you and your gang, wherever you are...

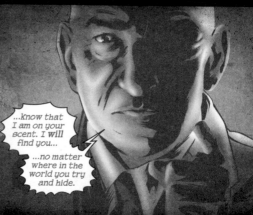

...know that I am on your scent. I will find you...

...no matter where in the world you try and hide.

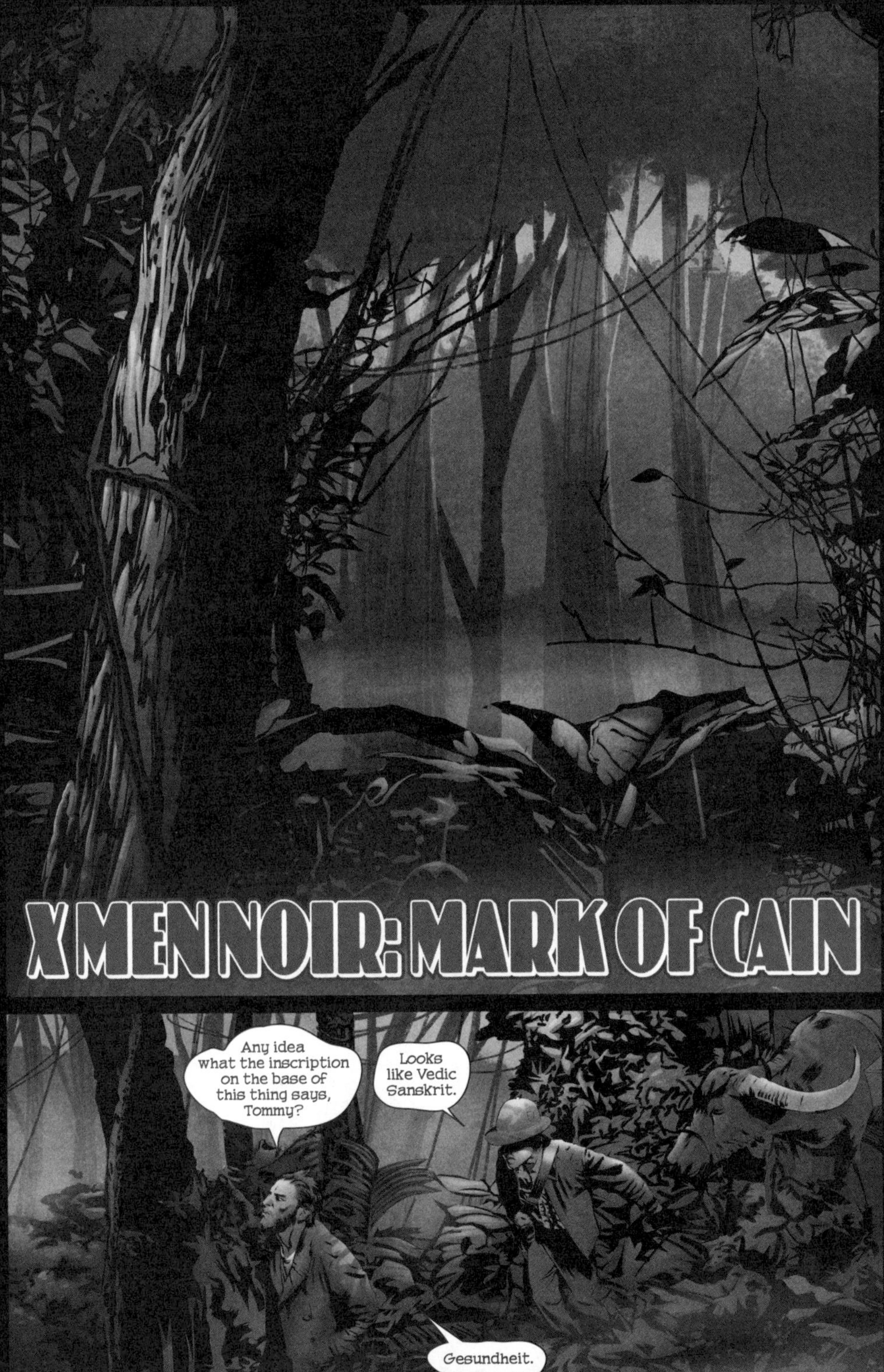
X MEN NOIR: MARK OF CAIN
Any idea what the inscription on the base of this thing says, Tommy?
Looks like Vedic Sanskrit.
Gesundheit.

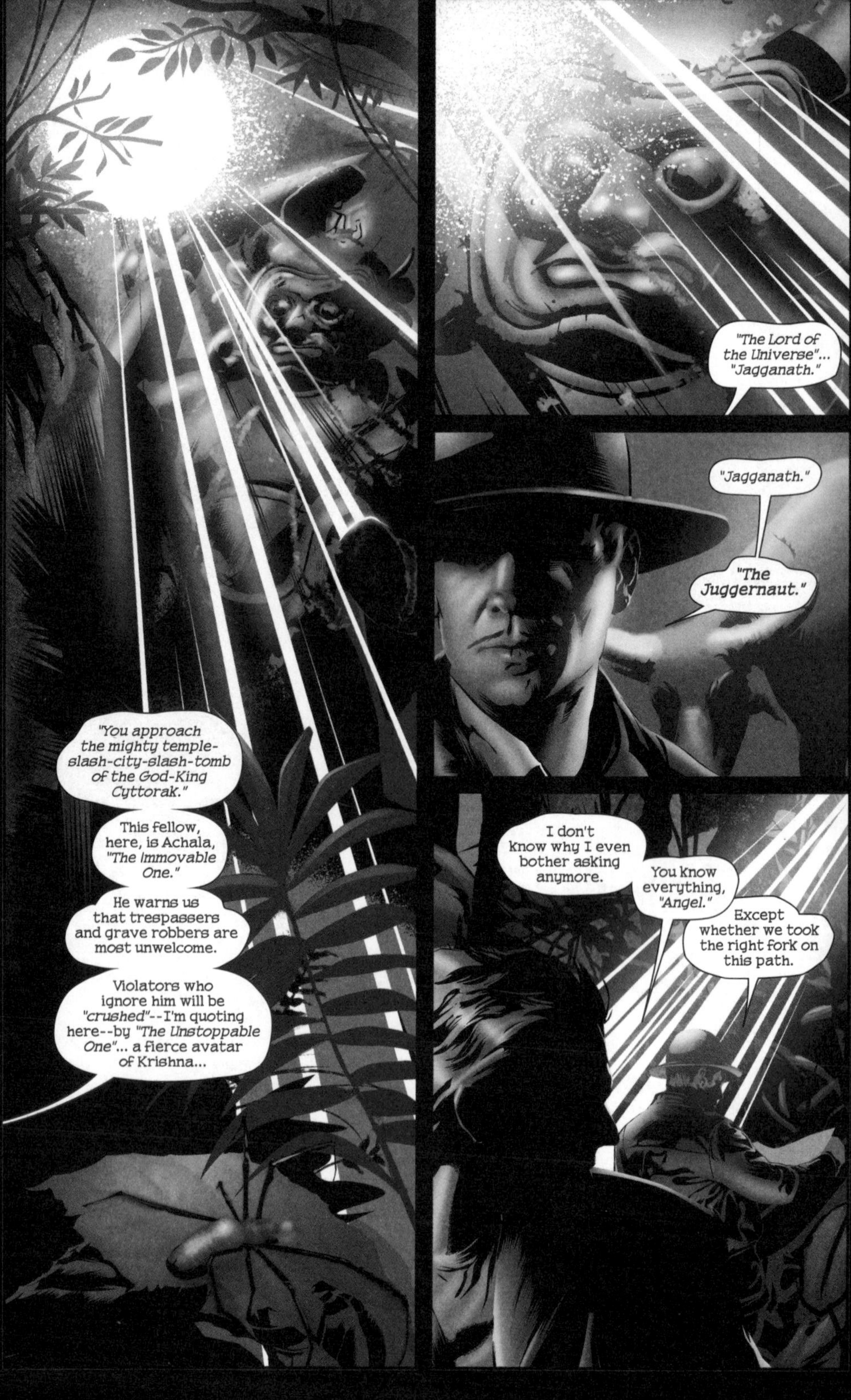
"You approach the mighty temple-slash-city-slash-tomb of the God-King Cyttorak."
This fellow, here, is Achala, "The Immovable One."
He warns us that trespassers and grave robbers are most unwelcome.
Violators who ignore him will be "crushed"--I'm quoting here--by "The Unstoppable One"... a fierce avatar of Krishna...
"The Lord of the Universe"... "Jagganath."
"Jagganath."
"The Juggernaut."
I don't know why I even bother asking anymore.
You know everything, "Angel."
Except whether we took the right fork on this path.

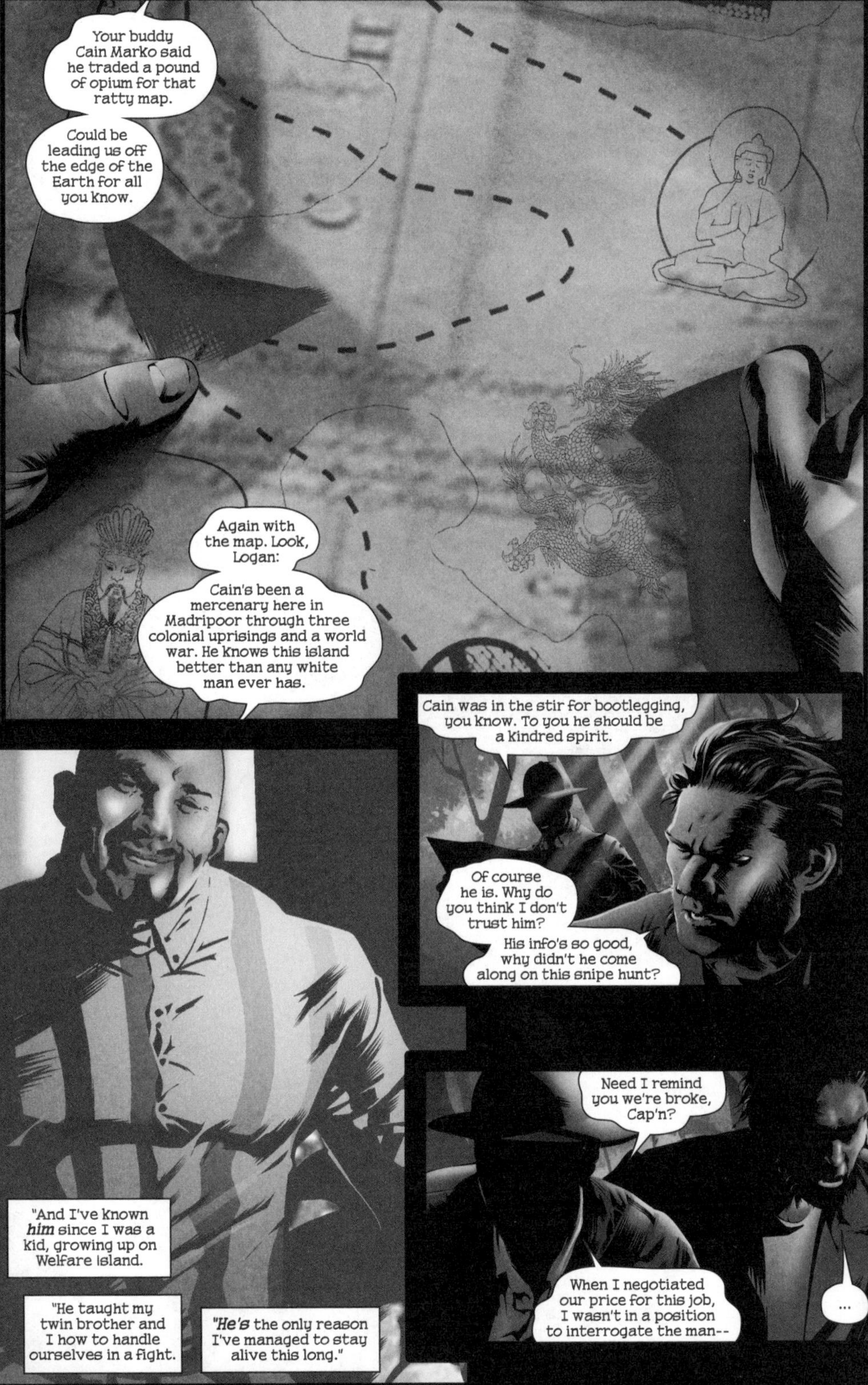
Your buddy Cain Marko said he traded a pound of opium for that ratty map.
Could be leading us off the edge of the Earth for all you know.
Again with the map. Look, Logan:
Cain's been a mercenary here in Madripoor through three colonial uprisings and a world war. He knows this island better than any white man ever has.
Cain was in the stir for bootlegging, you know. To you he should be a kindred spirit.
Of course he is. Why do you think I don't trust him?
His info's so good, why didn't he come along on this snipe hunt?
"And I've known *him* since I was a kid, growing up on Welfare Island.
"He taught my twin brother and I how to handle ourselves in a fight.
"*He's* the only reason I've managed to stay alive this long."
Need I remind you we're broke, Cap'n?
When I negotiated our price for this job, I wasn't in a position to interrogate the man--
...

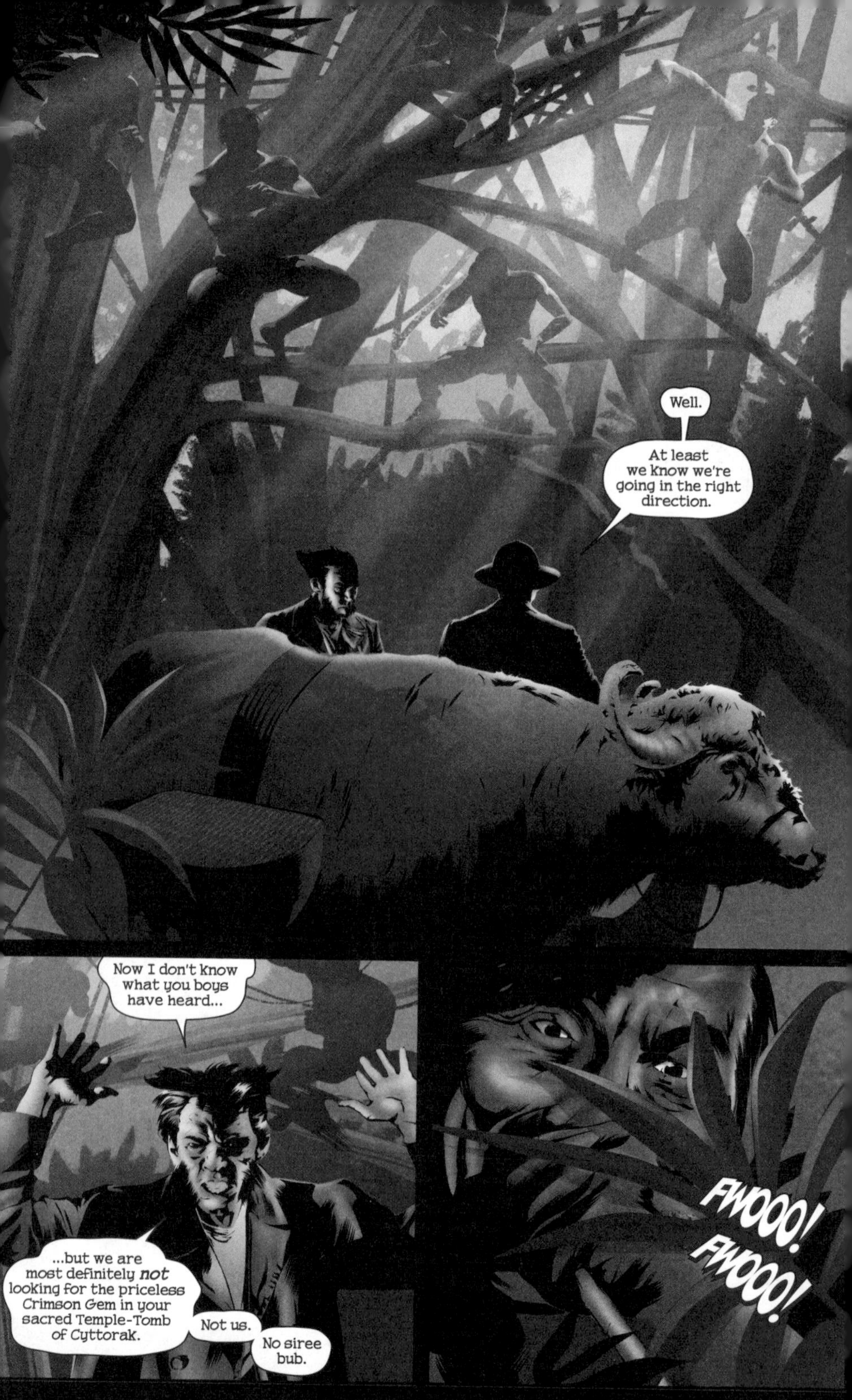
Well.
At least we know we're going in the right direction.
Now I don't know what you boys have heard...
...but we are most definitely *not* looking for the priceless Crimson Gem in your sacred Temple-Tomb of Cyttorak.
Not us.
No siree bub.
FWOOO! FWOOO!

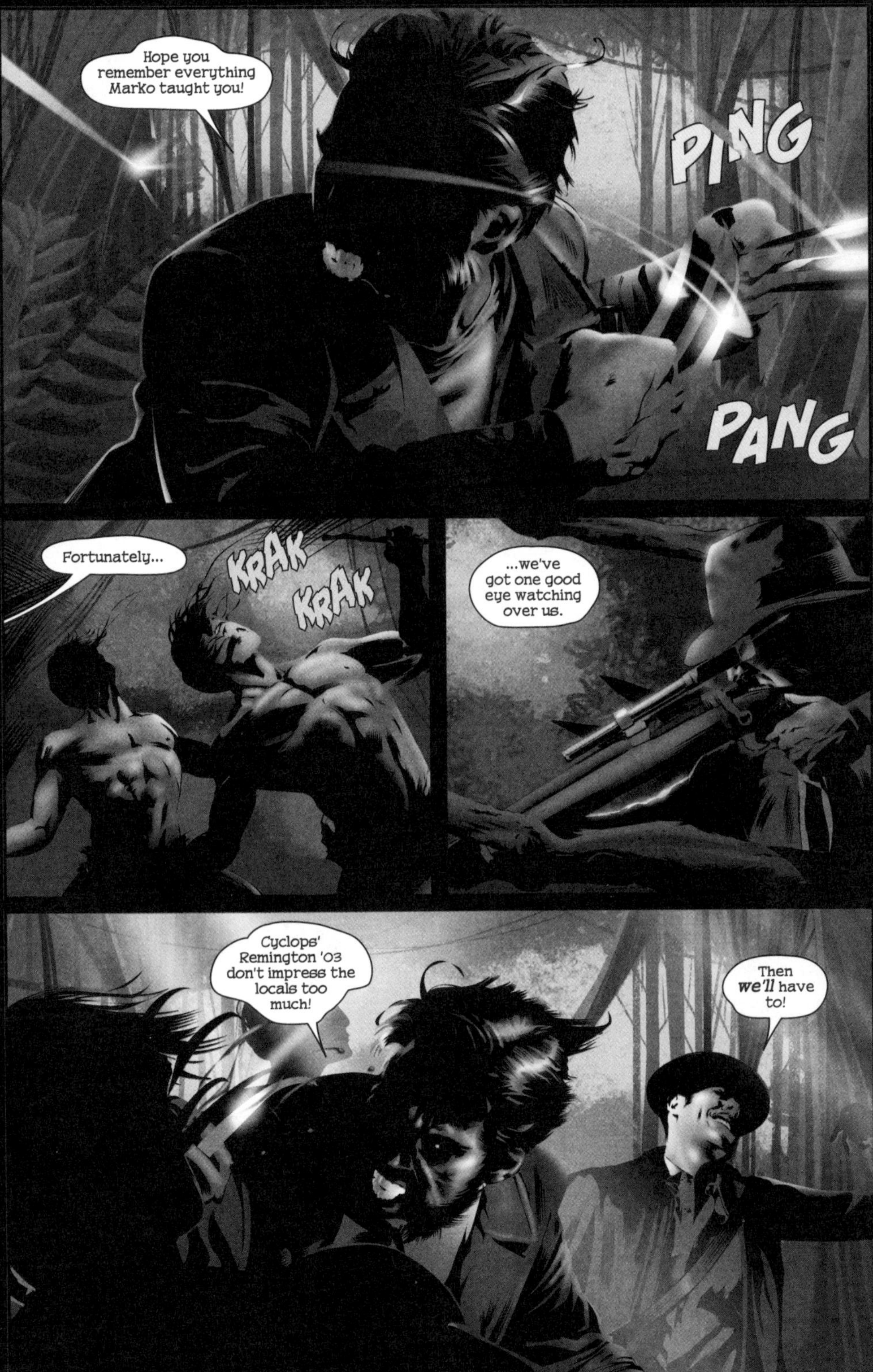
Hope you remember everything Marko taught you!
PING
PANG
Fortunately...
KRAK
KRAK
...we've got one good eye watching over us.
Cyclops' Remington '03 don't impress the locals too much!
Then we'll have to!

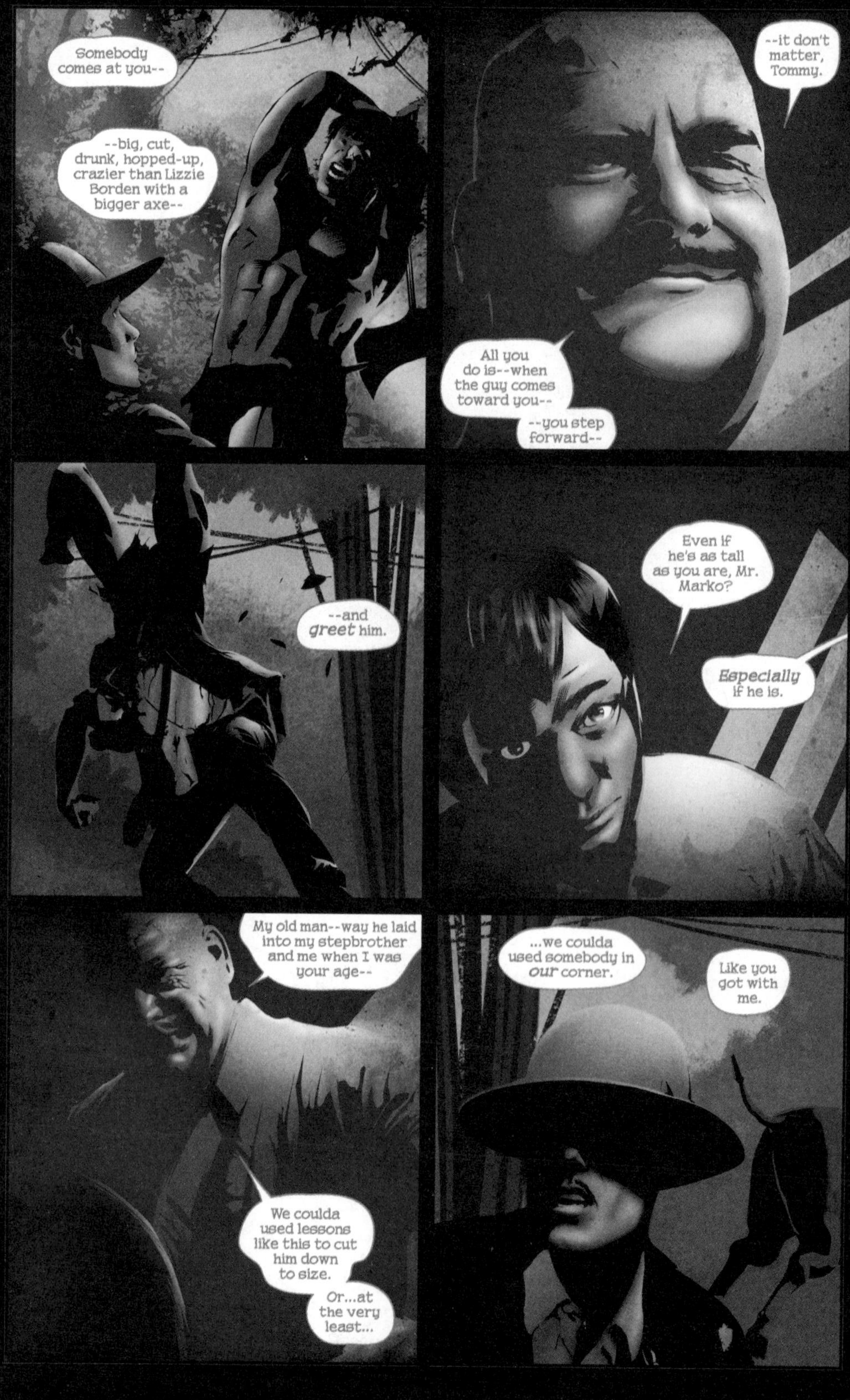
Somebody comes at you--
--big, cut, drunk, hopped-up, crazier than Lizzie Borden with a bigger axe--
--it don't matter, Tommy.
All you do is--when the guy comes toward you--
--you step forward--
--and *greet* him.
Even if he's as tall as you are, Mr. Marko?
Especially if he is.
My old man--way he laid into my stepbrother and me when I was your age--
We coulda used lessons like this to cut him down to size.
Or...at the very least...
...we coulda used somebody in *our* corner.
Like you got with me.

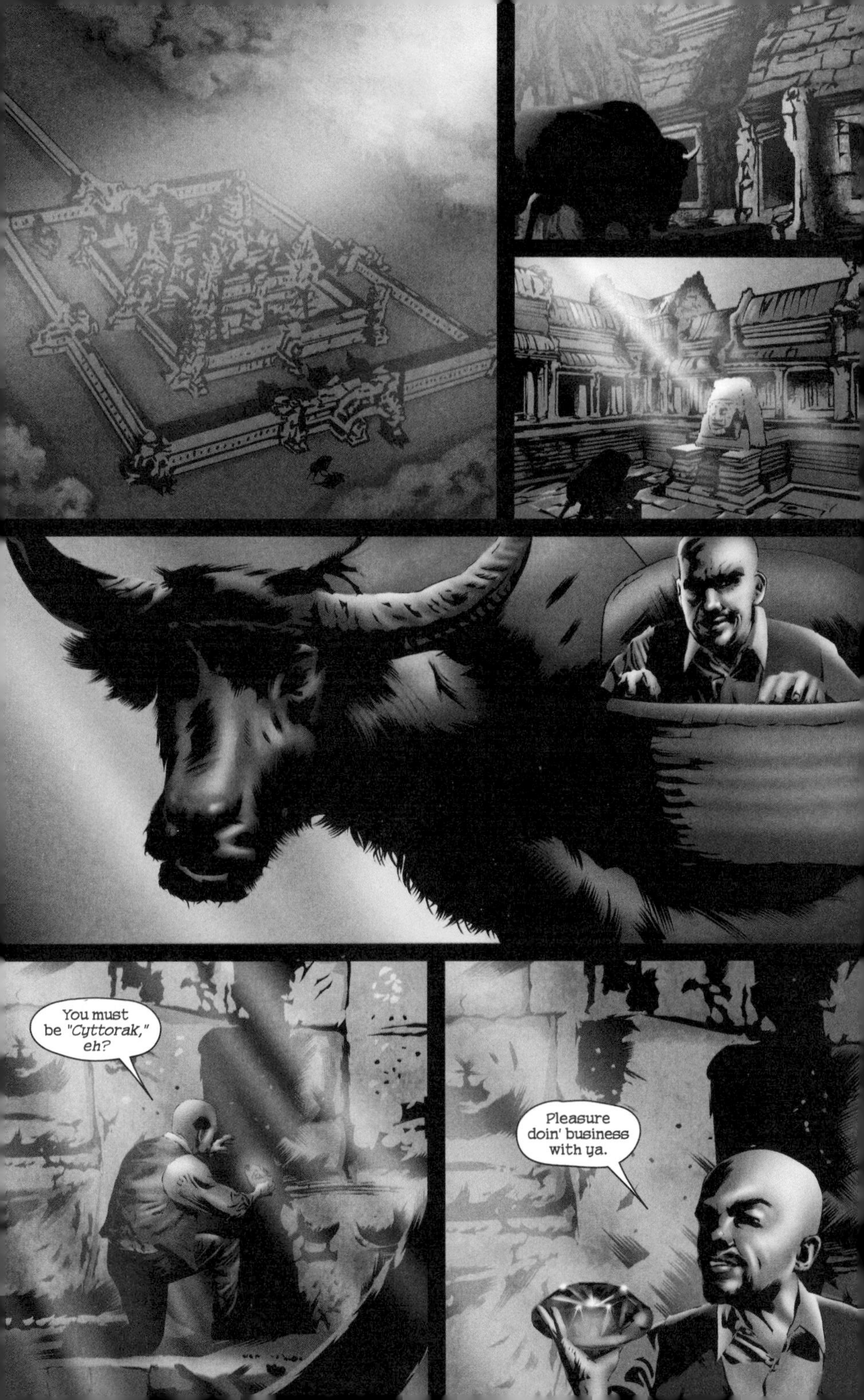
You must be "Cyttorak," eh?
Pleasure doin' business with ya.

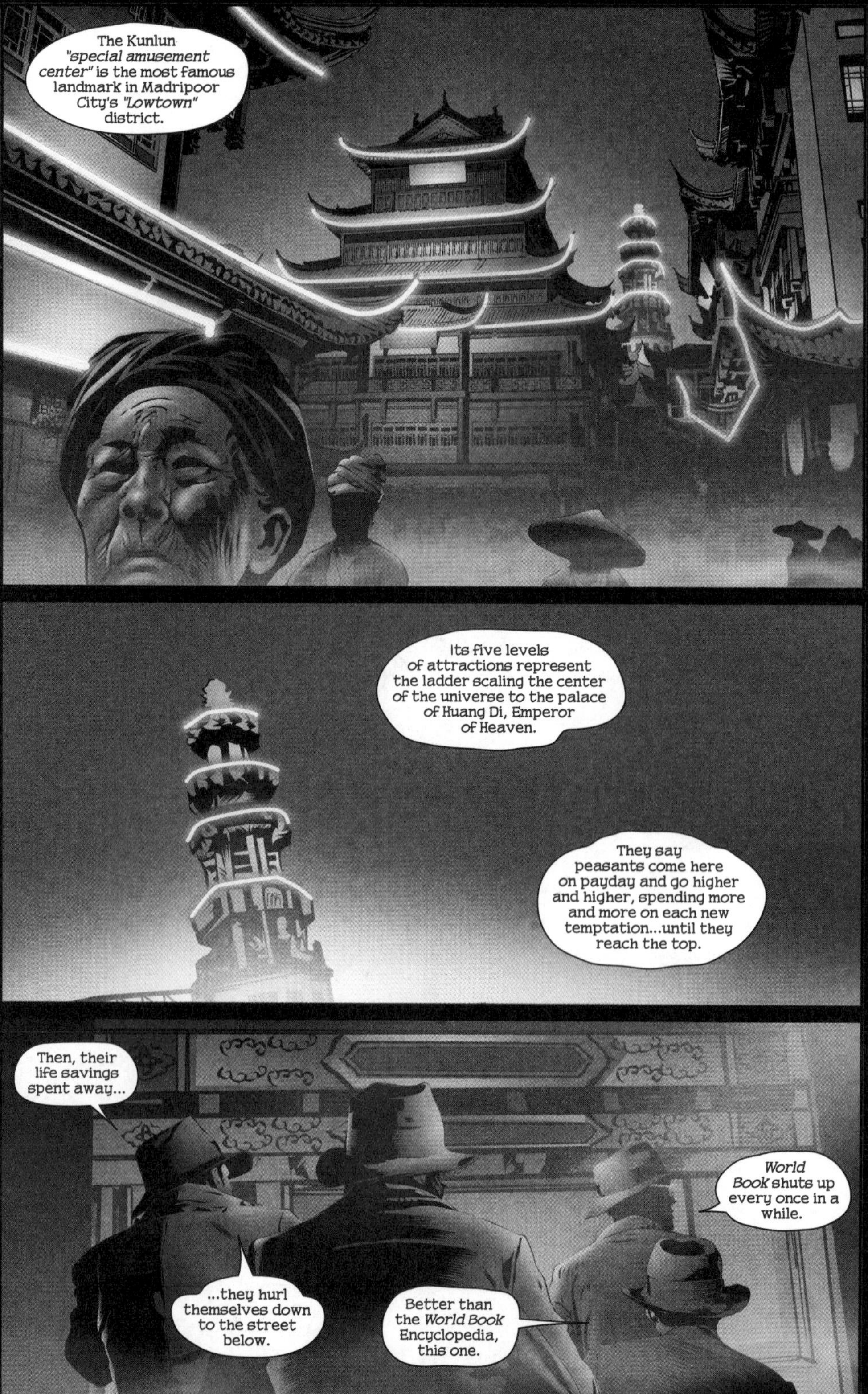

The Kunlun *"special amusement center"* is the most famous landmark in Madripoor City's *"Lowtown"* district.
Its five levels of attractions represent the ladder scaling the center of the universe to the palace of Huang Di, Emperor of Heaven.
They say peasants come here on payday and go higher and higher, spending more and more on each new temptation...until they reach the top.
Then, their life savings spent away...
...they hurl themselves down to the street below.
World Book shuts up every once in a while.
Better than the *World Book* Encyclopedia, this one.

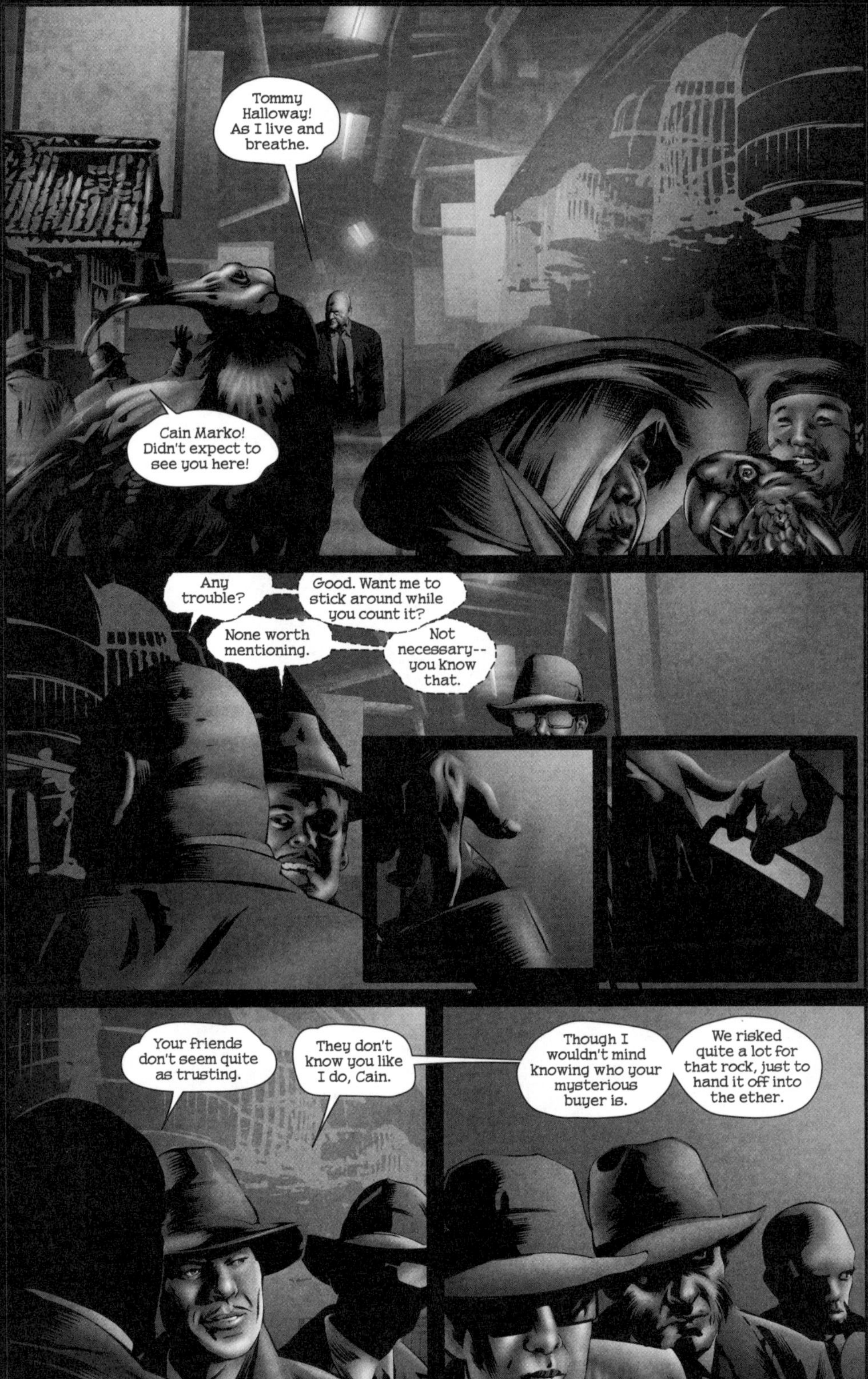
Tommy Halloway! As I live and breathe.
Cain Marko! Didn't expect to see you here!
Any trouble?
None worth mentioning.
Good. Want me to stick around while you count it?
Not necessary-- you know that.
Your friends don't seem quite as trusting.
They don't know you like I do, Cain.
Though I wouldn't mind knowing who your mysterious buyer is.
We risked quite a lot for that rock, just to hand it off into the ether.

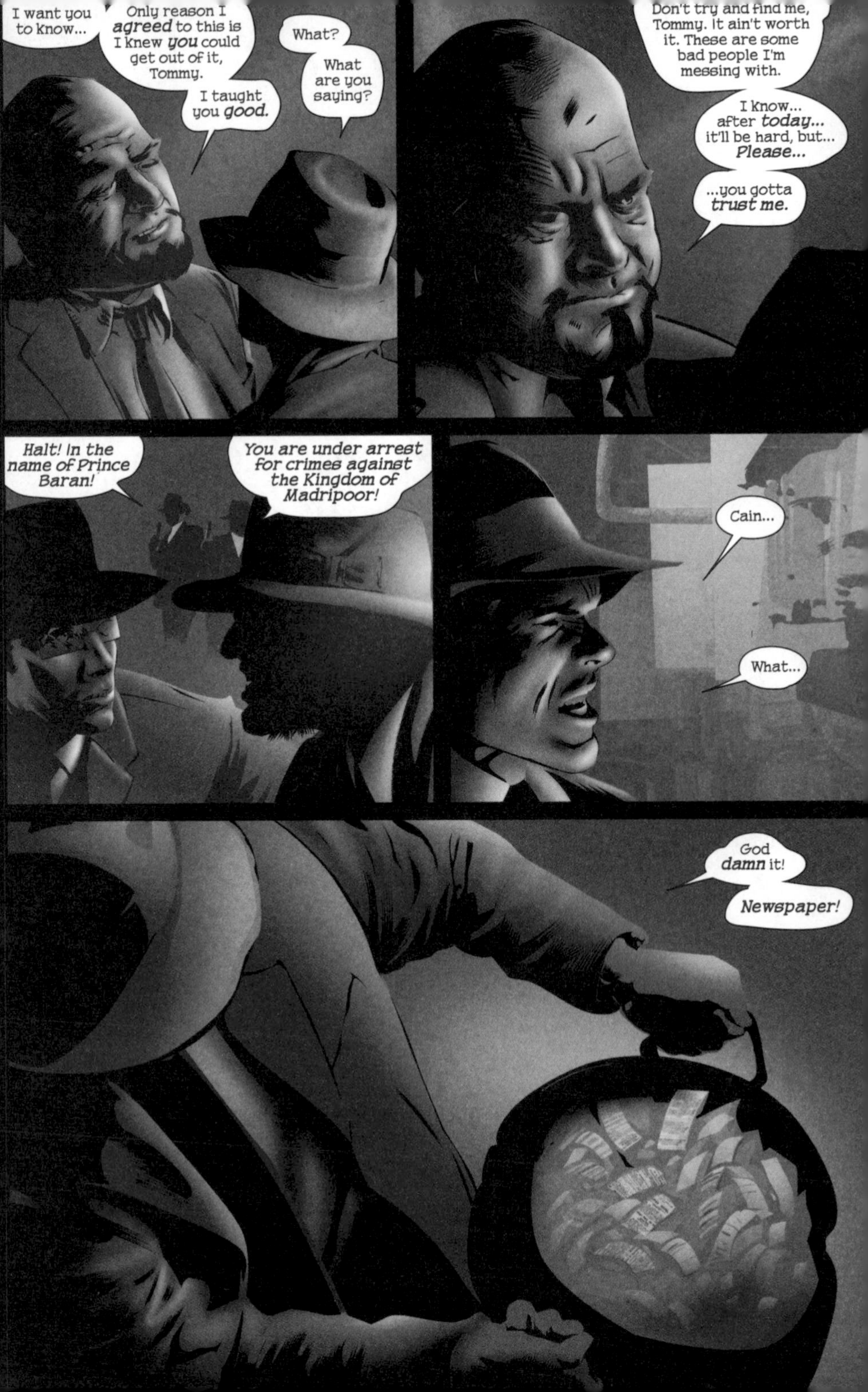
I want you to know...
Only reason I *agreed* to this is I knew *you* could get out of it, Tommy.
I taught you *good.*
What?
What are you saying?
Don't try and find me, Tommy. It ain't worth it. These are some bad people I'm messing with.
I know... after *today...* it'll be hard, but... *Please...*
...you gotta *trust me.*
Halt! In the name of Prince Baran!
You are under arrest for crimes against the Kingdom of Madripoor!
Cain...
What...
God *damn* it!
Newspaper!

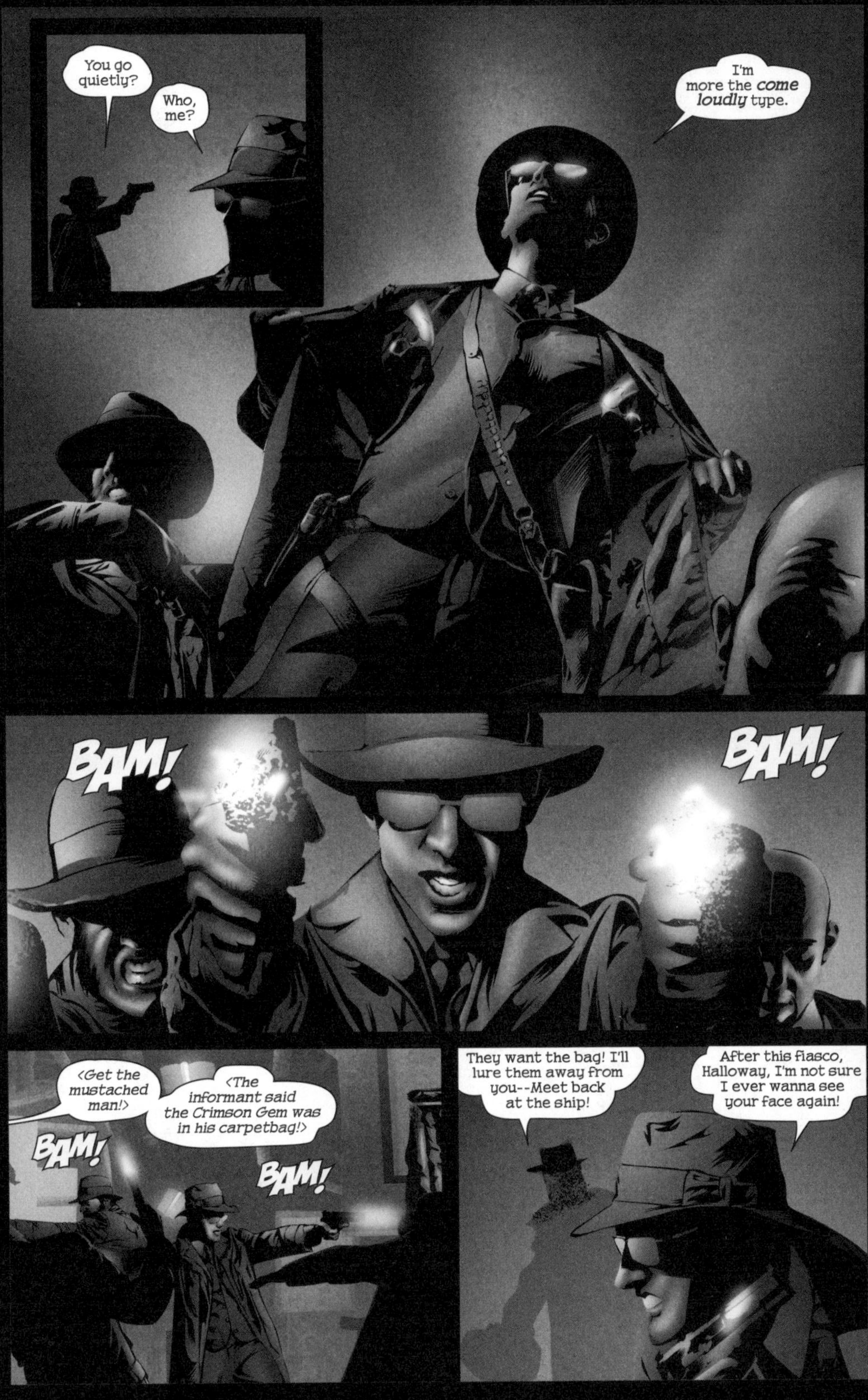
You go quietly?
Who, me?
I'm more the come loudly type.
BAM!
BAM!
<Get the mustached man!>
<The informant said the Crimson Gem was in his carpetbag!>
BAM!
BAM!
They want the bag! I'll lure them away from you--Meet back at the ship!
After this fiasco, Halloway, I'm not sure I ever wanna see your face again!

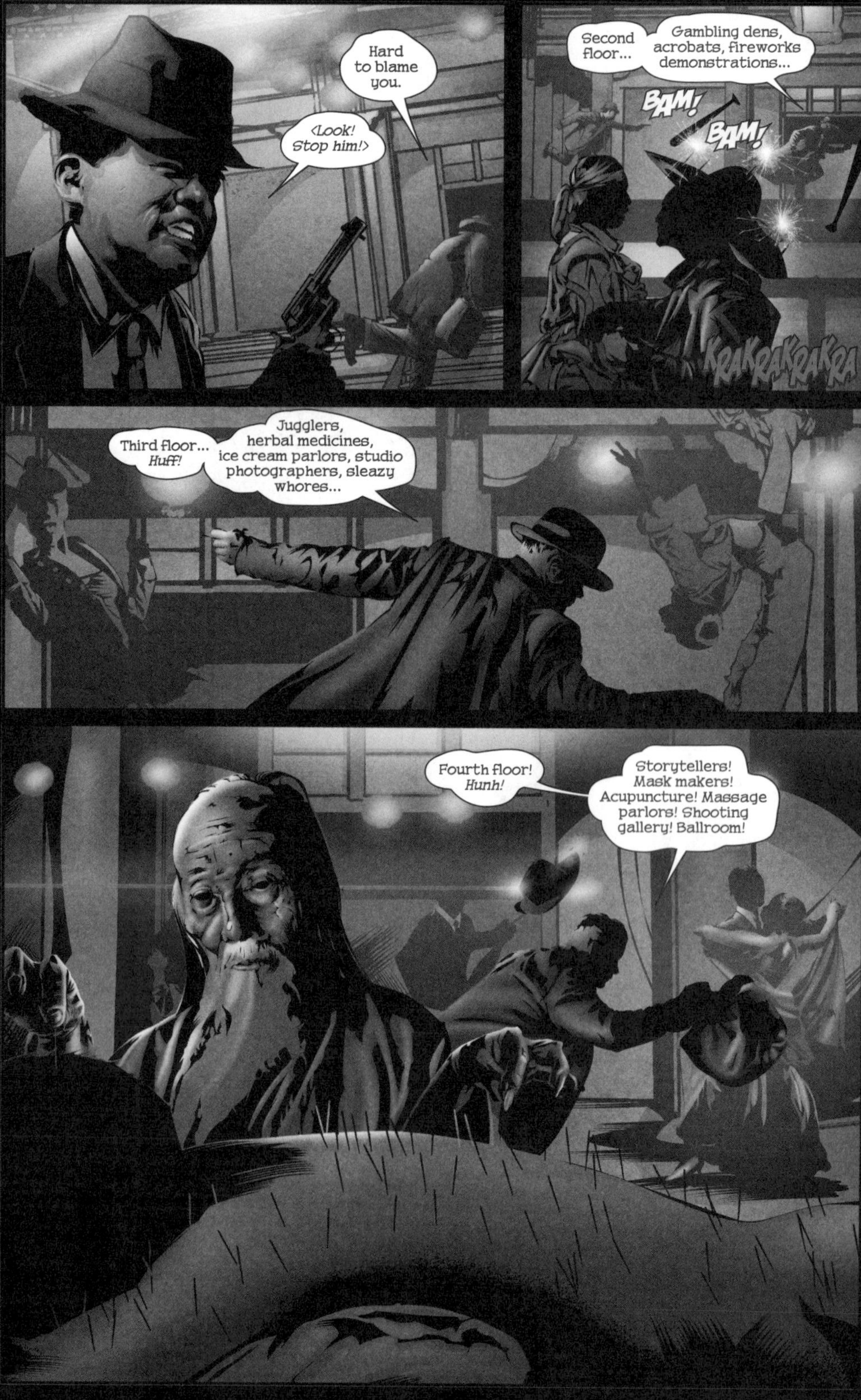
Hard to blame you.
<Look! Stop him!>
Second floor...
Gambling dens, acrobats, fireworks demonstrations...
BAM!
BAM!
KRAKRAKRAKRA
Third floor... Huff!
Jugglers, herbal medicines, ice cream parlors, studio photographers, sleazy whores...
Fourth floor! Hunh!
Storytellers! Mask makers! Acupuncture! Massage parlors! Shooting gallery! Ballroom!

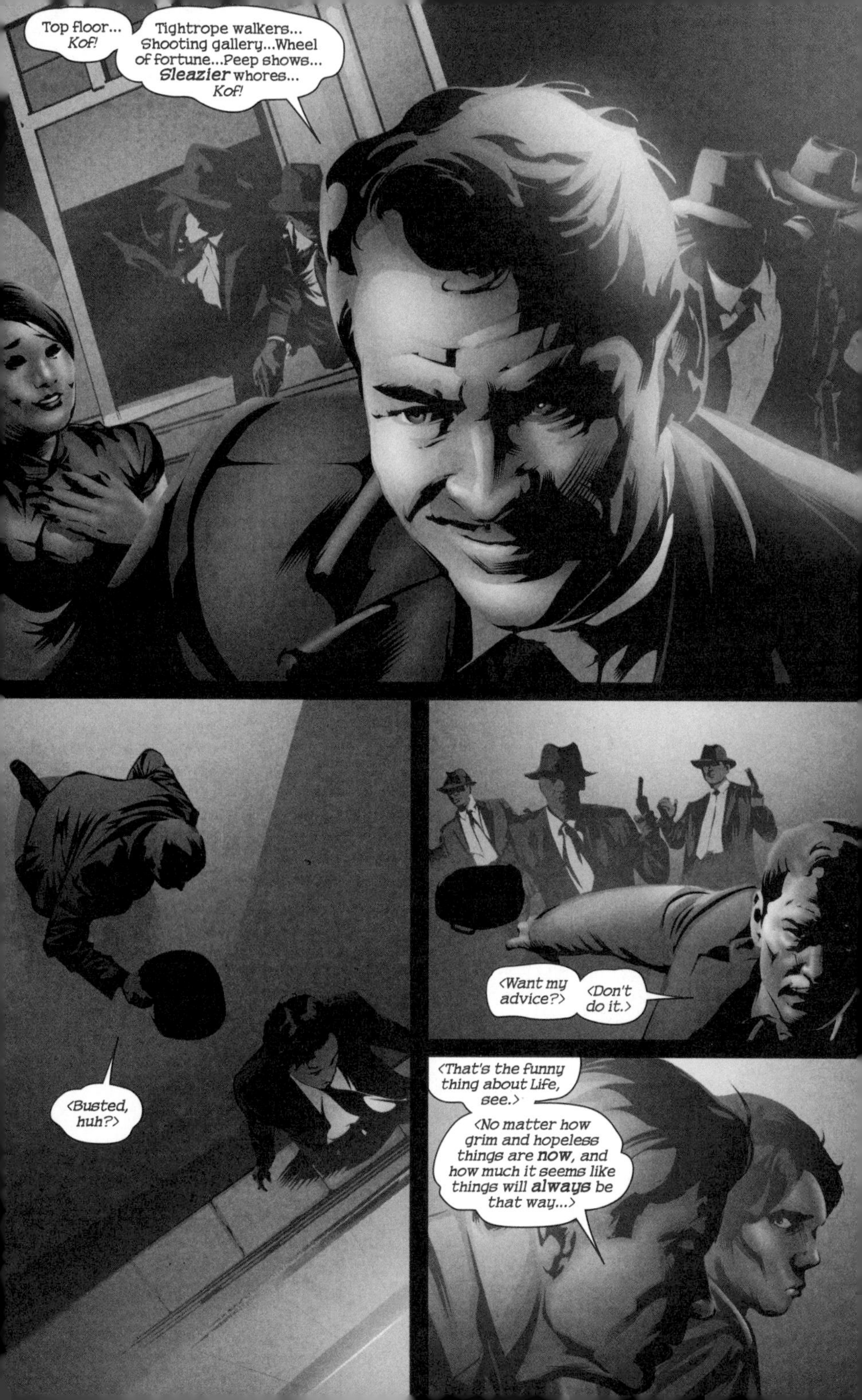

Top floor... Kof!
Tightrope walkers... Shooting gallery...Wheel of fortune...Peep shows... **Sleazier** whores... Kof!
<Busted, huh?>
<Want my advice?>
<Don't do it.>
<That's the funny thing about Life, see.>
<No matter how grim and hopeless things are **now**, and how much it seems like things will **always** be that way...>

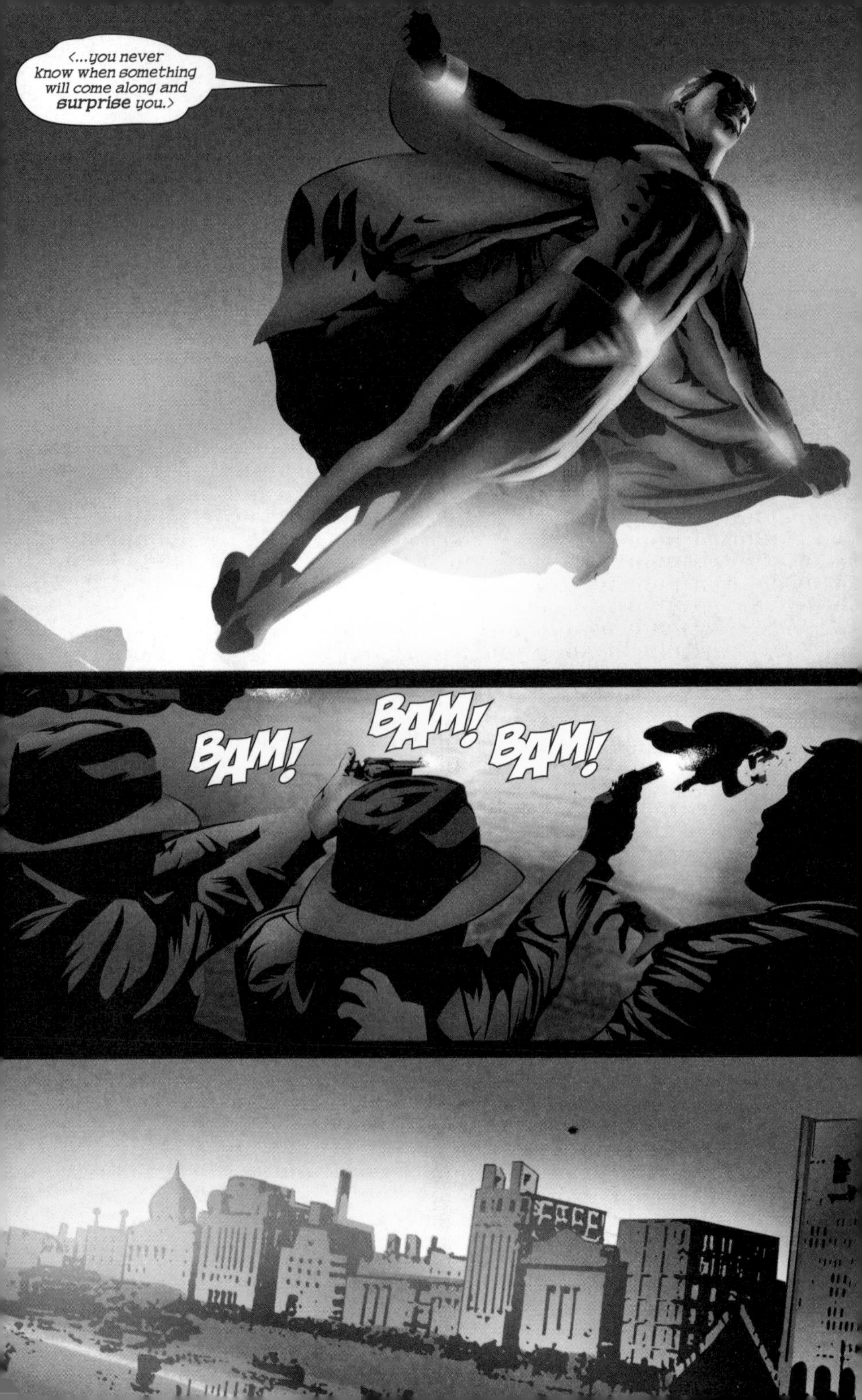

<...you never know when something will come along and surprise you.>
BAM!
BAM!
BAM!

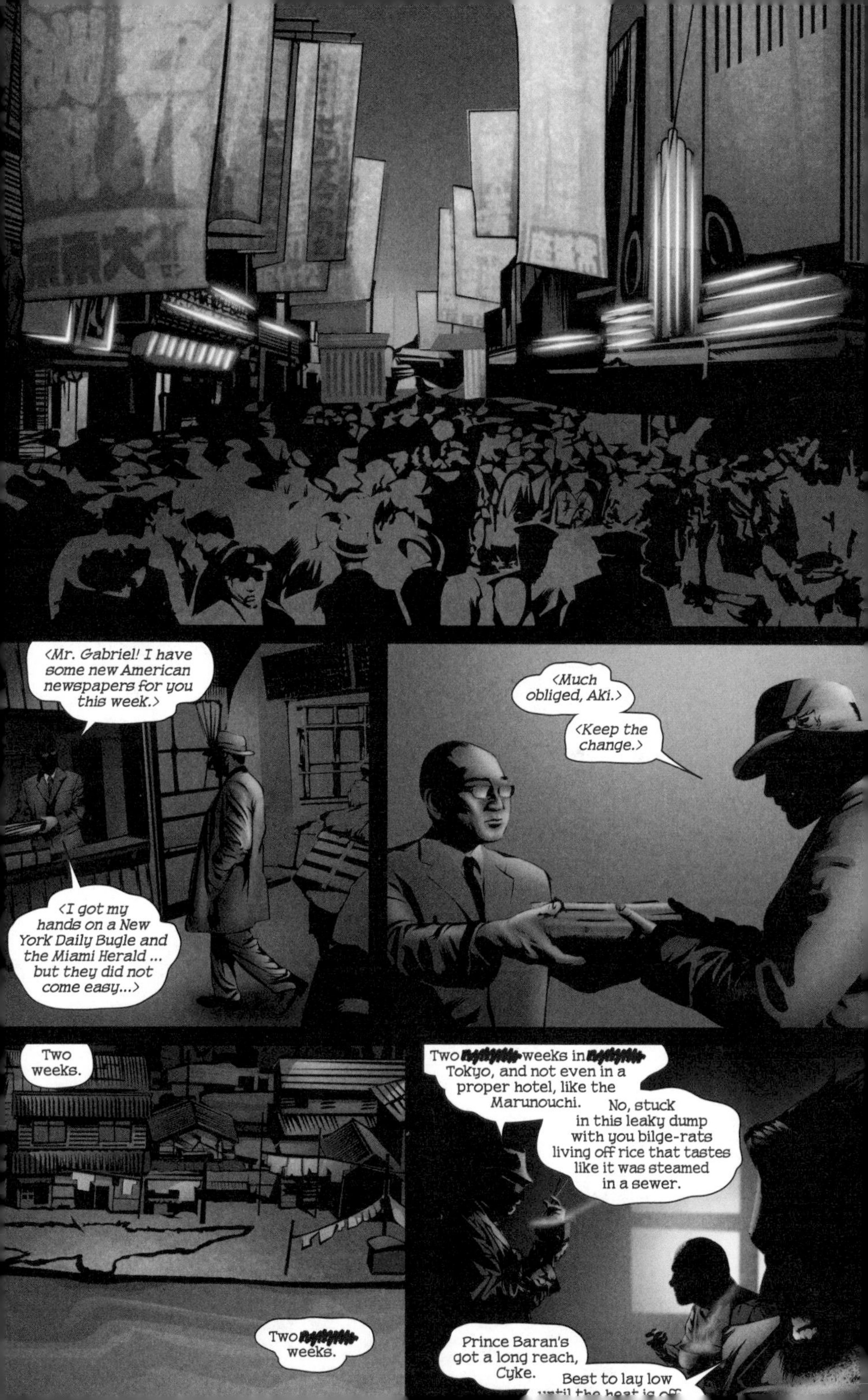
<Mr. Gabriel! I have some new American newspapers for you this week.>
<I got my hands on a New York Daily Bugle and the Miami Herald ... but they did not come easy...>
<Much obliged, Aki.>
<Keep the change.>
Two weeks.
Two [redacted] weeks in [redacted] Tokyo, and not even in a proper hotel, like the Marunouchi.
No, stuck in this leaky dump with you bilge-rats living off rice that tastes like it was steamed in a sewer.
Two [redacted] weeks.
Prince Baran's got a long reach, Cyke.
Best to lay low

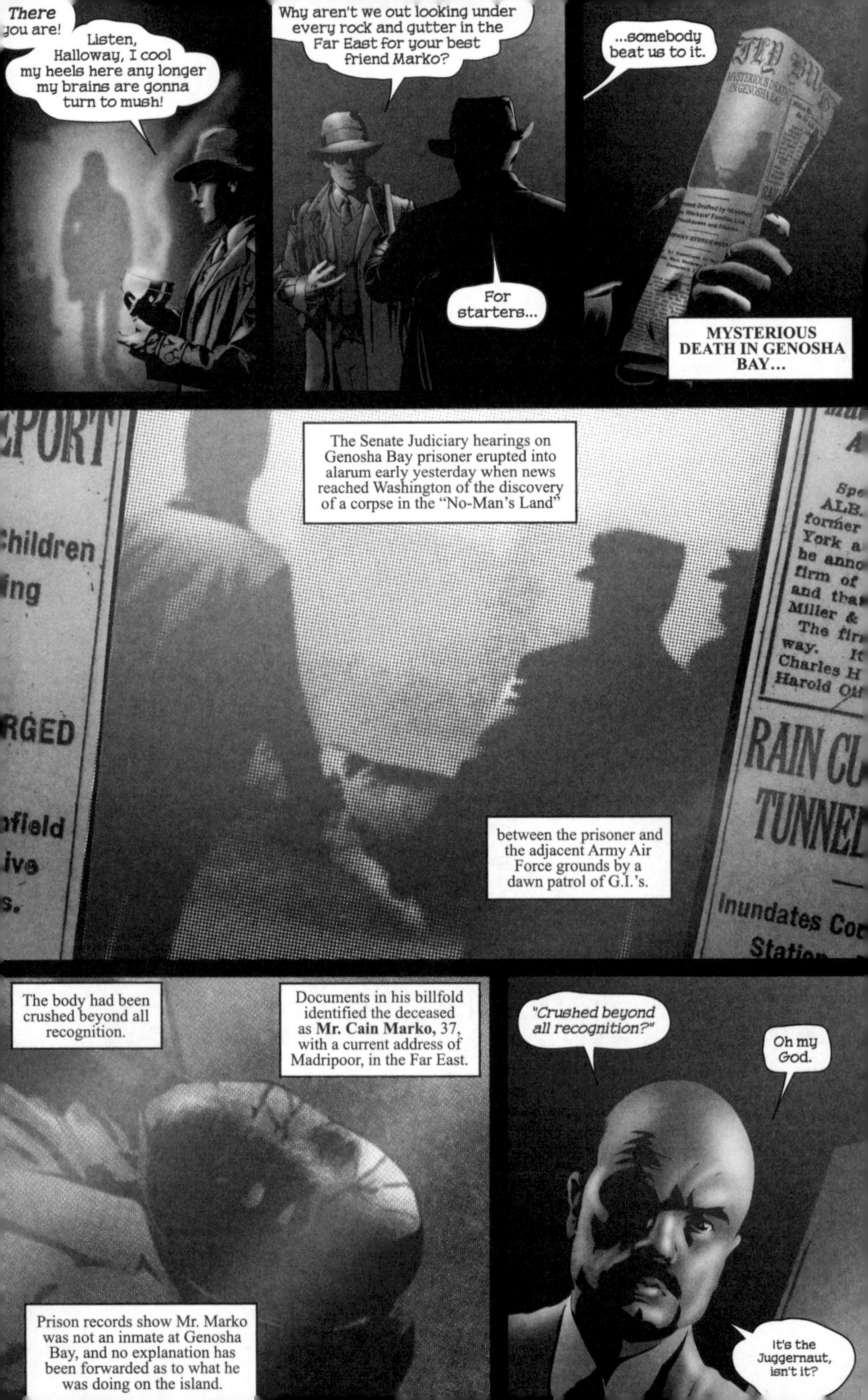
There you are!
Listen, Halloway, I cool my heels here any longer my brains are gonna turn to mush!
Why aren't we out looking under every rock and gutter in the Far East for your best friend Marko?
For starters...
...somebody beat us to it.
MYSTERIOUS DEATH IN GENOSHA BAY
MYSTERIOUS DEATH IN GENOSHA BAY...
The Senate Judiciary hearings on Genosha Bay prisoner erupted into alarum early yesterday when news reached Washington of the discovery of a corpse in the "No-Man's Land"
between the prisoner and the adjacent Army Air Force grounds by a dawn patrol of G.I.'s.
The body had been crushed beyond all recognition.
Documents in his billfold identified the deceased as **Mr. Cain Marko,** 37, with a current address of Madripoor, in the Far East.
Prison records show Mr. Marko was not an inmate at Genosha Bay, and no explanation has been forwarded as to what he was doing on the island.
"Crushed beyond all recognition?"
Oh my God.
It's the Juggernaut, isn't it?

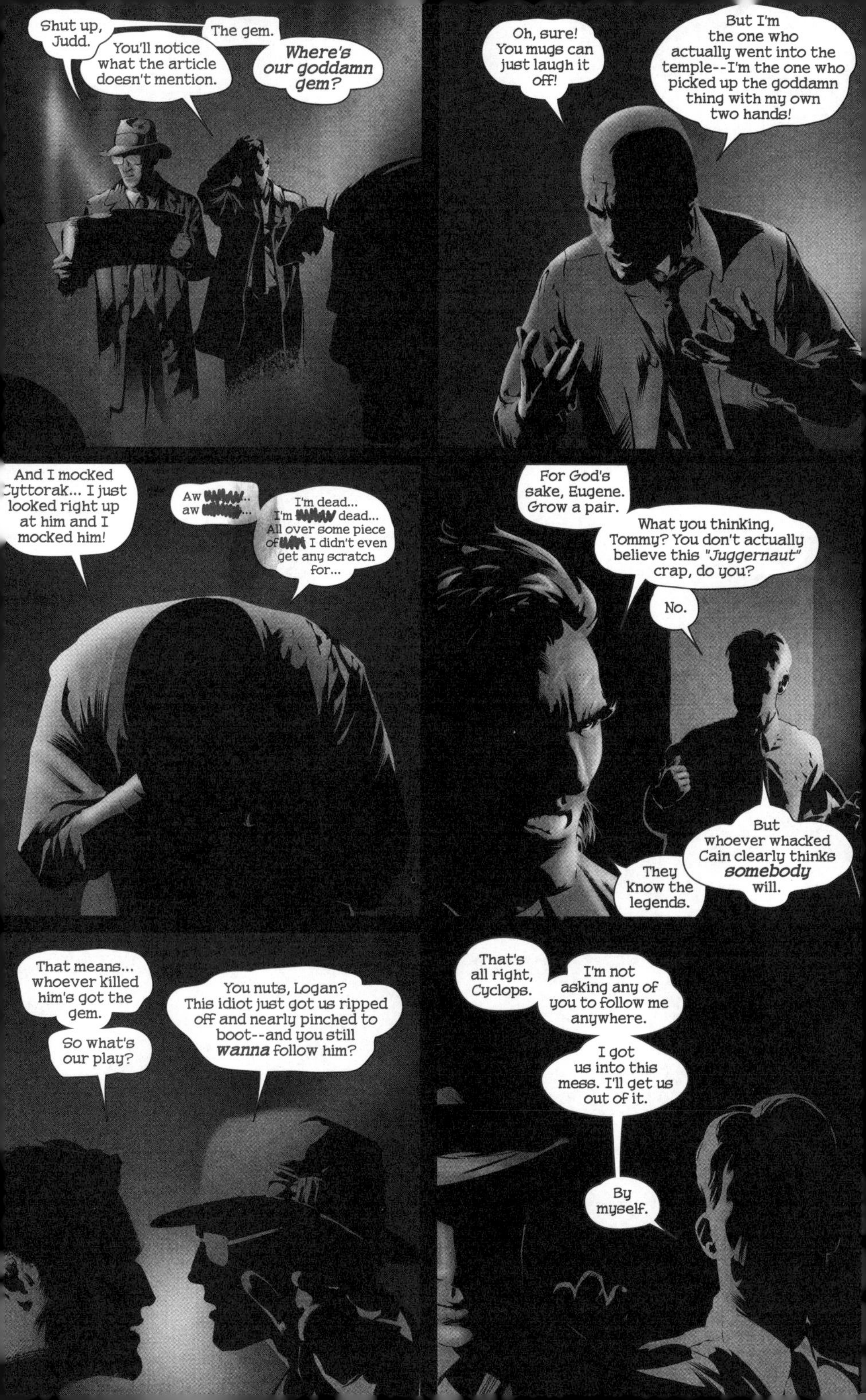
Shut up, Judd.
The gem.
You'll notice what the article doesn't mention.
Where's our goddamn gem?
Oh, sure! You mugs can just laugh it off!
But I'm the one who actually went into the temple--I'm the one who picked up the goddamn thing with my own two hands!
And I mocked Cyttorak... I just looked right up at him and I mocked him!
Aw [redacted]... aw [redacted]...
I'm dead... I'm [redacted] dead... All over some piece of [redacted] I didn't even get any scratch for...
For God's sake, Eugene. Grow a pair.
What you thinking, Tommy? You don't actually believe this "*Juggernaut*" crap, do you?
No.
But whoever whacked Cain clearly thinks *somebody* will.
They know the legends.
That means... whoever killed him's got the gem.
So what's our play?
You nuts, Logan? This idiot just got us ripped off and nearly pinched to boot--and you still *wanna* follow him?
That's all right, Cyclops.
I'm not asking any of you to follow me anywhere.
I got us into this mess. I'll get us out of it.
By myself.

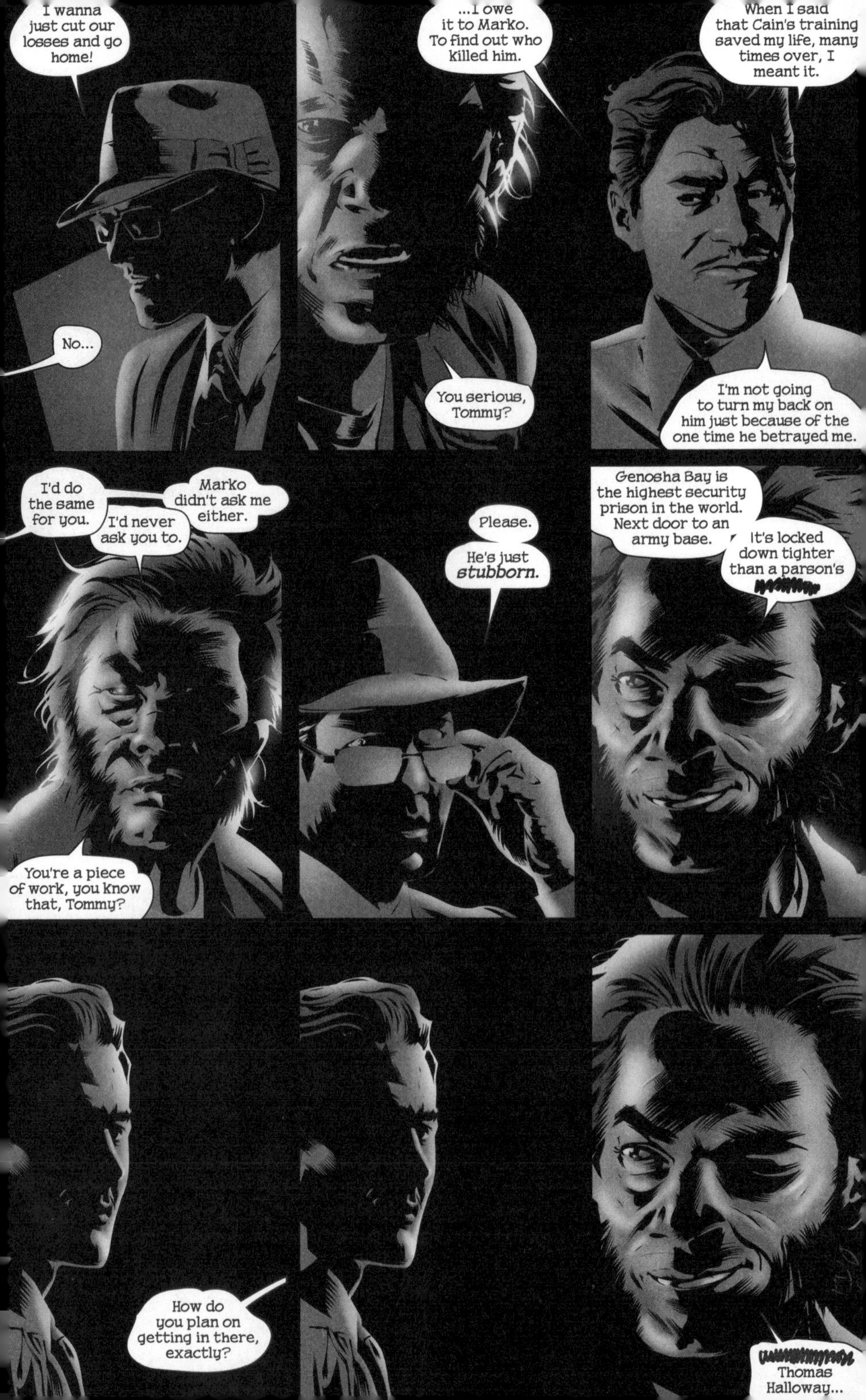
I wanna just cut our losses and go home!
No...
...I owe it to Marko. To find out who killed him.
You serious, Tommy?
When I said that Cain's training saved my life, many times over, I meant it.
I'm not going to turn my back on him just because of the one time he betrayed me.
I'd do the same for you.
I'd never ask you to.
Marko didn't ask me either.
You're a piece of work, you know that, Tommy?
Please.
He's just *stubborn.*
Genosha Bay is the highest security prison in the world. Next door to an army base.
It's locked down tighter than a parson's
How do you plan on getting in there, exactly?
Thomas Halloway...

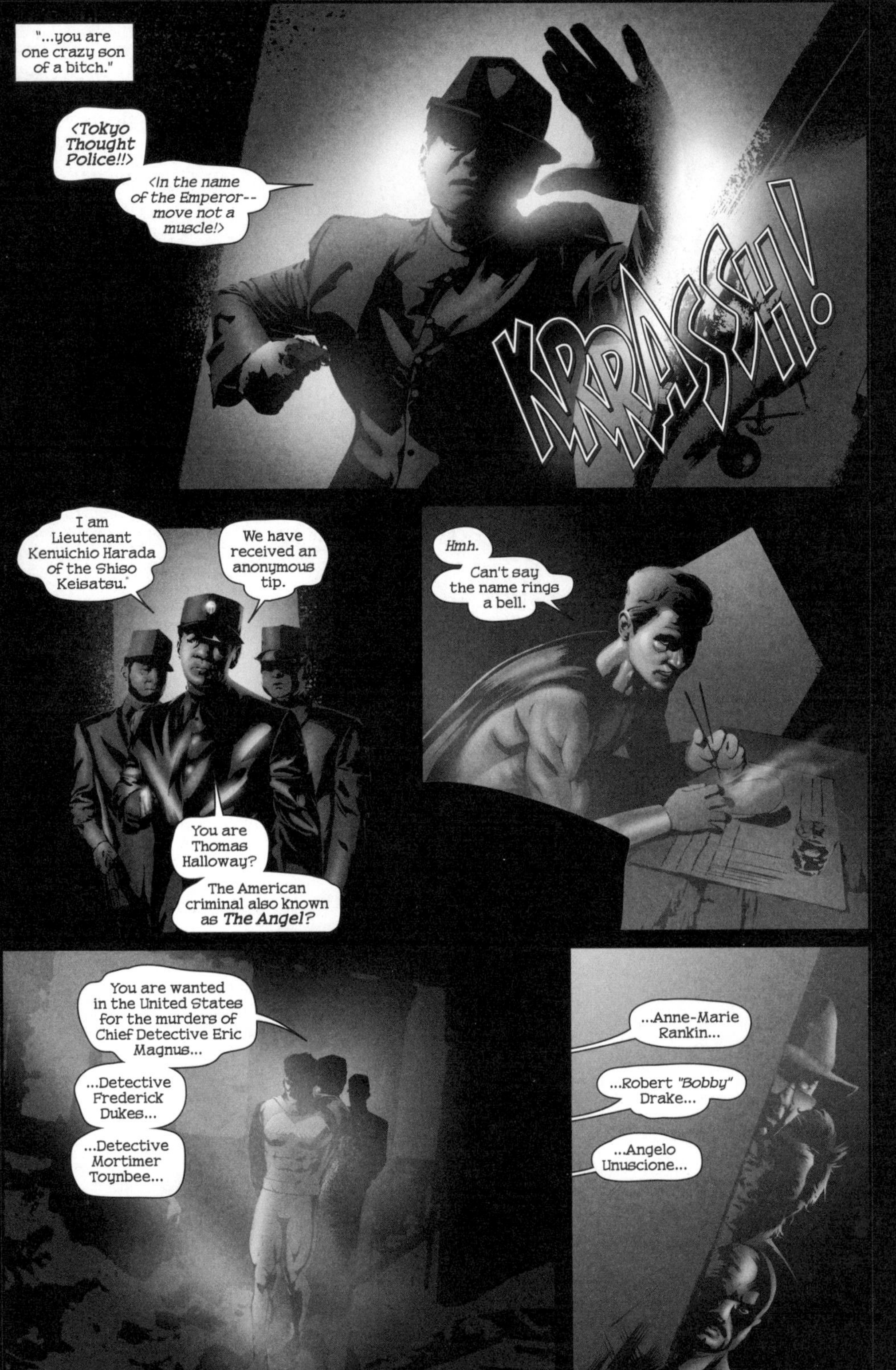
"...you are one crazy son of a bitch."
<Tokyo Thought Police!!>
<In the name of the Emperor--move not a muscle!>
KRRASSHH!
I am Lieutenant Kenuichio Harada of the Shiso Keisatsu.*
We have received an anonymous tip.
You are Thomas Halloway?
The American criminal also known as The Angel?
Hmh.
Can't say the name rings a bell.
You are wanted in the United States for the murders of Chief Detective Eric Magnus...
...Detective Frederick Dukes...
...Detective Mortimer Toynbee...
...Anne-Marie Rankin...
...Robert "Bobby" Drake...
...Angelo Unuscione...

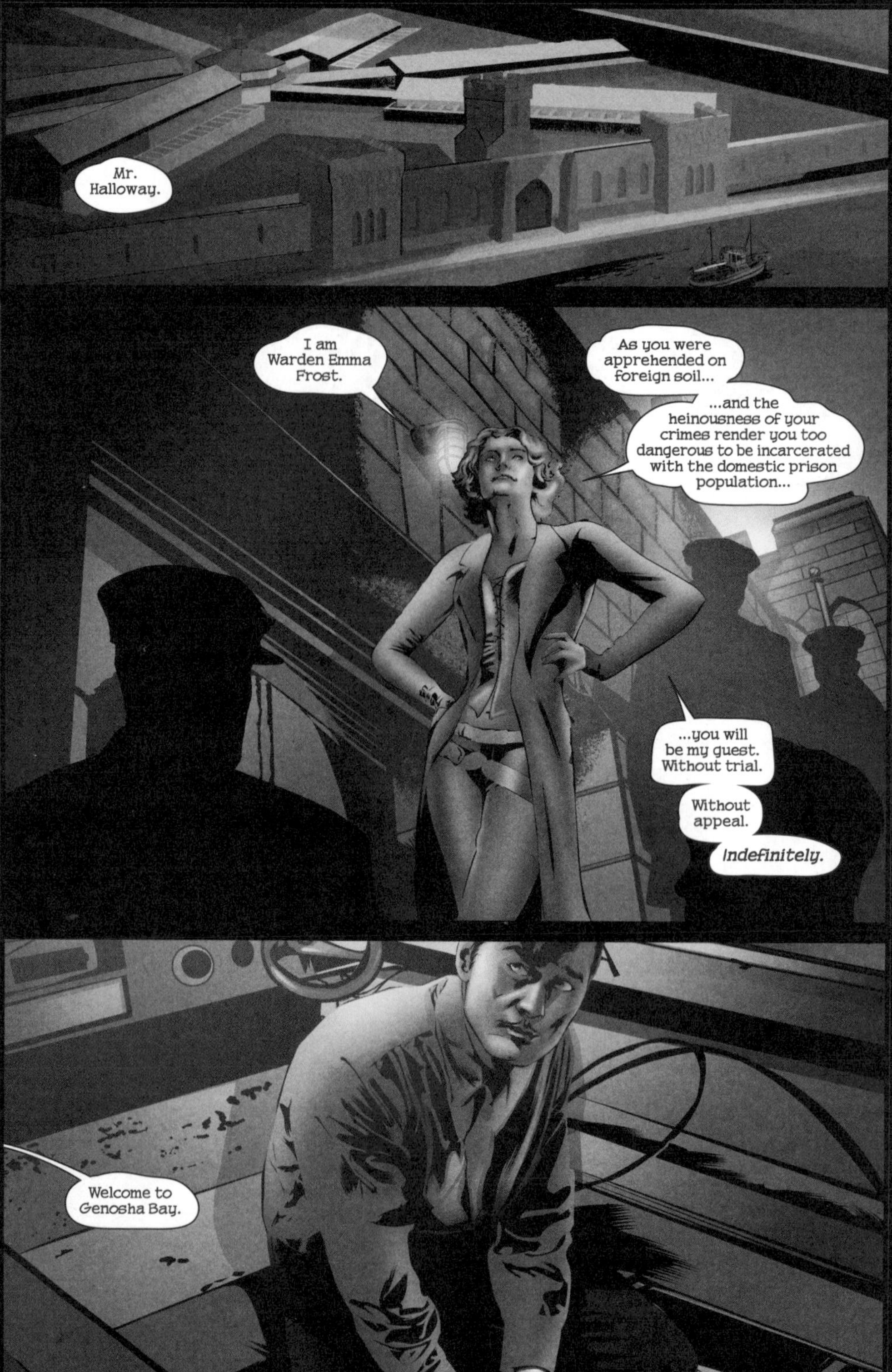
Mr. Halloway.
I am Warden Emma Frost.
As you were apprehended on foreign soil...
...and the heinousness of your crimes render you too dangerous to be incarcerated with the domestic prison population...
...you will be my guest. Without trial.
Without appeal.
Indefinitely.
Welcome to Genosha Bay.

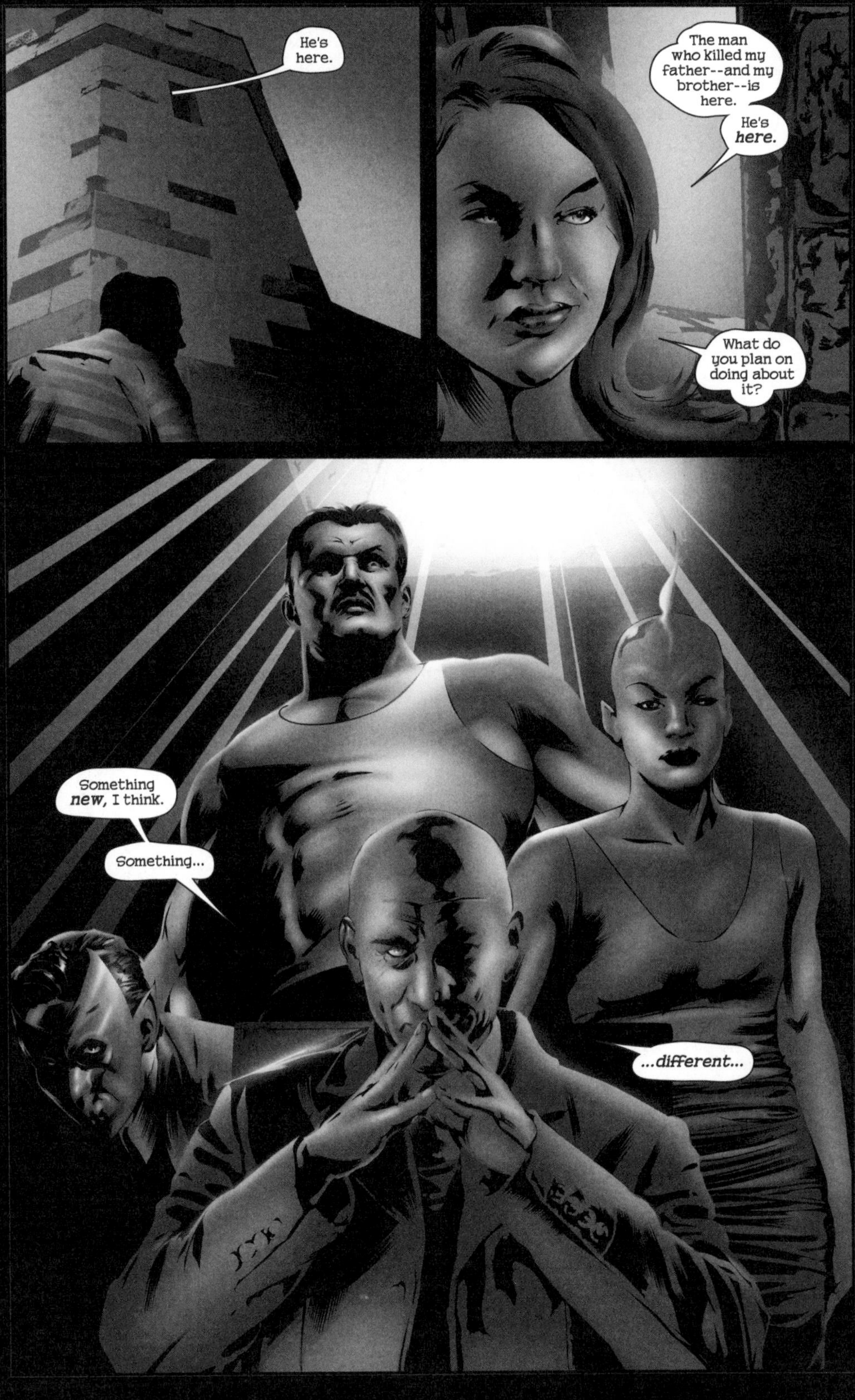
He's here.
The man who killed my father--and my brother--is here.
He's *here.*
What do you plan on doing about it?
Something *new,* I think.
Something...
...*different*...

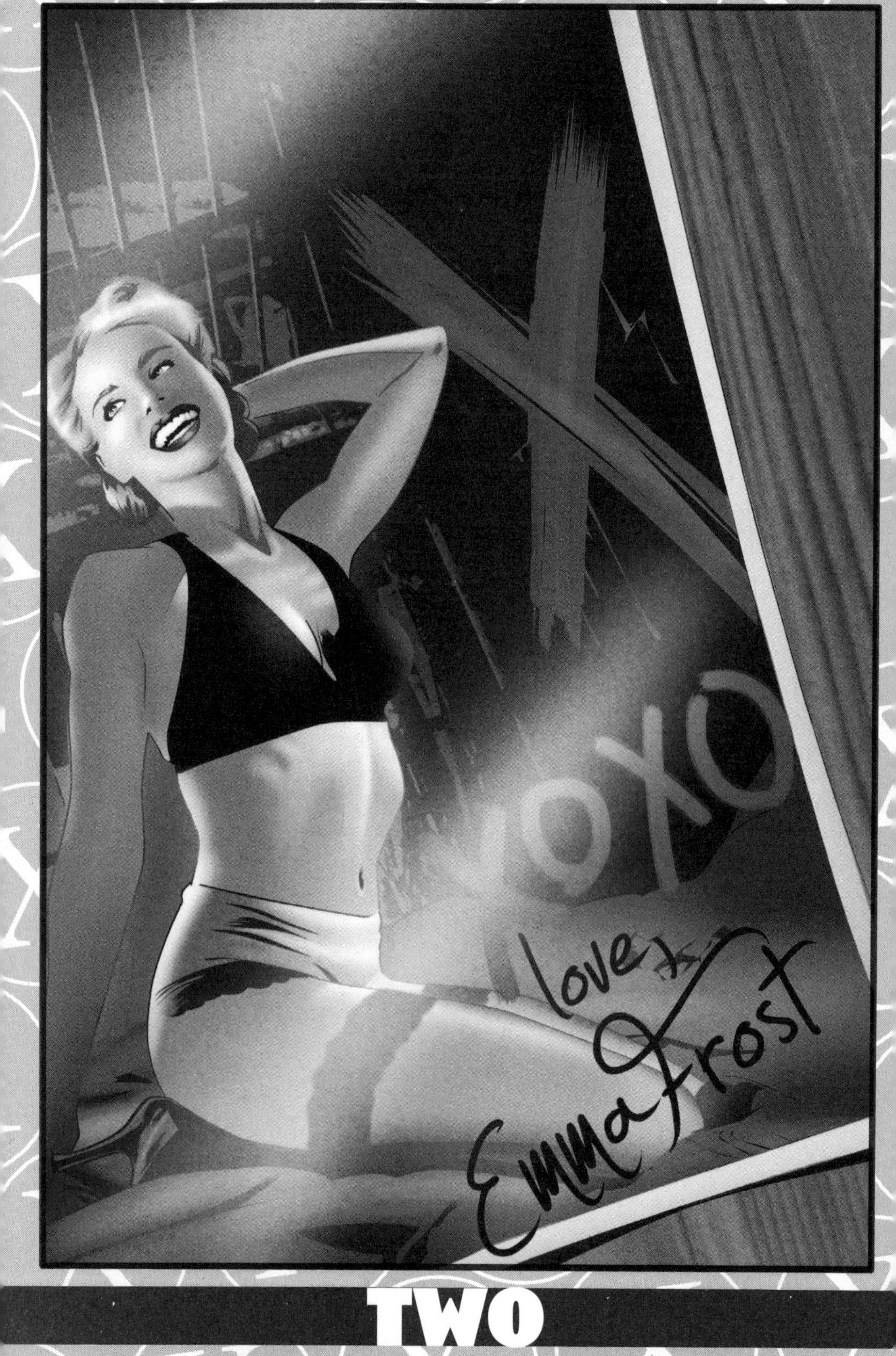
XOXO
love xx
Emma Frost

TWO

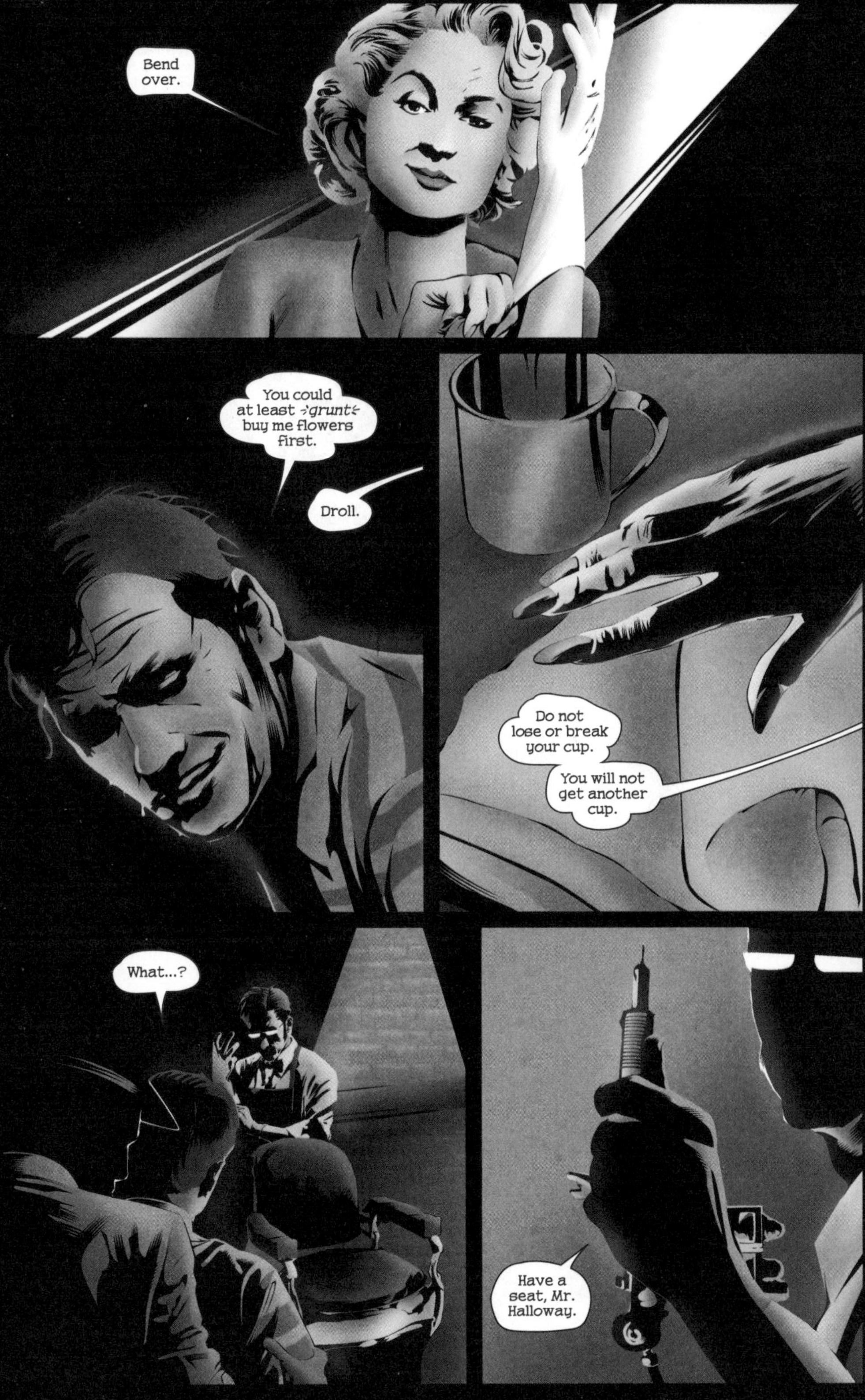
Bend over.
You could at least -:grunt:- buy me flowers first.
Droll.
Do not lose or break your cup.
You will not get another cup.
What...?
Have a seat, Mr. Halloway.

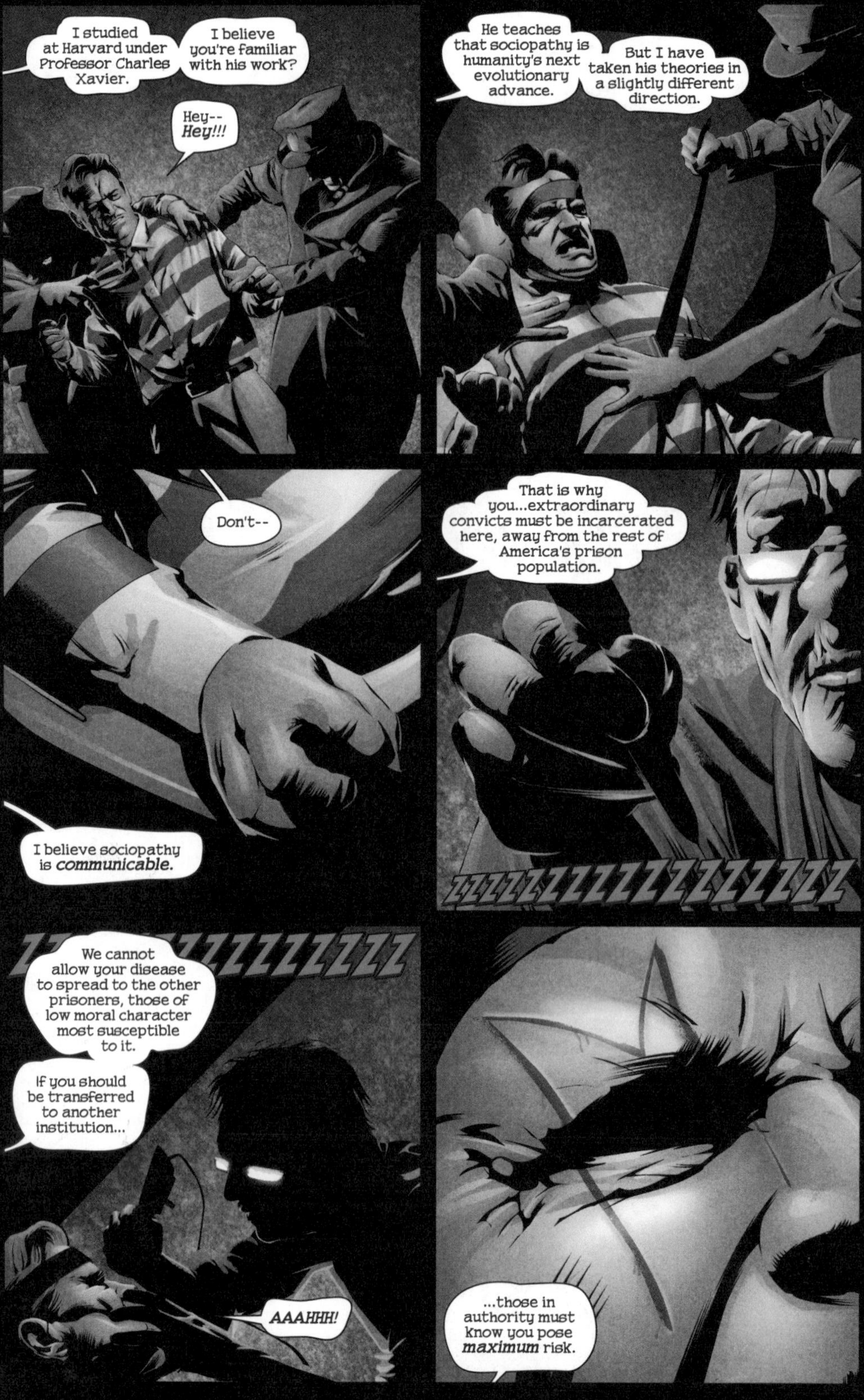

I studied at Harvard under Professor Charles Xavier.
I believe you're familiar with his work?
Hey-- Hey!!!
He teaches that sociopathy is humanity's next evolutionary advance.
But I have taken his theories in a slightly different direction.
Don't--
I believe sociopathy is communicable.
That is why you...extraordinary convicts must be incarcerated here, away from the rest of America's prison population.
ZZZZZZZZZZZZZZZZZ
ZZZZZZZZZZZZZZZ
We cannot allow your disease to spread to the other prisoners, those of low moral character most susceptible to it.
If you should be transferred to another institution...
AAAHHH!
...those in authority must know you pose maximum risk.

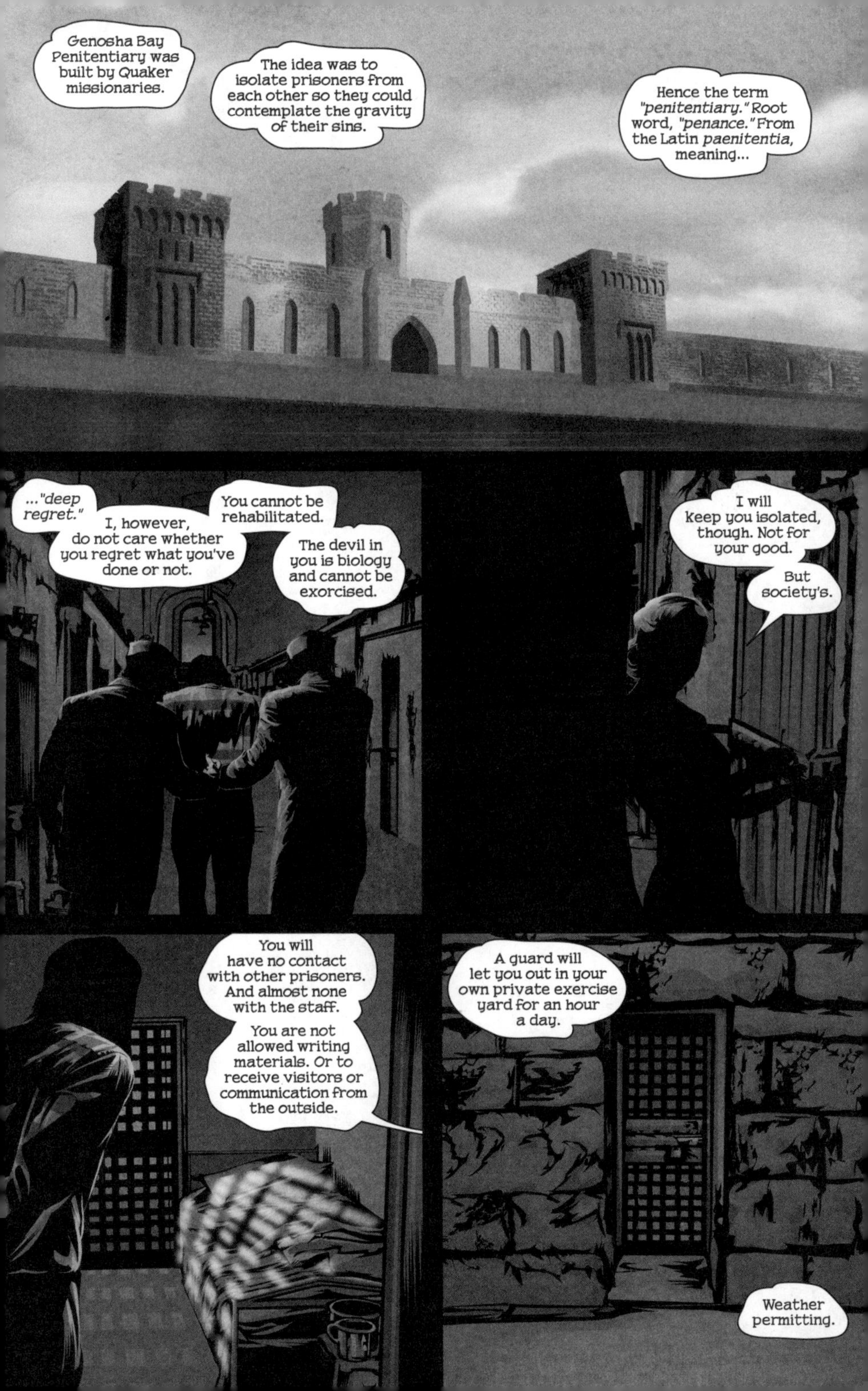
Genosha Bay Penitentiary was built by Quaker missionaries.
The idea was to isolate prisoners from each other so they could contemplate the gravity of their sins.
Hence the term *"penitentiary."* Root word, *"penance."* From the Latin *paenitentia*, meaning...
...*"deep regret."*
I, however, do not care whether you regret what you've done or not.
You cannot be rehabilitated.
The devil in you is biology and cannot be exorcised.
I will keep you isolated, though. Not for your good.
But society's.
You will have no contact with other prisoners. And almost none with the staff.
You are not allowed writing materials. Or to receive visitors or communication from the outside.
A guard will let you out in your own private exercise yard for an hour a day.
Weather permitting.

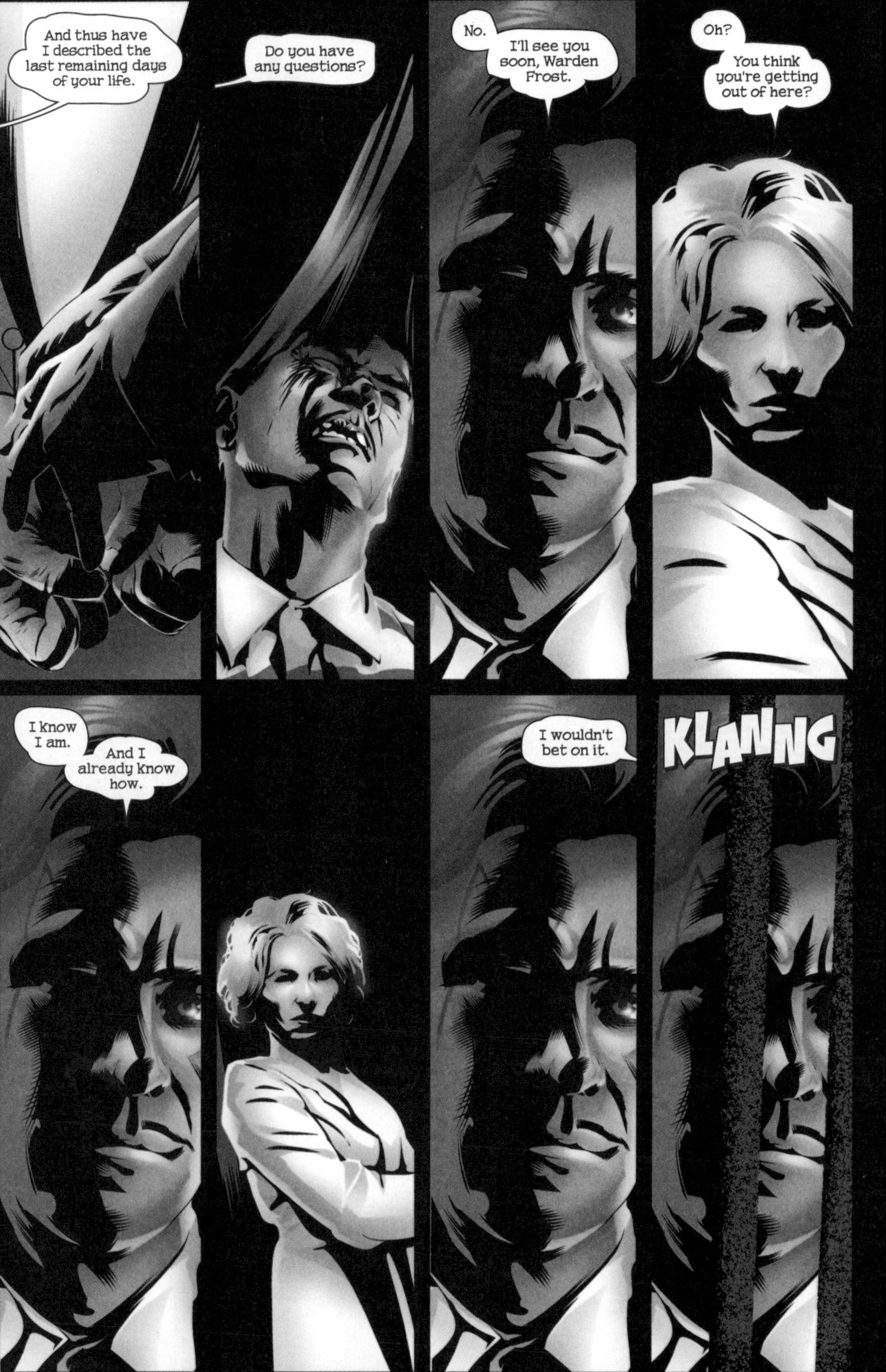
And thus have I described the last remaining days of your life.
Do you have any questions?
No.
I'll see you soon, Warden Frost.
Oh?
You think you're getting out of here?
I know I am.
And I already know how.
I wouldn't bet on it.
KLANNG

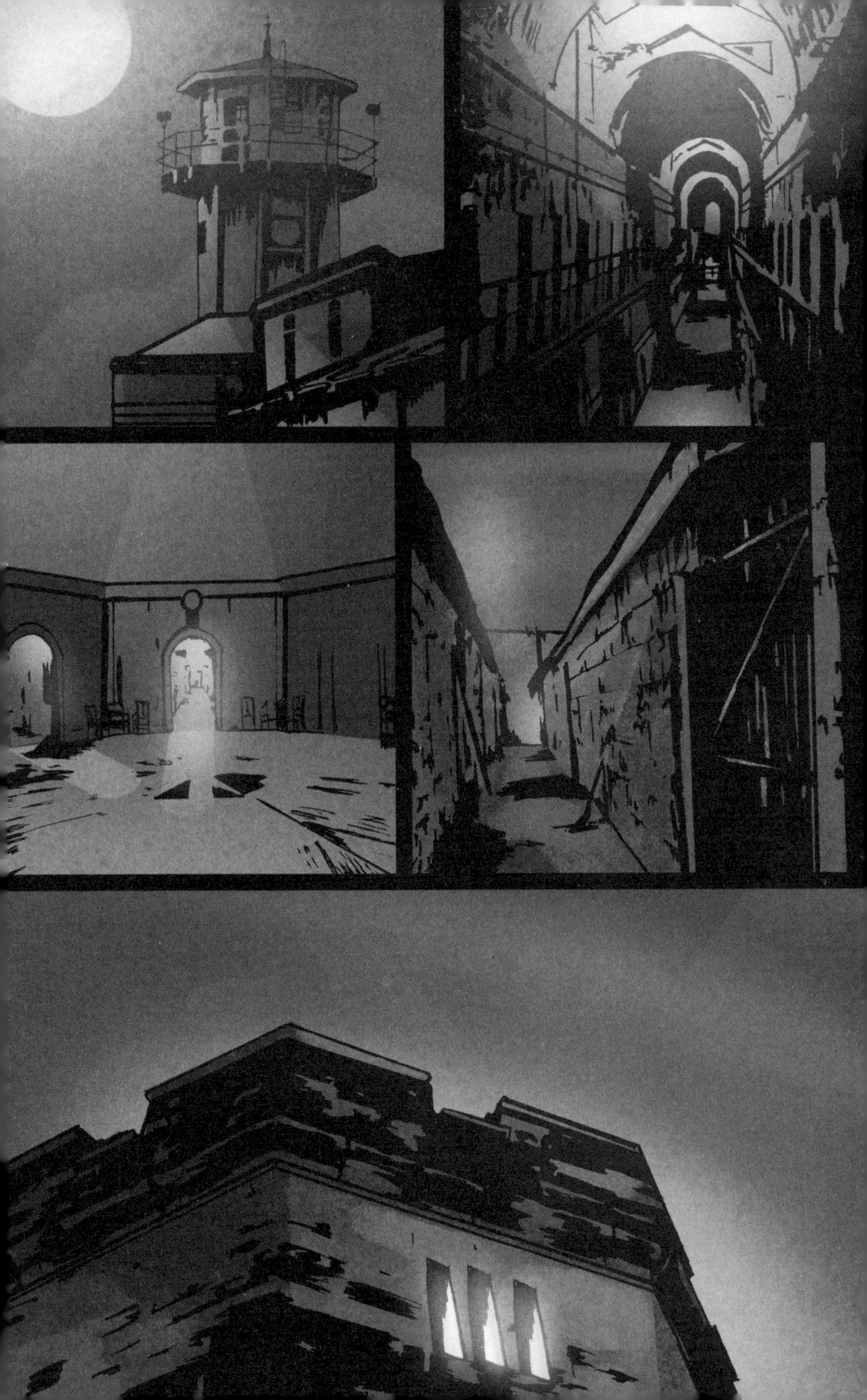

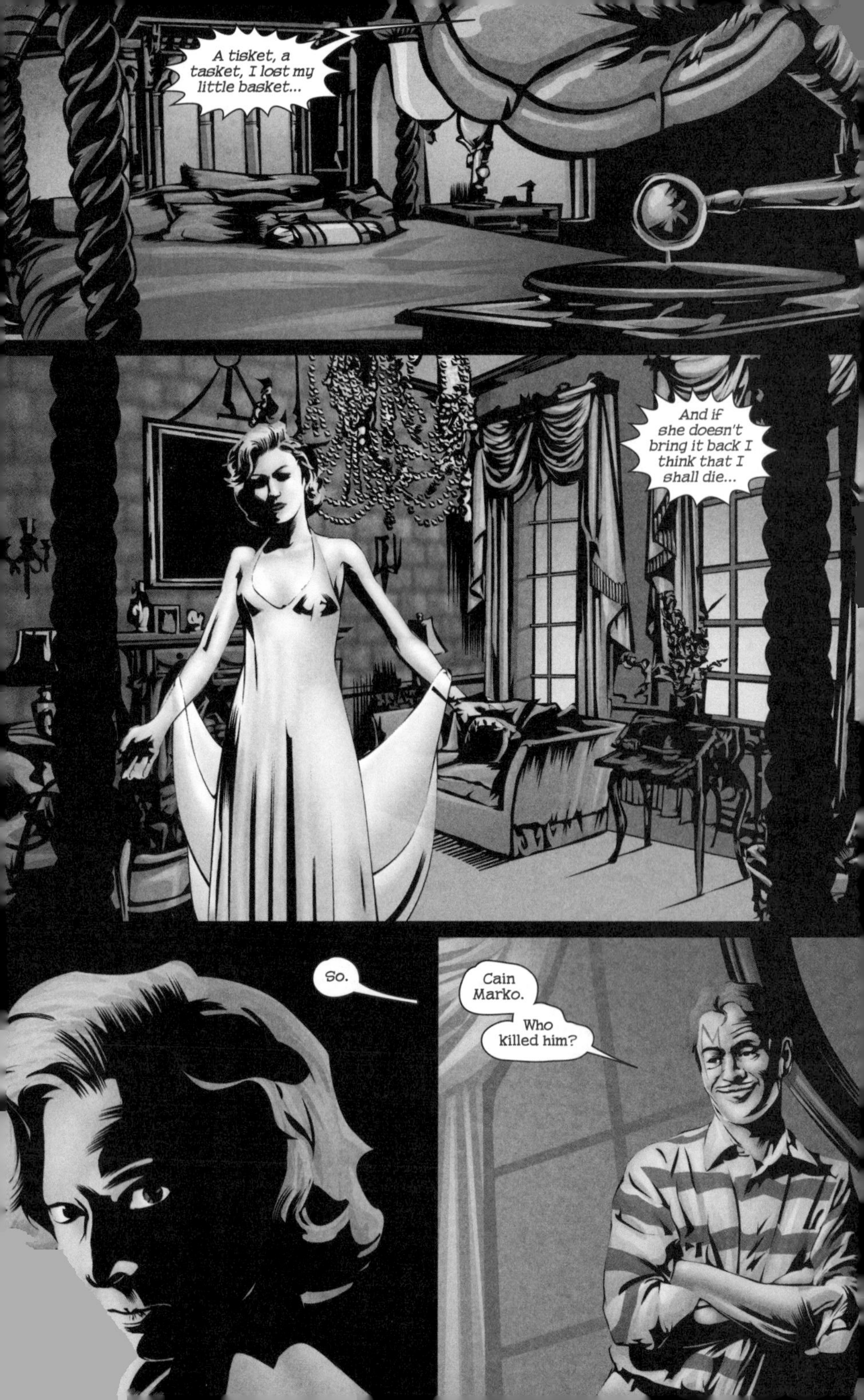
A tisket, a tasket, I lost my little basket...
And if she doesn't bring it back I think that I shall die...
So.
Cain Marko.
Who killed him?

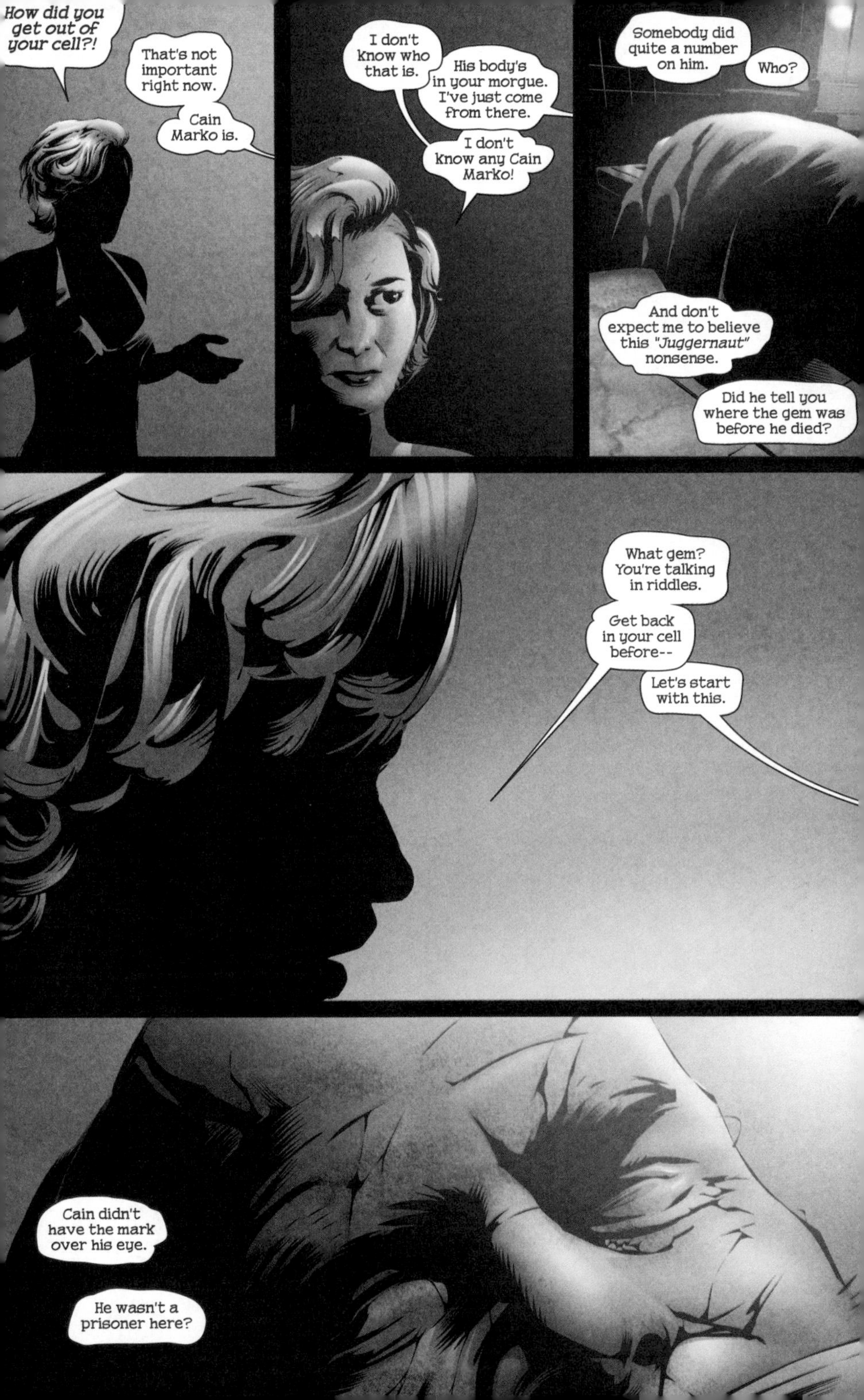
How did you get out of your cell?!
That's not important right now.
Cain Marko is.
I don't know who that is.
His body's in your morgue. I've just come from there.
I don't know any Cain Marko!
Somebody did quite a number on him.
Who?
And don't expect me to believe this "Juggernaut" nonsense.
Did he tell you where the gem was before he died?
What gem? You're talking in riddles.
Get back in your cell before--
Let's start with this.
Cain didn't have the mark over his eye.
He wasn't a prisoner here?

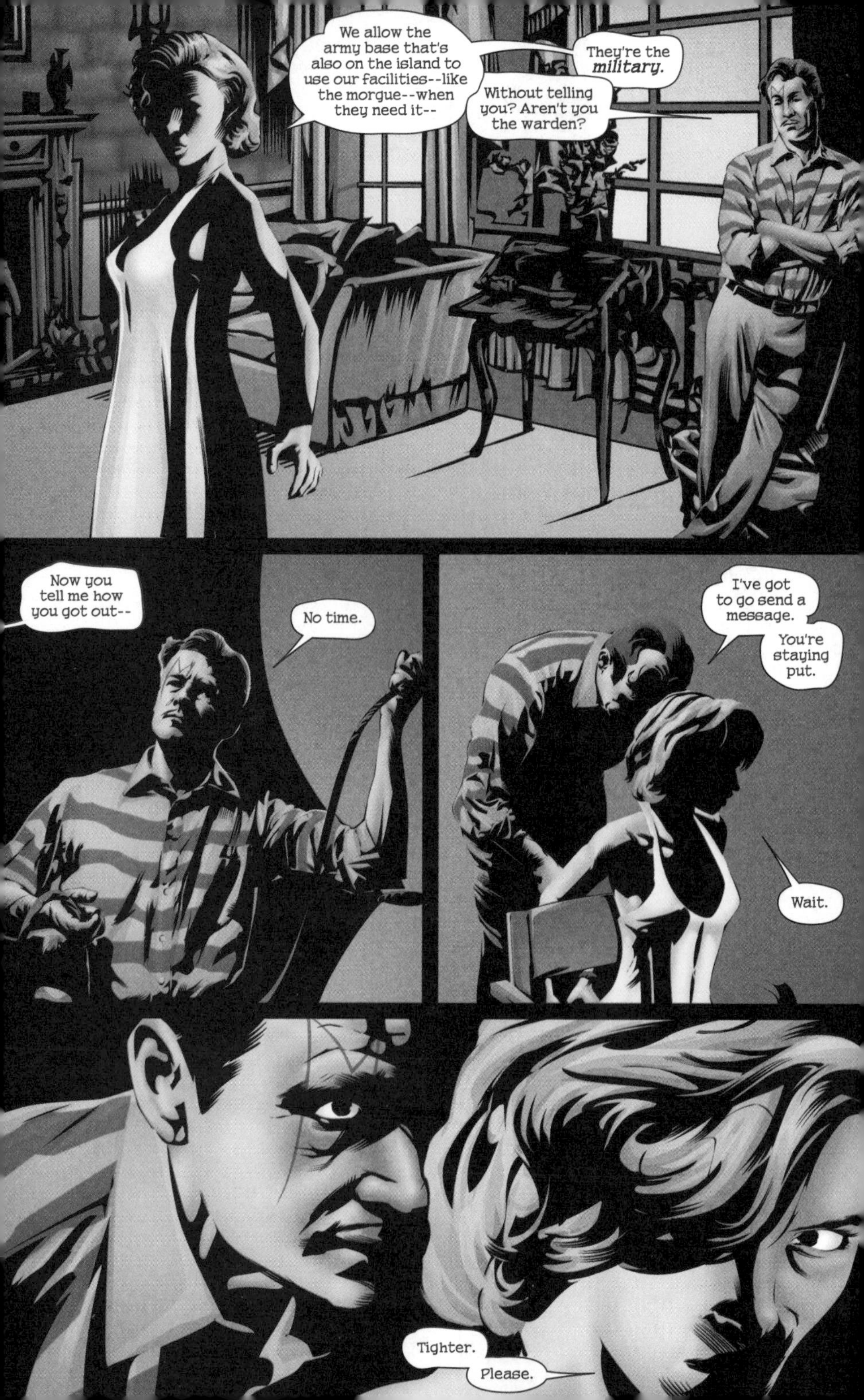
We allow the army base that's also on the island to use our facilities--like the morgue--when they need it--
They're the *military*.
Without telling you? Aren't you the warden?
Now you tell me how you got out--
No time.
I've got to go send a message.
You're staying put.
Wait.
Tighter.
Please.

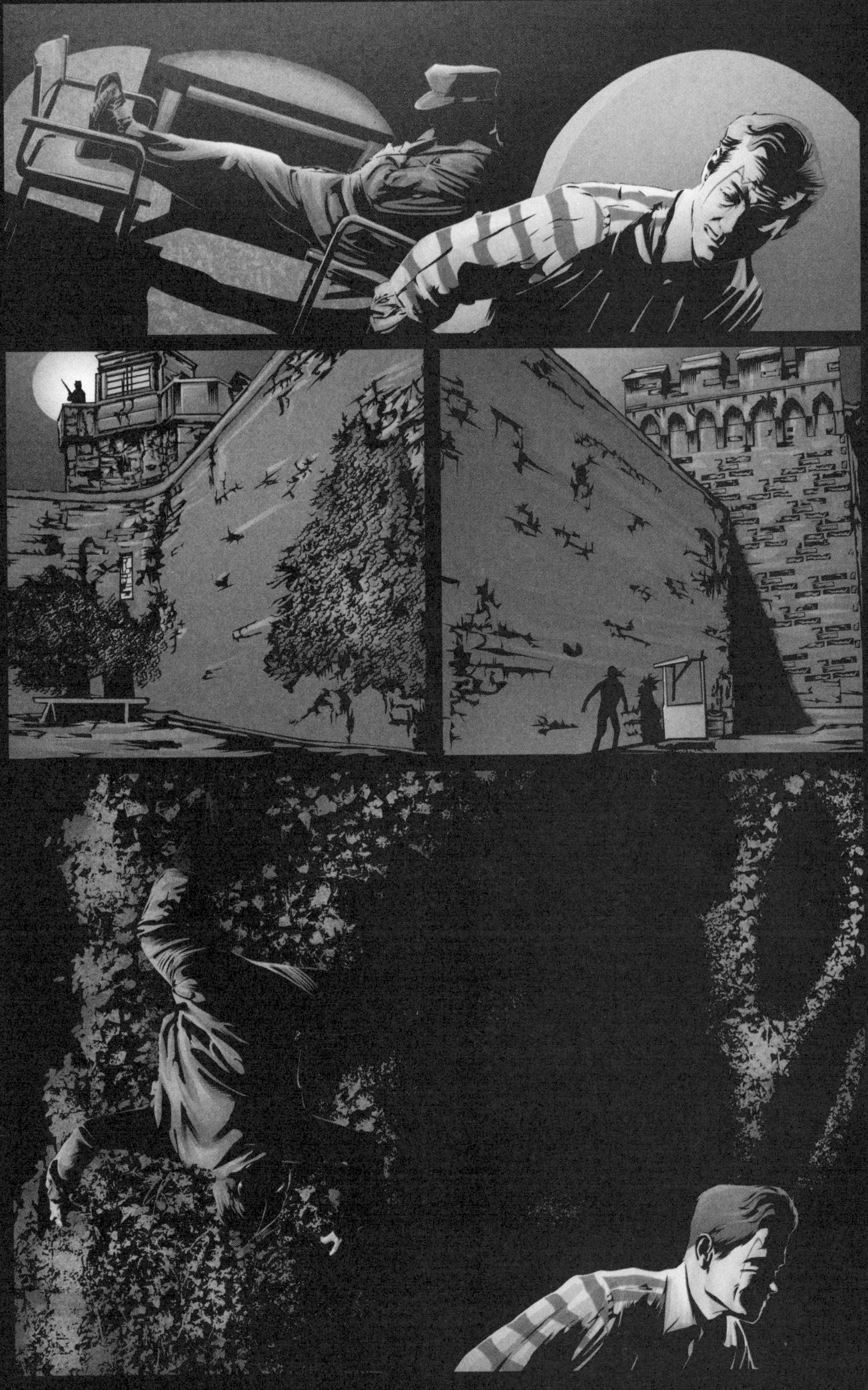

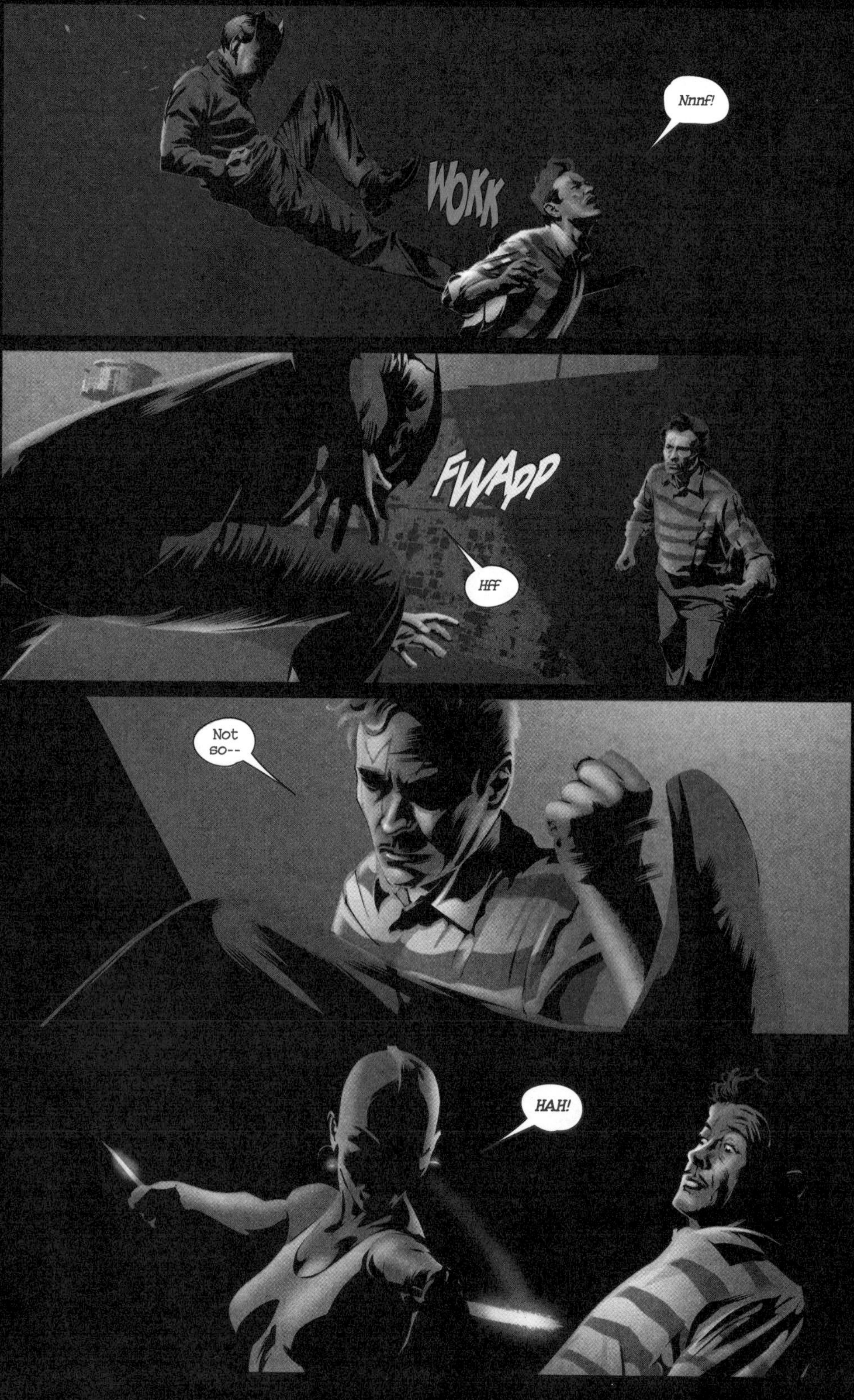
Nnnf!
WOKK
FWAPP
Hff
Not so--
HAH!

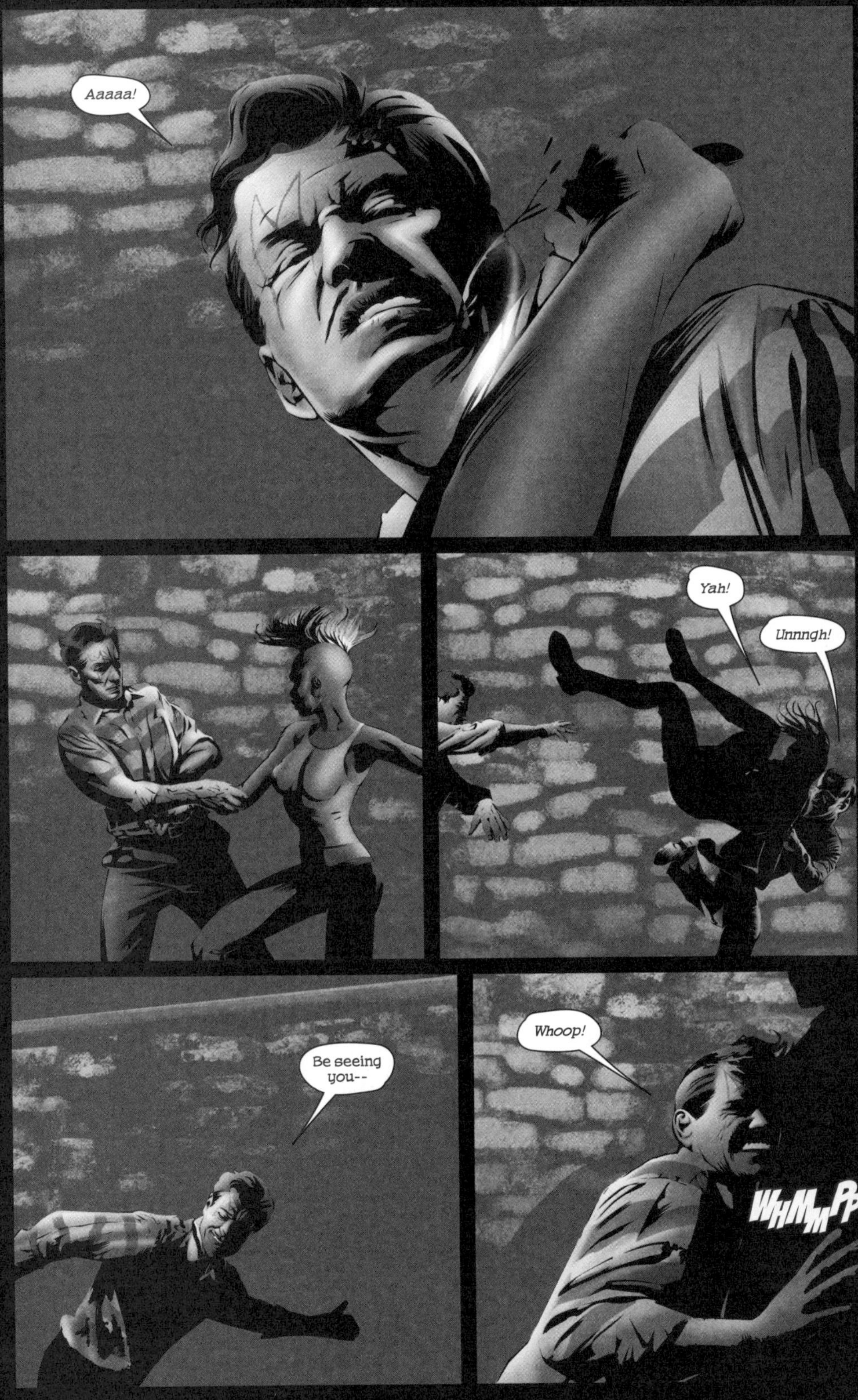
Aaaaa!
Yah!
Unnngh!
Be seeing you--
Whoop!
WHMMPP

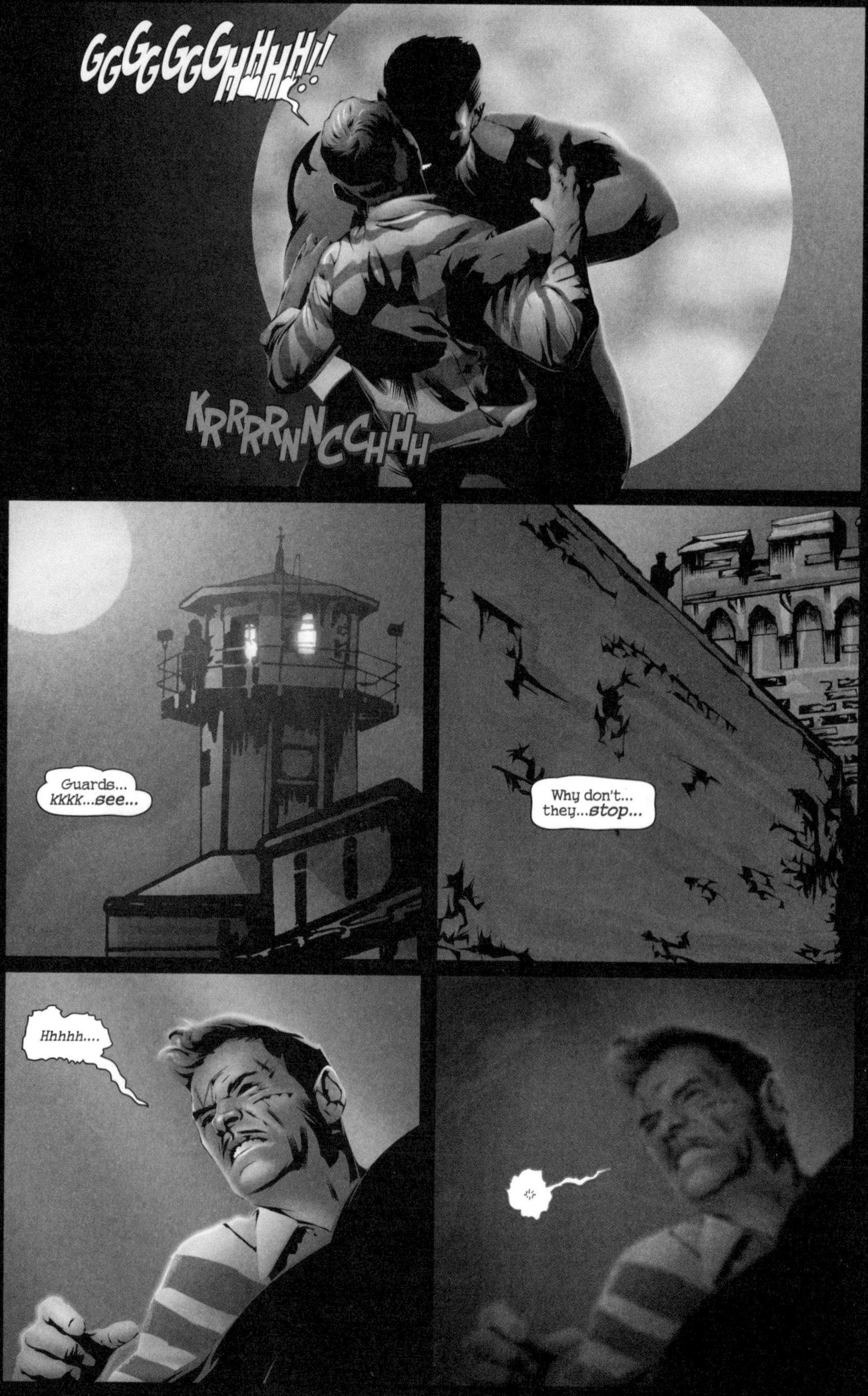
GGGGGGHHHH!!
KRRRRNNCCHHHH
Guards... kkkk...see...
Why don't... they...stop...
Hhhhh....

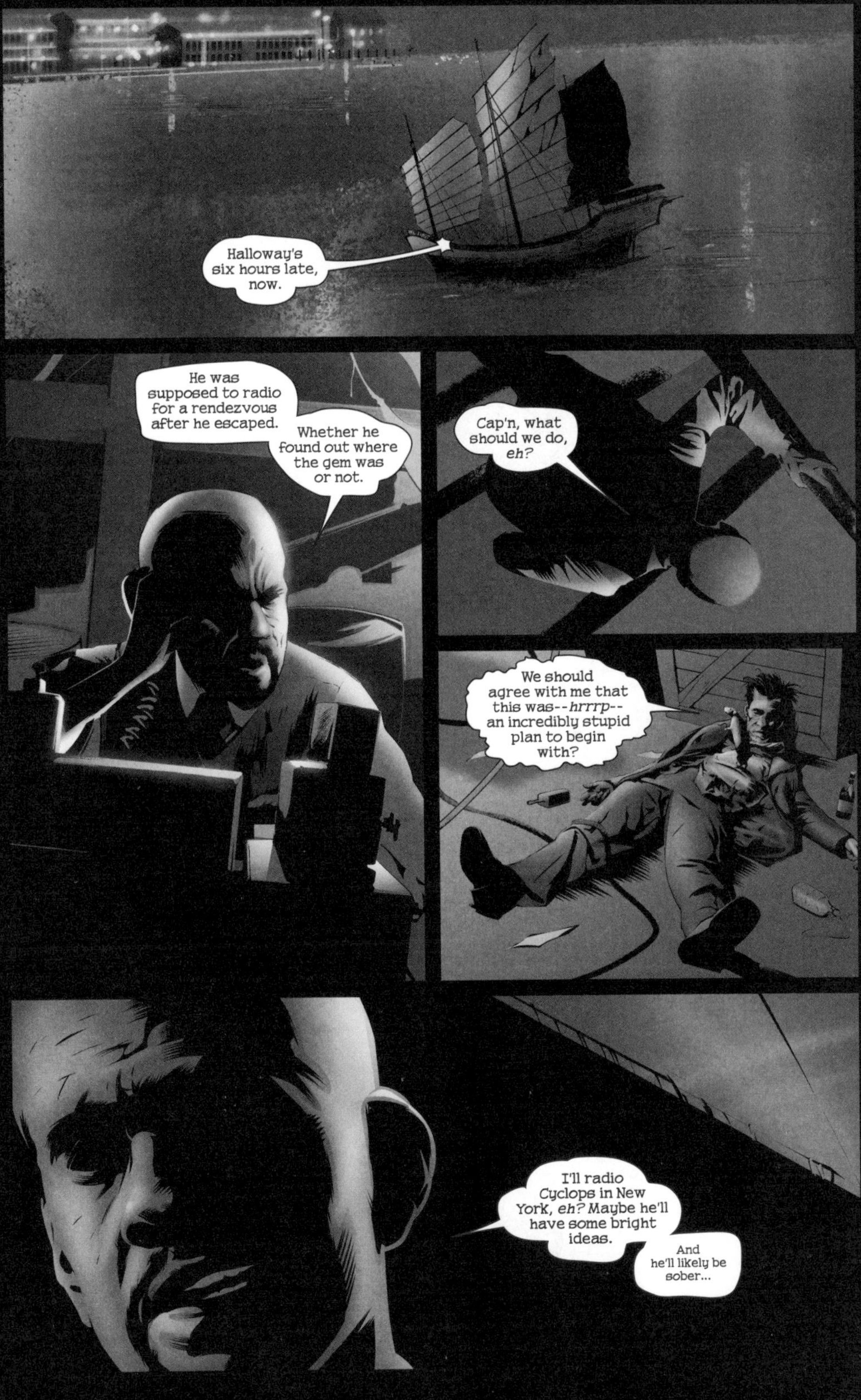
Halloway's six hours late, now.
He was supposed to radio for a rendezvous after he escaped.
Whether he found out where the gem was or not.
Cap'n, what should we do, *eh?*
We should agree with me that this was--*hrrrp*--an incredibly stupid plan to begin with?
I'll radio Cyclops in New York, *eh?* Maybe he'll have some bright ideas.
And he'll likely be sober...

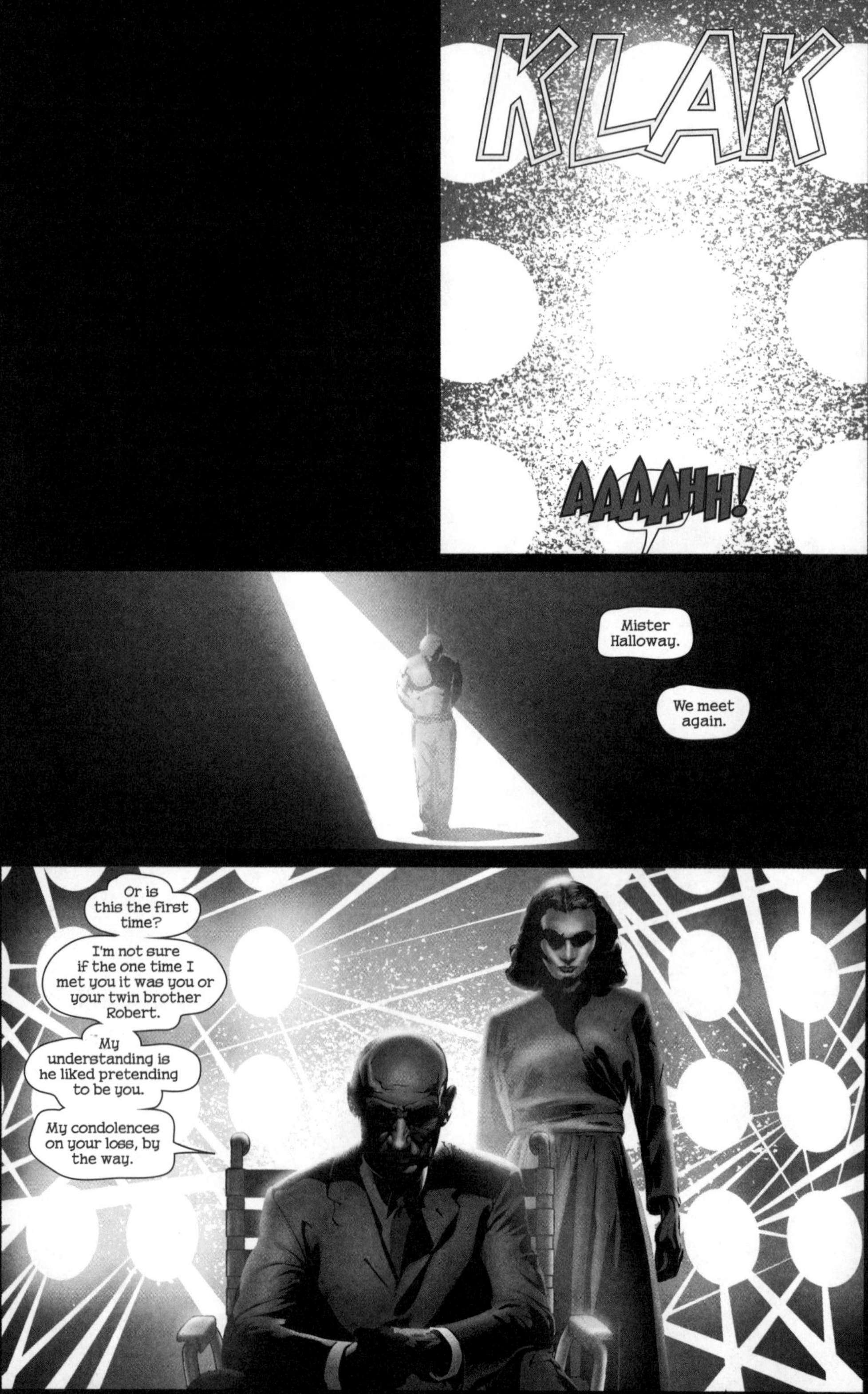
KLAK
AAAAHH!
Mister Halloway.
We meet again.
Or is this the first time?
I'm not sure if the one time I met you it was you or your twin brother Robert.
My understanding is he liked pretending to be you.
My condolences on your loss, by the way.

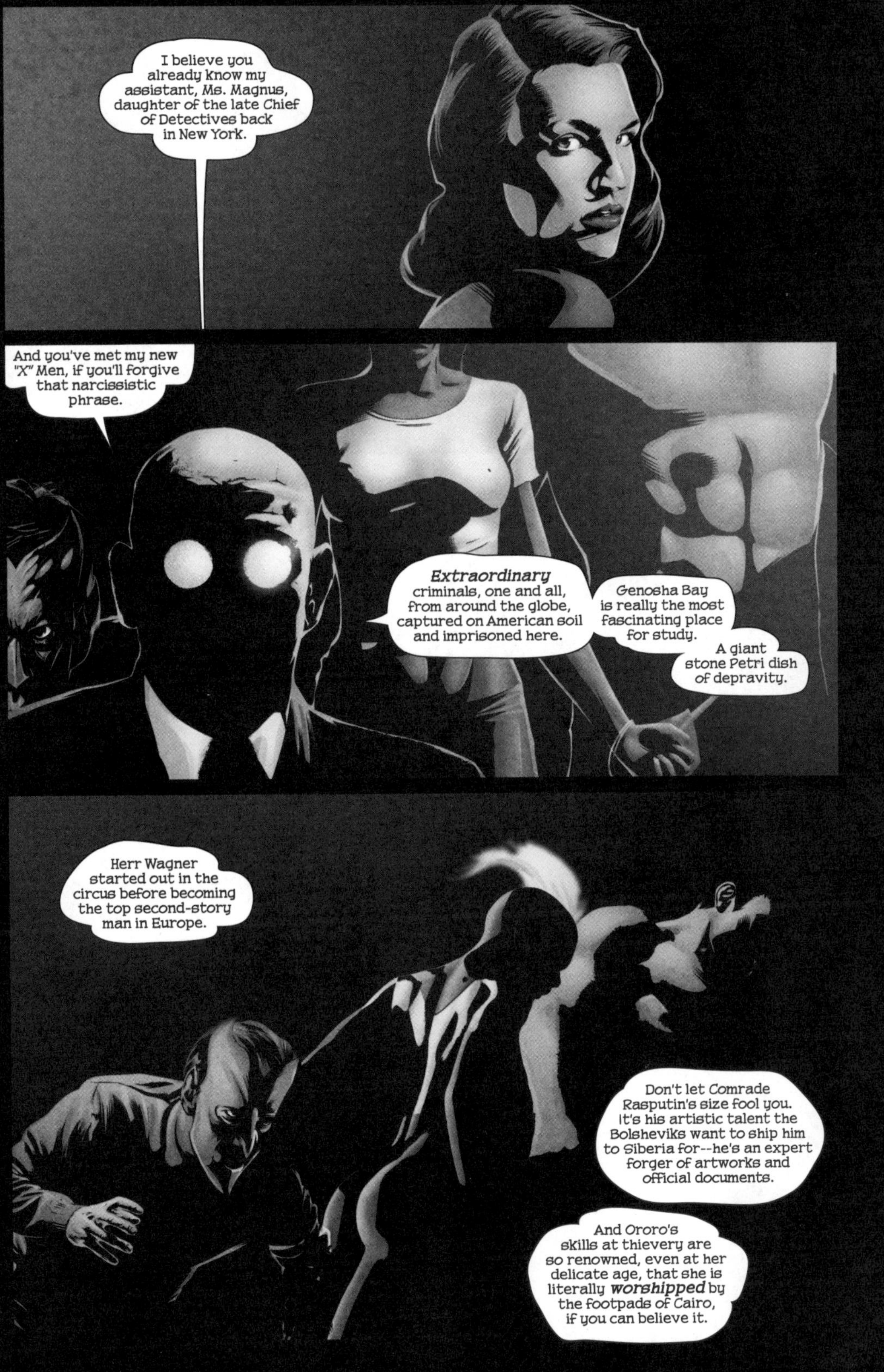

I believe you already know my assistant, Ms. Magnus, daughter of the late Chief of Detectives back in New York.
And you've met my new "X" Men, if you'll forgive that narcissistic phrase.
Extraordinary criminals, one and all, from around the globe, captured on American soil and imprisoned here.
Genosha Bay is really the most fascinating place for study.
A giant stone Petri dish of depravity.
Herr Wagner started out in the circus before becoming the top second-story man in Europe.
Don't let Comrade Rasputin's size fool you. It's his artistic talent the Bolsheviks want to ship him to Siberia for--he's an expert forger of artworks and official documents.
And Ororo's skills at thievery are so renowned, even at her delicate age, that she is literally *worshipped* by the footpads of Cairo, if you can believe it.

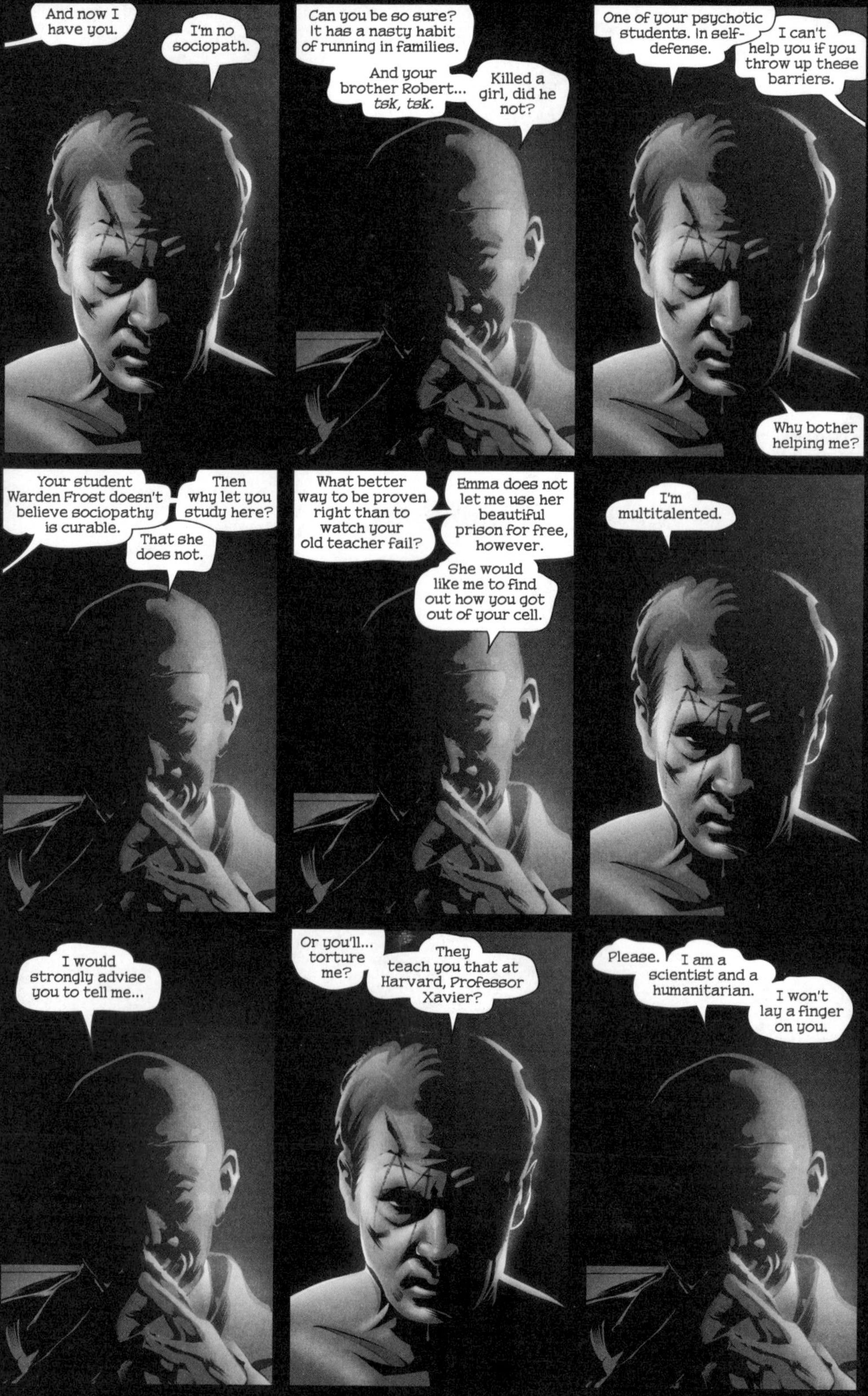
And now I have you.
I'm no sociopath.
Can you be so sure? It has a nasty habit of running in families.
And your brother Robert... *tsk, tsk.*
Killed a girl, did he not?
One of your psychotic students. In self-defense.
I can't help you if you throw up these barriers.
Why bother helping me?
Your student Warden Frost doesn't believe sociopathy is curable.
Then why let you study here?
That she does not.
What better way to be proven right than to watch your old teacher fail?
Emma does not let me use her beautiful prison for free, however.
She would like me to find out how you got out of your cell.
I'm multitalented.
I would strongly advise you to tell me...
Or you'll... torture me?
They teach you that at Harvard, Professor Xavier?
Please.
I am a scientist and a humanitarian.
I won't lay a finger on you.

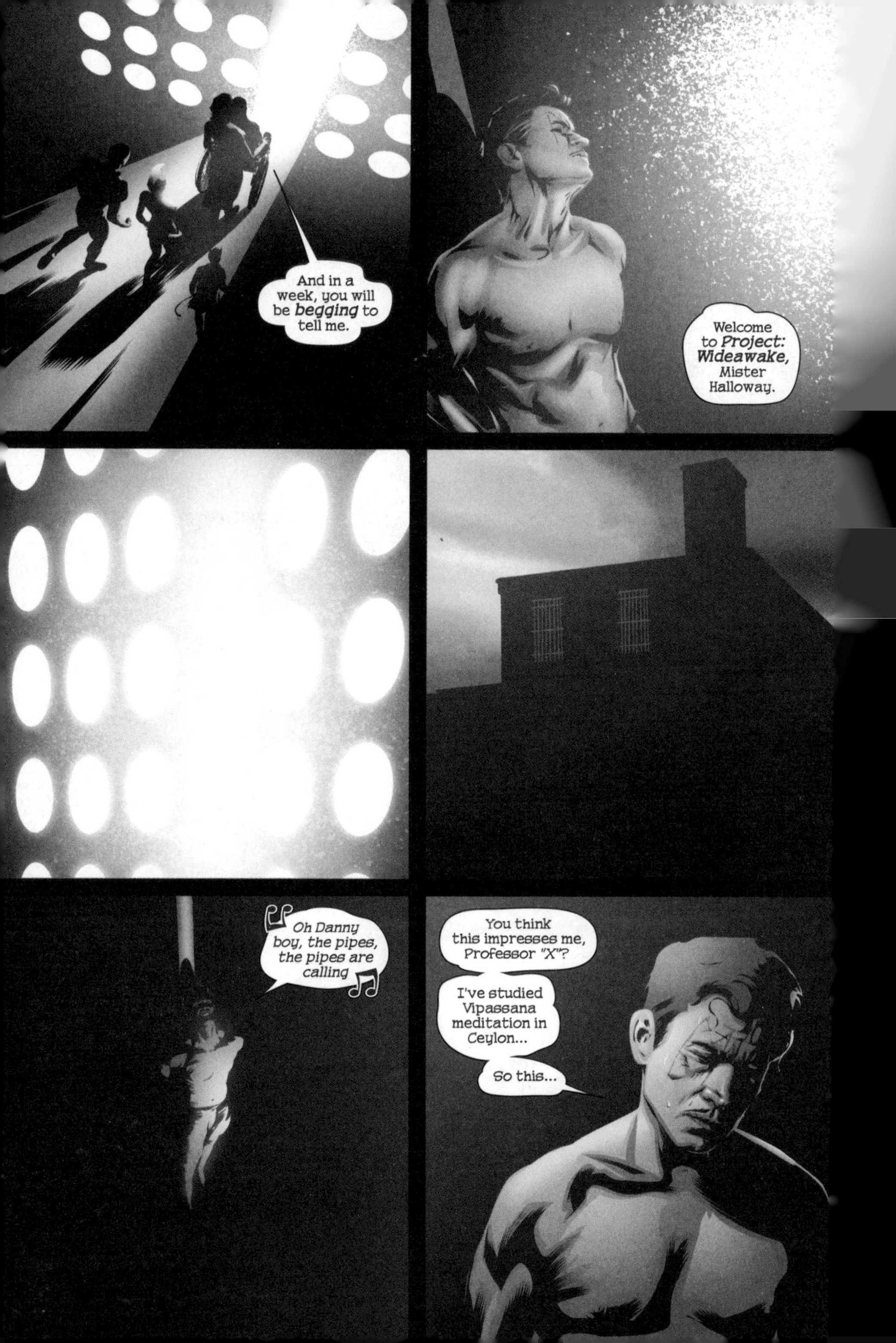
And in a week, you will be *begging* to tell me.
Welcome to *Project: Wideawake,* Mister Halloway.
Oh Danny boy, the pipes, the pipes are calling
You think this impresses me, Professor "X"?
I've studied Vipassana meditation in Ceylon...
So this...

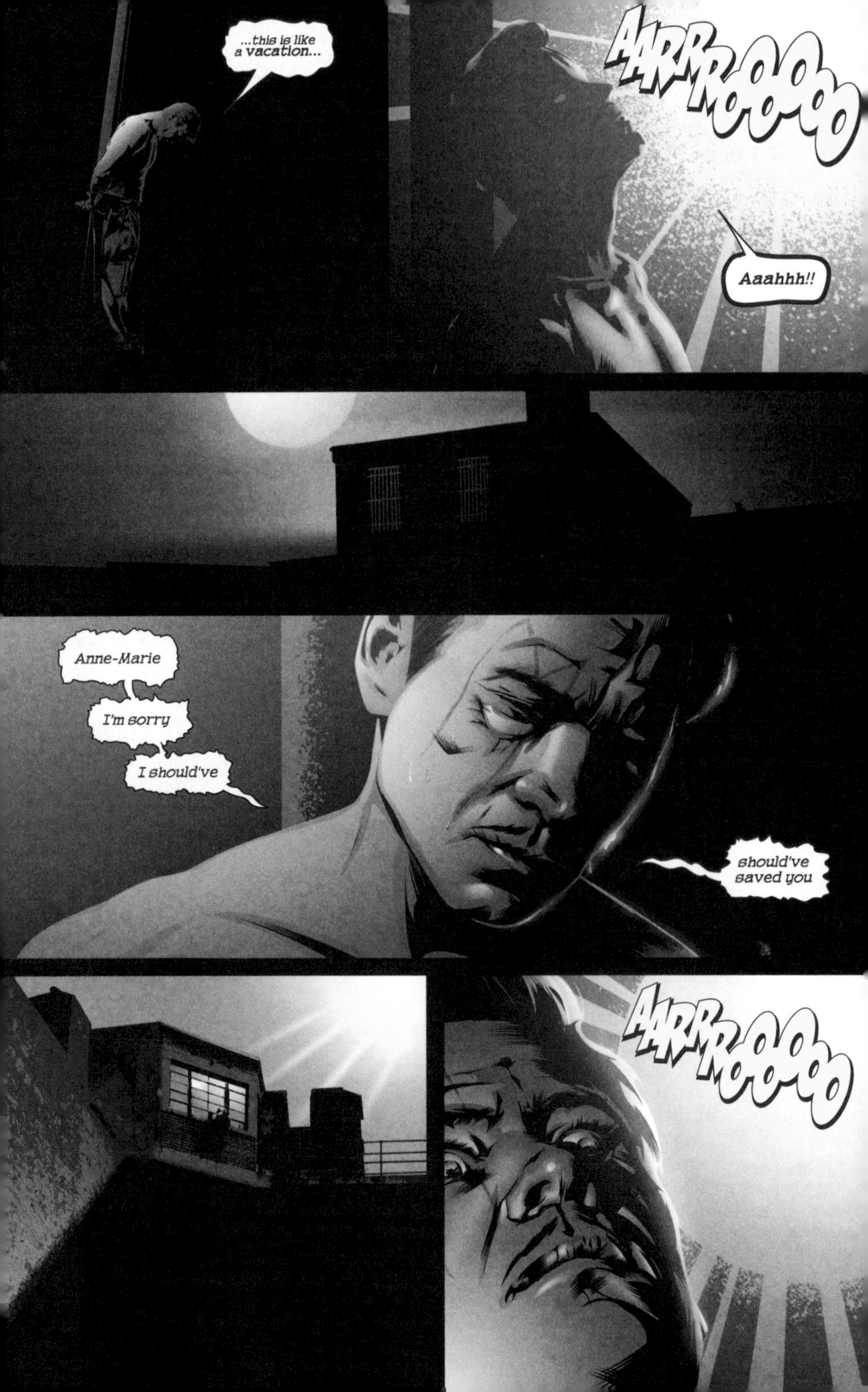
...this is like a vacation...
AARRROOOOOO
Aaahhh!!
Anne-Marie
I'm sorry
I should've
should've saved you
AARRROOOOOO

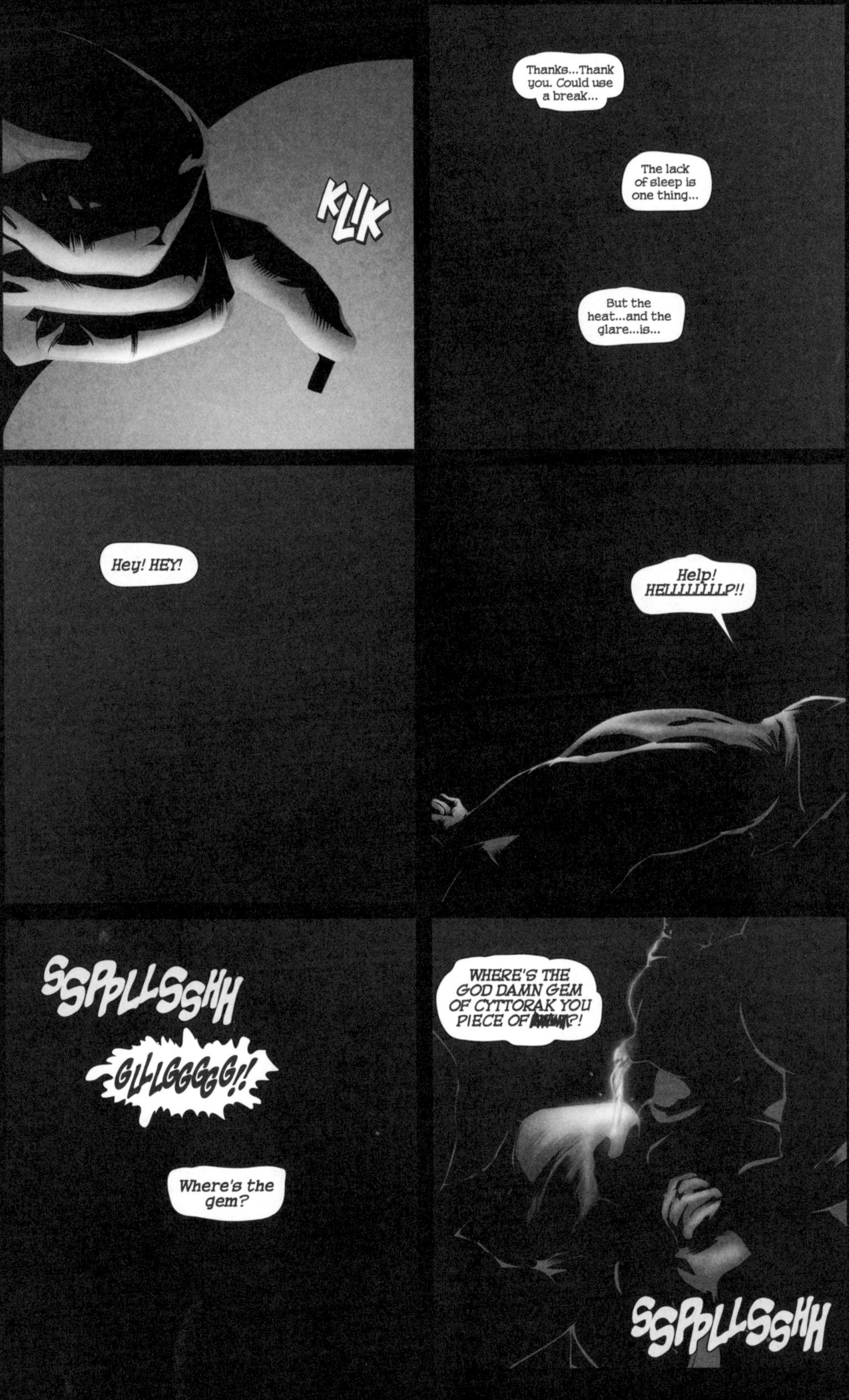
KLIK
Thanks...Thank you. Could use a break...
The lack of sleep is one thing...
But the heat...and the glare...is...
Hey! HEY!
Help! HELLLLLLLLP!!
SSPPLLSSHH
GLLLGGGGG!!
Where's the gem?
WHERE'S THE GOD DAMN GEM OF CYTTORAK YOU PIECE OF [redacted]?!
SSPPLLSSHH

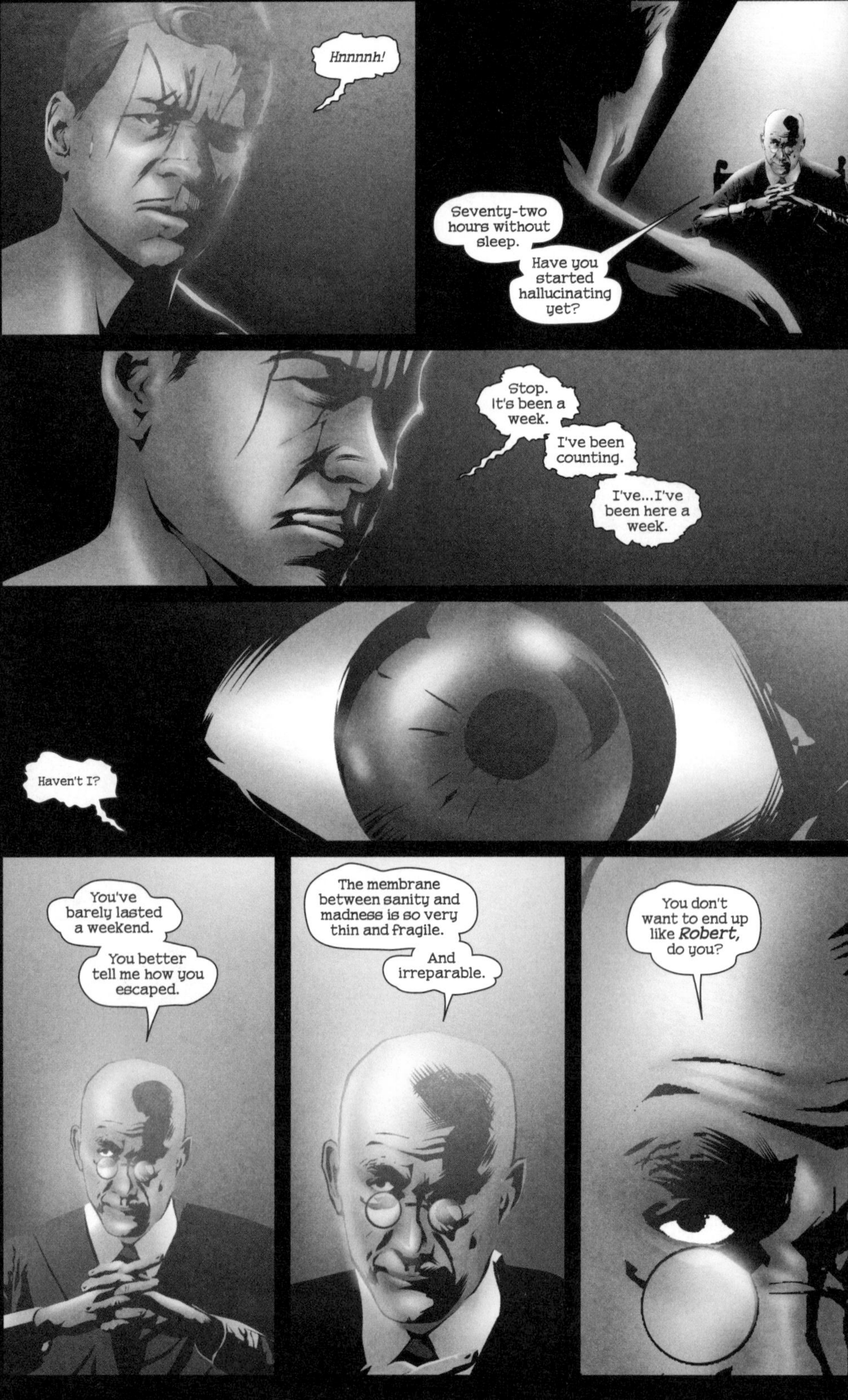
Hnnnnh!
Seventy-two hours without sleep.
Have you started hallucinating yet?
Stop. It's been a week.
I've been counting.
I've...I've been here a week.
Haven't I?
You've barely lasted a weekend.
You better tell me how you escaped.
The membrane between sanity and madness is so very thin and fragile.
And irreparable.
You don't want to end up like *Robert,* do you?

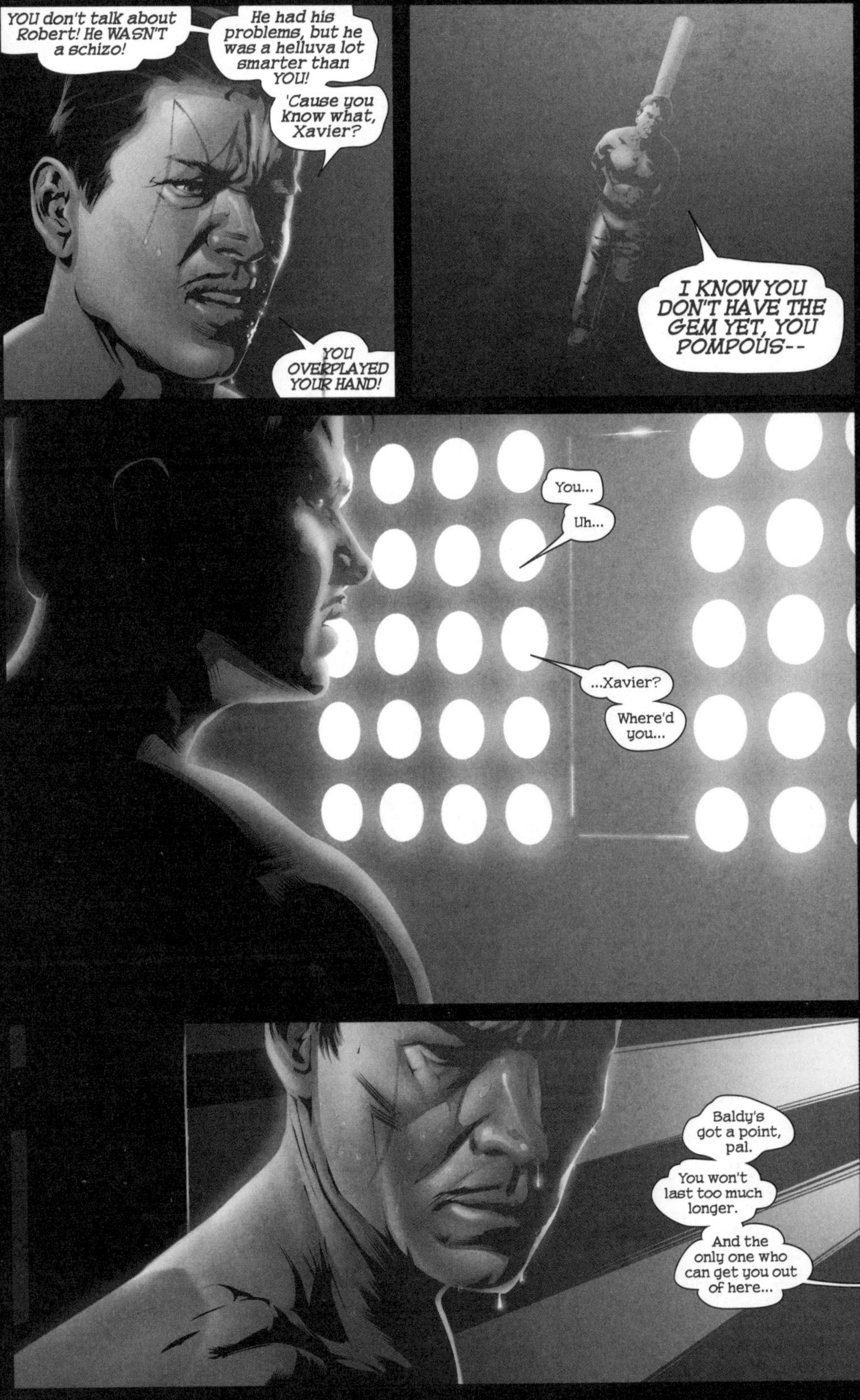
YOU don't talk about Robert! He WASN'T a schizo!
He had his problems, but he was a helluva lot smarter than YOU!
'Cause you know what, Xavier?
YOU OVERPLAYED YOUR HAND!
I KNOW YOU DON'T HAVE THE GEM YET, YOU POMPOUS--
You...
Uh...
...Xavier?
Where'd you...
Baldy's got a point, pal.
You won't last too much longer.
And the only one who can get you out of here...

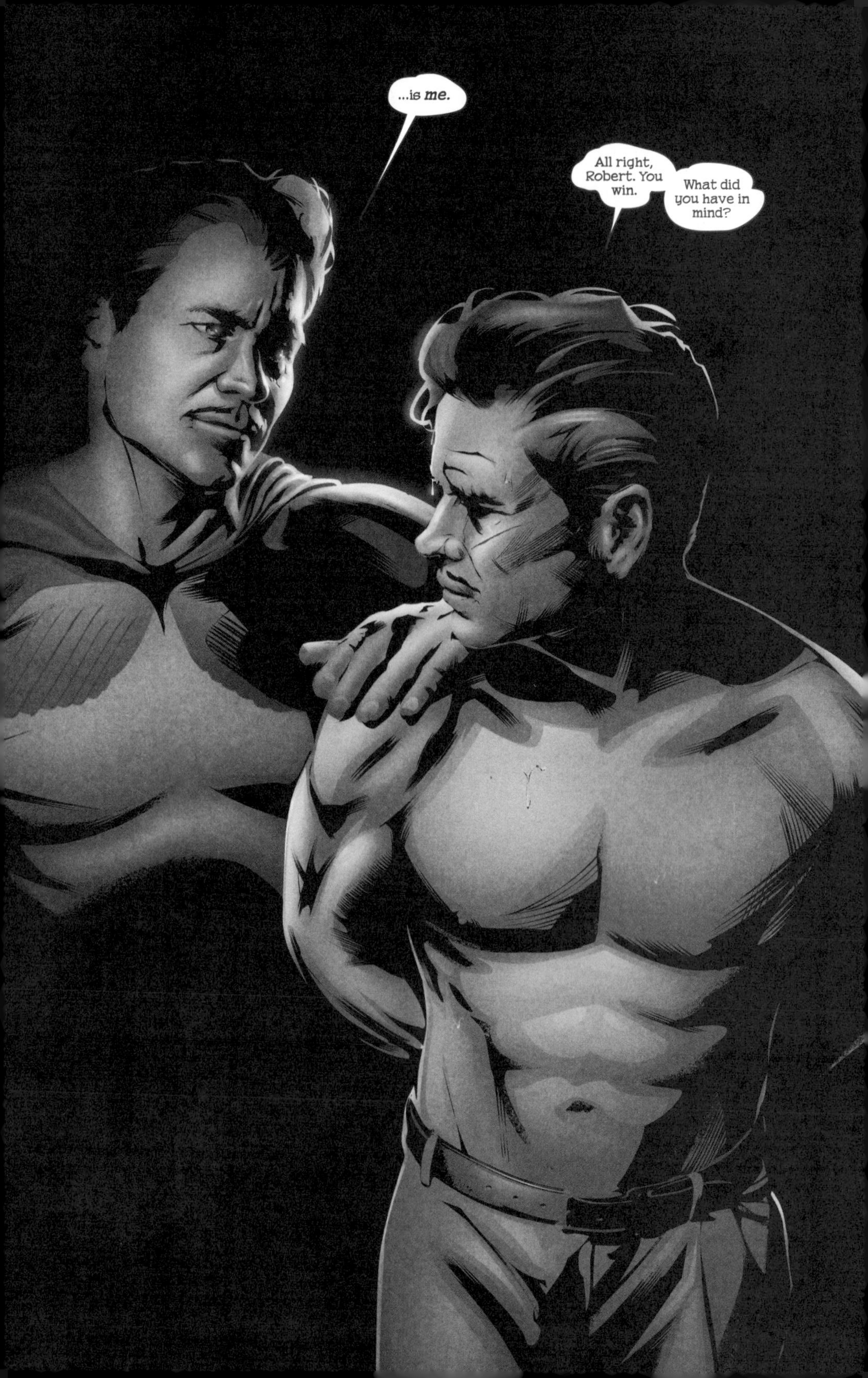
...is *me.*
All right, Robert. You win.
What did you have in mind?

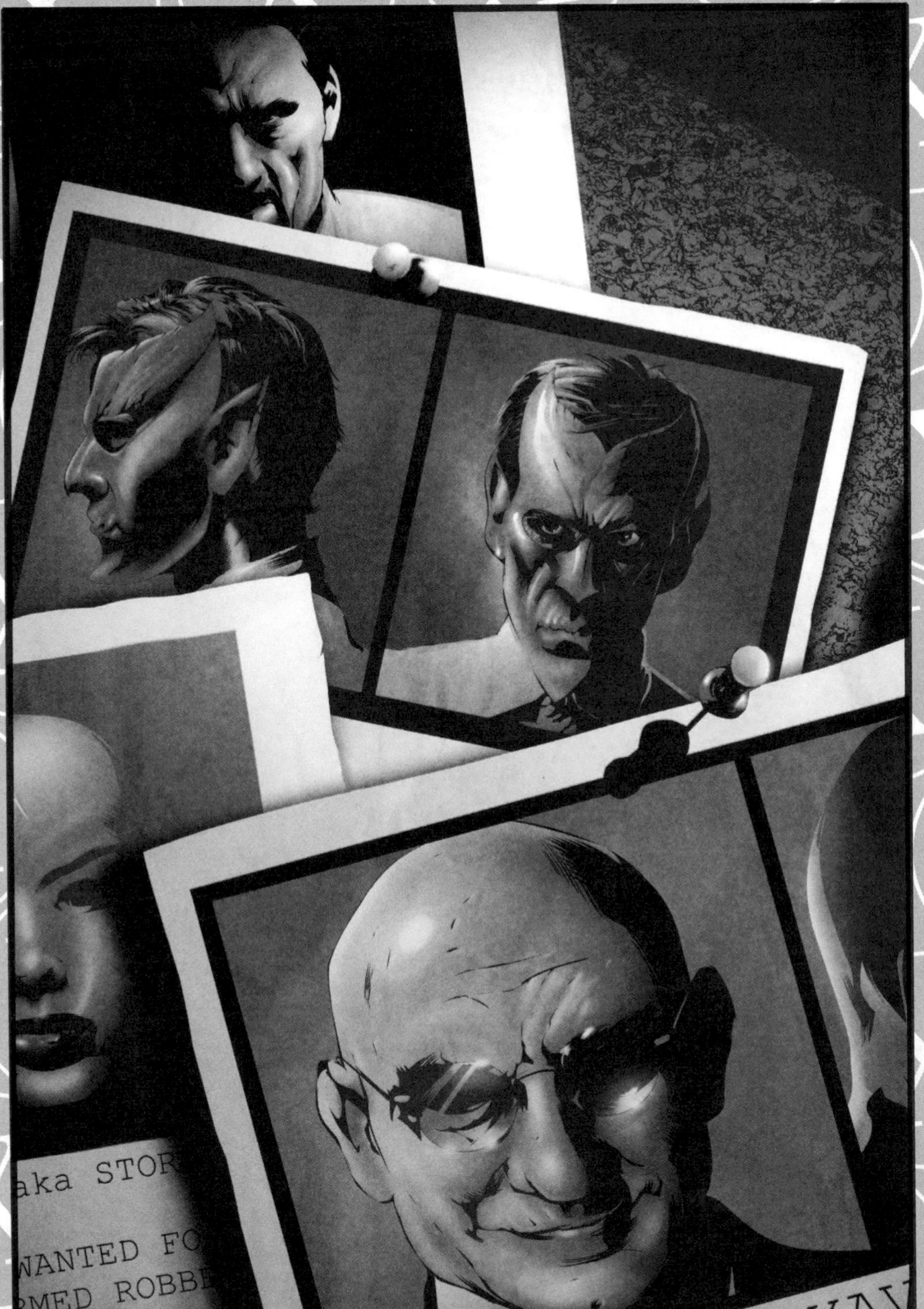
aka STOR
WANTED FO
RMED ROBBE
SOR XAV

THREE

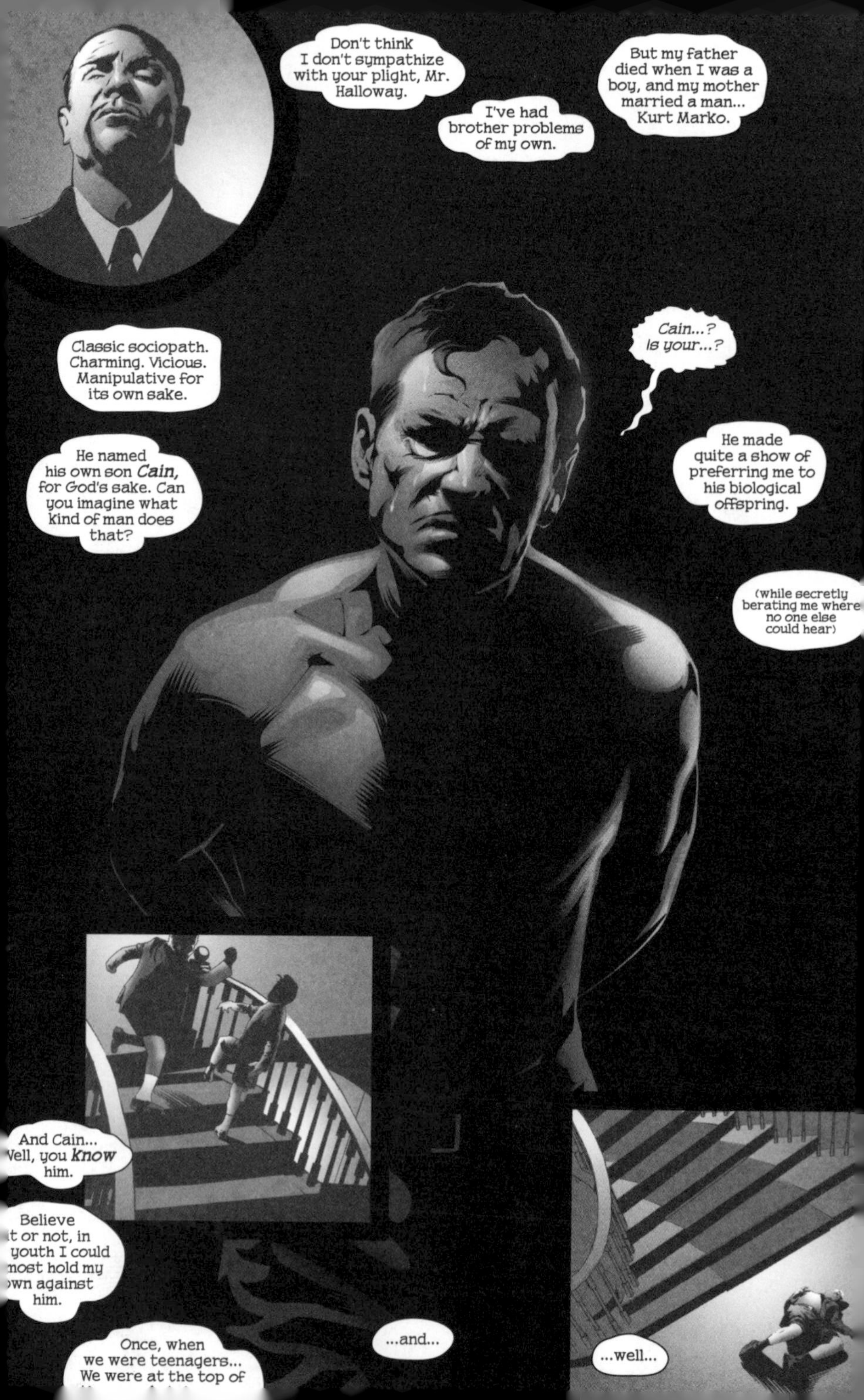

Don't think I don't sympathize with your plight, Mr. Halloway.
I've had brother problems of my own.
But my father died when I was a boy, and my mother married a man... Kurt Marko.
Classic sociopath. Charming. Vicious. Manipulative for its own sake.
He named his own son *Cain,* for God's sake. Can you imagine what kind of man does that?
Cain...? Is your...?
He made quite a show of preferring me to his biological offspring.
(while secretly berating me where no one else could hear)
And Cain... ell, you *know* him.
Believe t or not, in youth I could most hold my wn against him.
Once, when we were teenagers... We were at the top of
...and...
...well...

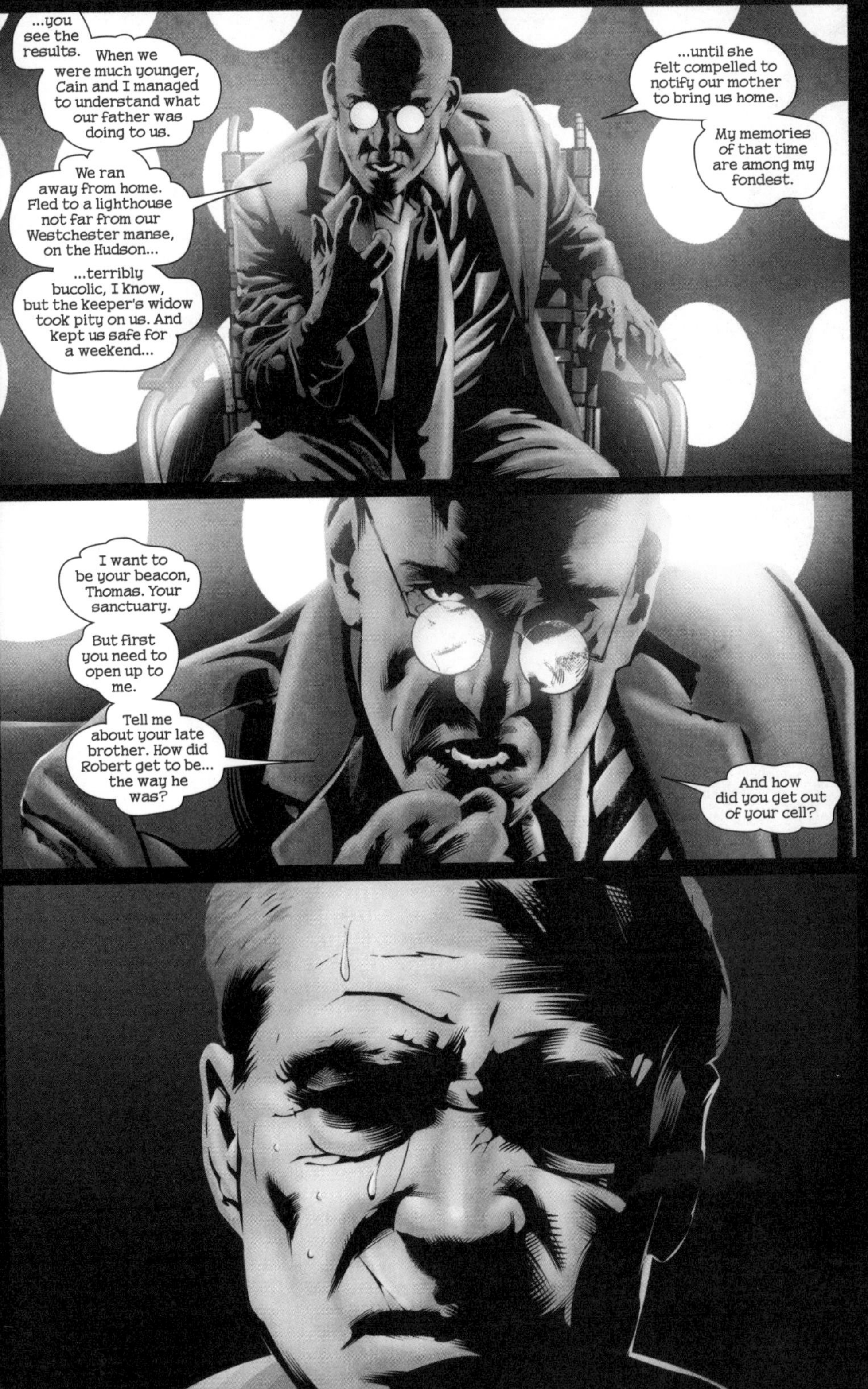
...you see the results.
When we were much younger, Cain and I managed to understand what our father was doing to us.
We ran away from home. Fled to a lighthouse not far from our Westchester manse, on the Hudson...
...terribly bucolic, I know, but the keeper's widow took pity on us. And kept us safe for a weekend...
...until she felt compelled to notify our mother to bring us home.
My memories of that time are among my fondest.
I want to be your beacon, Thomas. Your sanctuary.
But first you need to open up to me.
Tell me about your late brother. How did Robert get to be... the way he was?
And how did you get out of your cell?

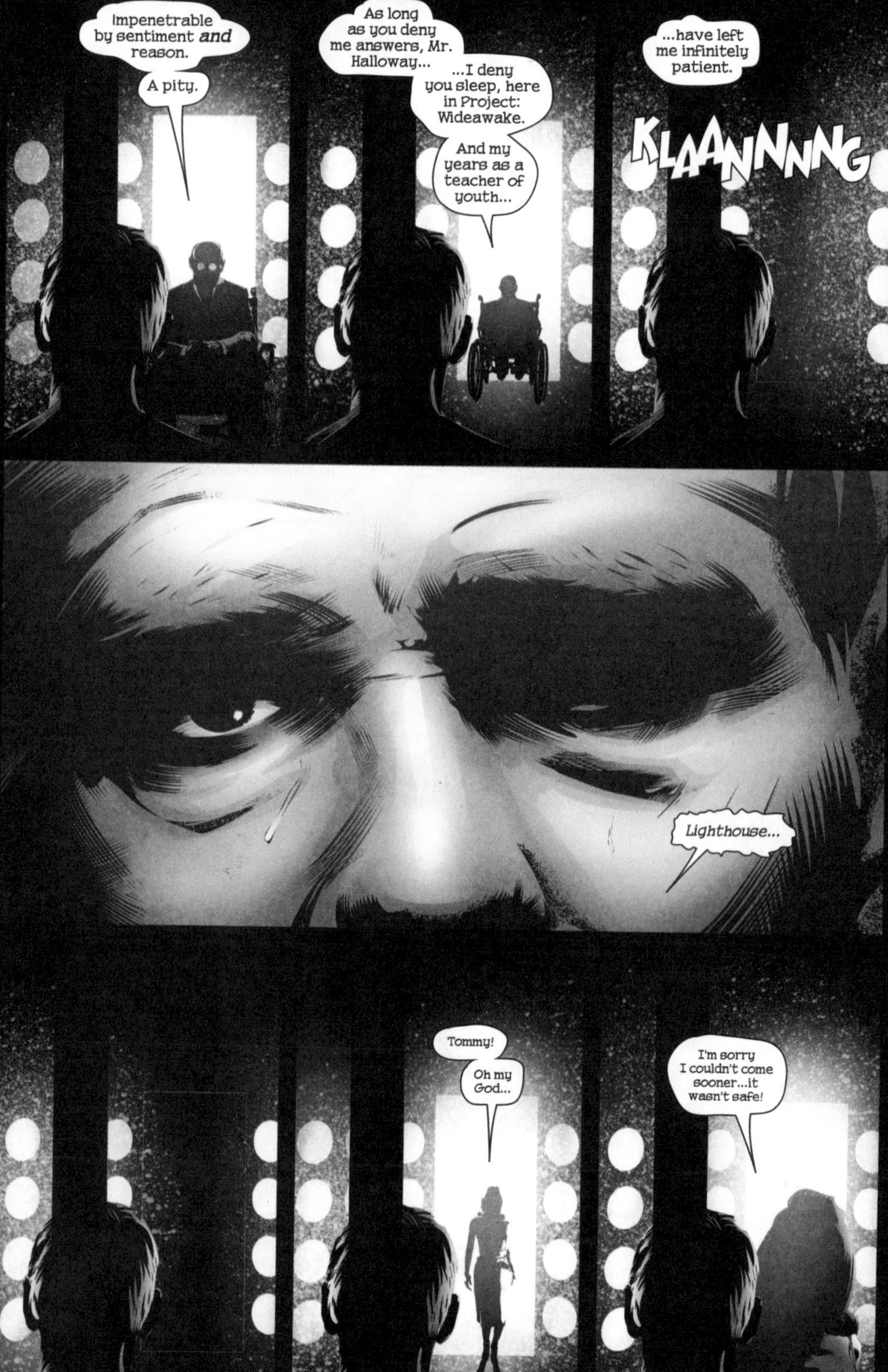
Impenetrable by sentiment *and* reason.
A pity.
As long as you deny me answers, Mr. Halloway...
...I deny you sleep, here in Project: Wideawake.
And my years as a teacher of youth...
...have left me infinitely patient.
KLAANNNNG
Lighthouse...
Tommy!
Oh my God...
I'm sorry I couldn't come sooner...it wasn't safe!

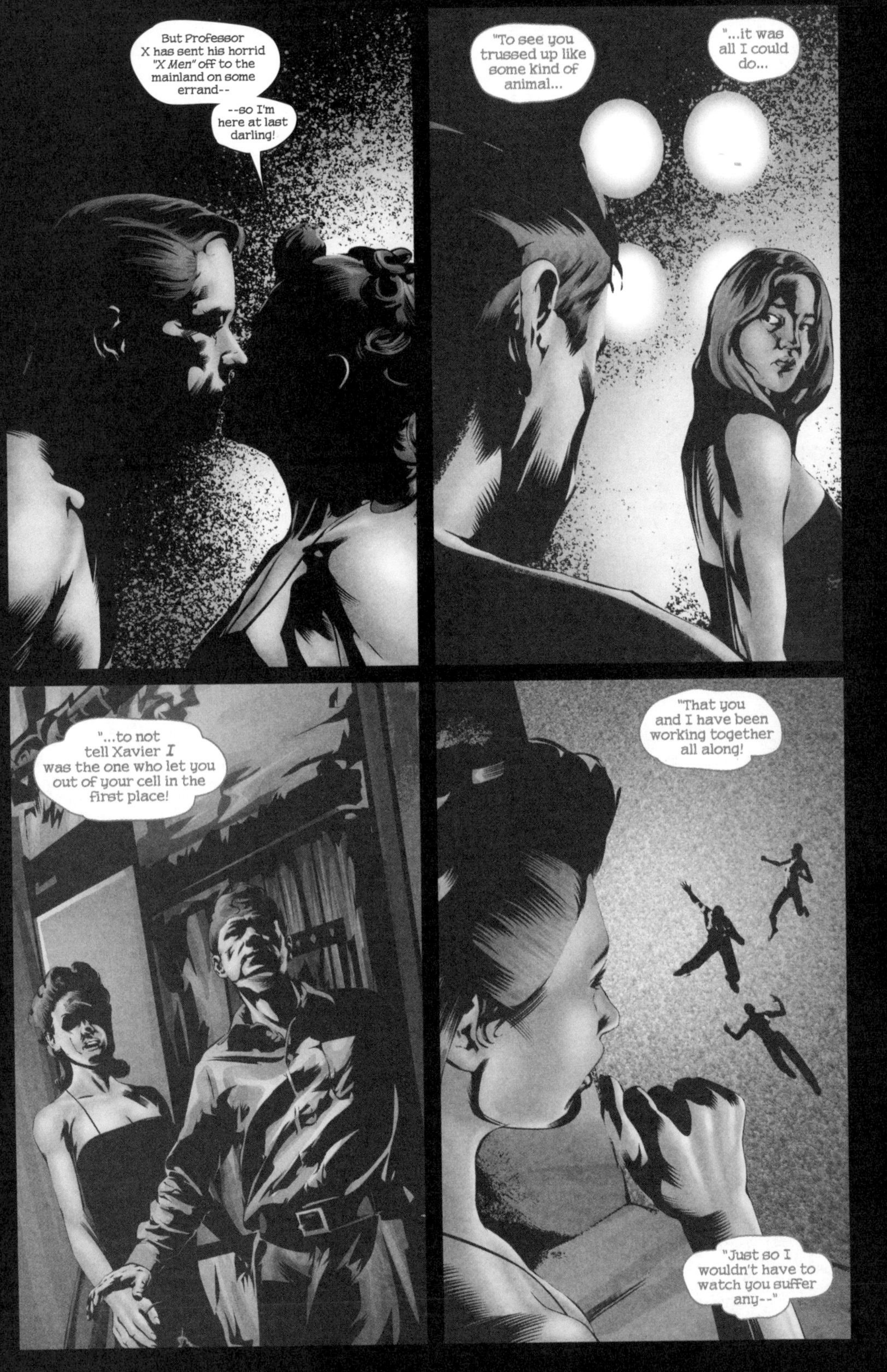

But Professor X has sent his horrid "X Men" off to the mainland on some errand--
--so I'm here at last darling!
"To see you trussed up like some kind of animal...
"...it was all I could do...
"...to not tell Xavier I was the one who let you out of your cell in the first place!
"That you and I have been working together all along!
"Just so I wouldn't have to watch you suffer any--"

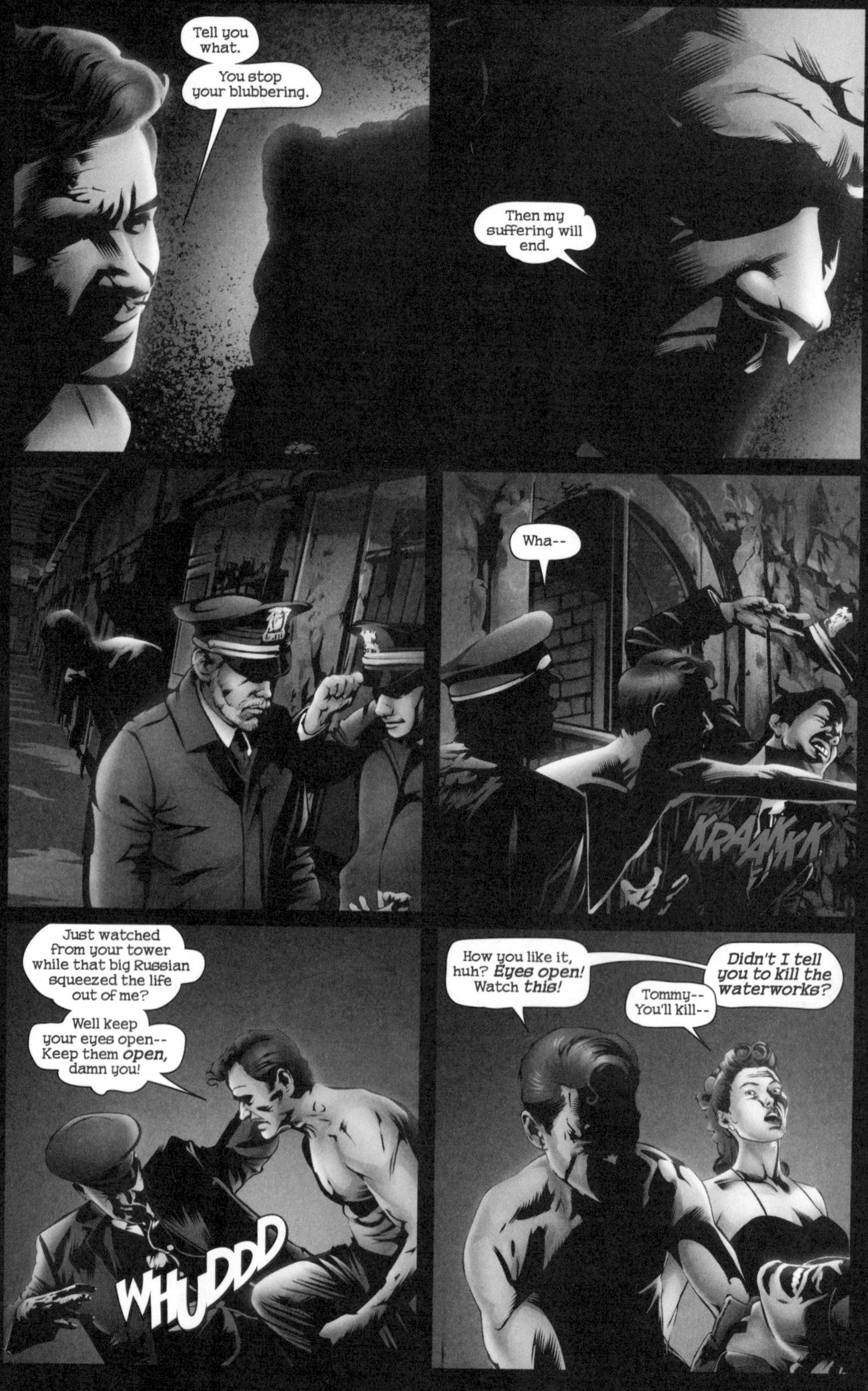
Tell you what.
You stop your blubbering.
Then my suffering will end.
Wha--
KRAAKKK
Just watched from your tower while that big Russian squeezed the life out of me?
Well keep your eyes open-- Keep them *open,* damn you!
WHUDDD
How you like it, huh? *Eyes open!* Watch *this!*
Didn't I tell you to kill the waterworks?
Tommy-- You'll kill--

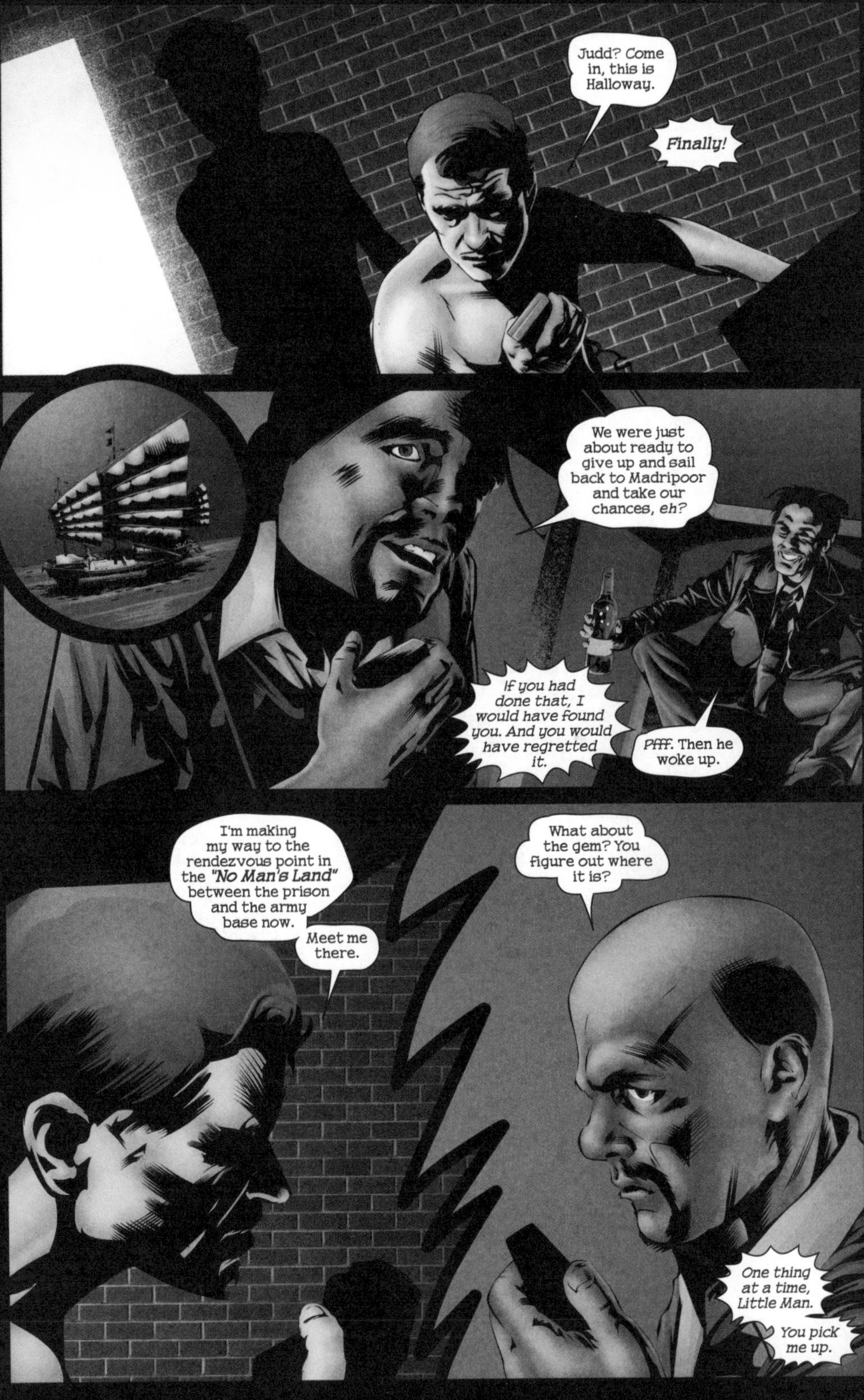
Judd? Come in, this is Halloway.
Finally!
We were just about ready to give up and sail back to Madripoor and take our chances, *eh?*
If you had done that, I would have found you. And you would have regretted it.
Pfff. Then he woke up.
I'm making my way to the rendezvous point in the *"No Man's Land"* between the prison and the army base now.
Meet me there.
What about the gem? You figure out where it is?
One thing at a time, Little Man.
You pick me up.

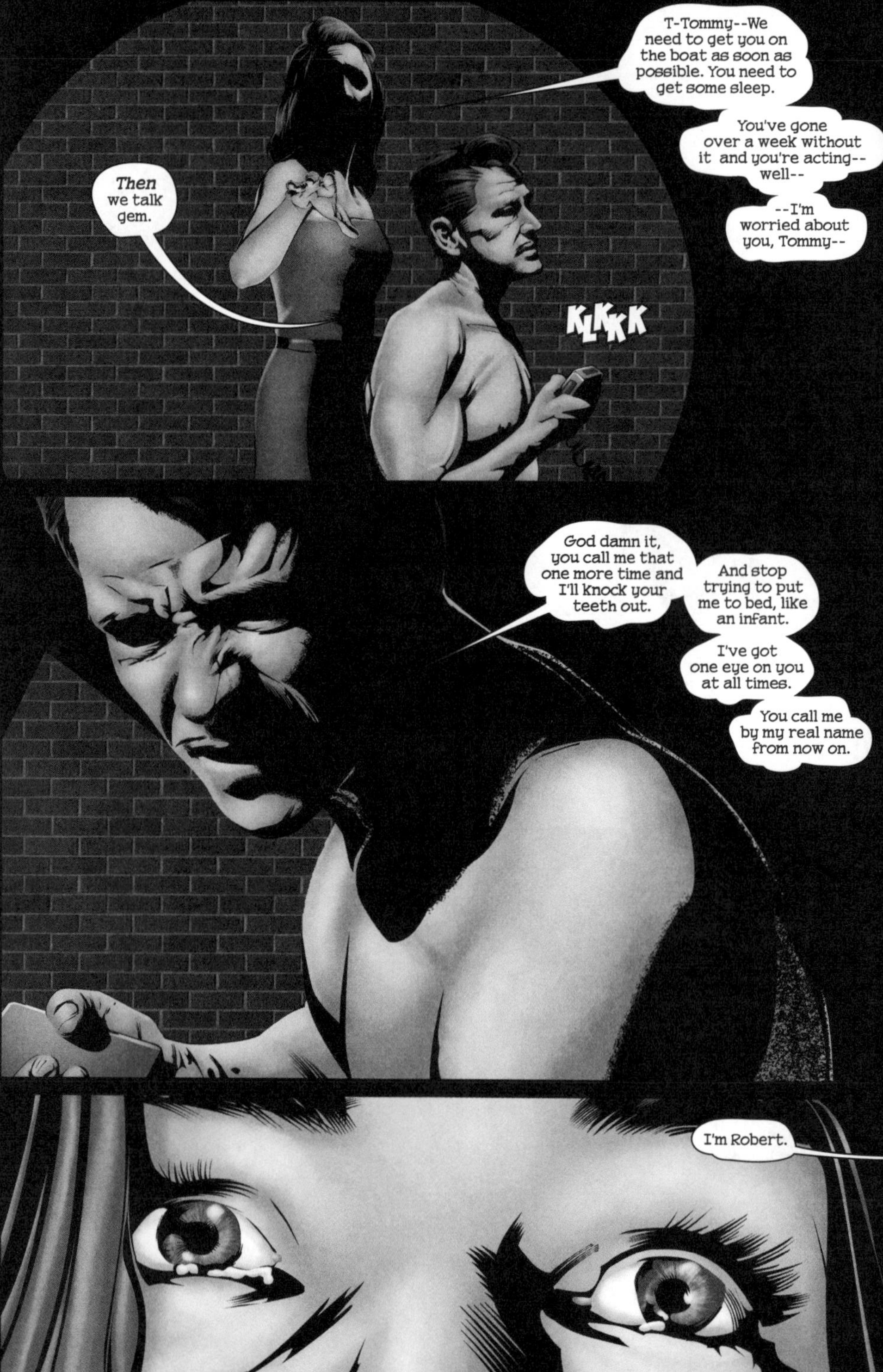
T-Tommy--We need to get you on the boat as soon as possible. You need to get some sleep.
You've gone over a week without it and you're acting--well--
--I'm worried about you, Tommy--
Then we talk gem.
KLKKK
God damn it, you call me that one more time and I'll knock your teeth out.
And stop trying to put me to bed, like an infant.
I've got one eye on you at all times.
You call me by my real name from now on.
I'm Robert.

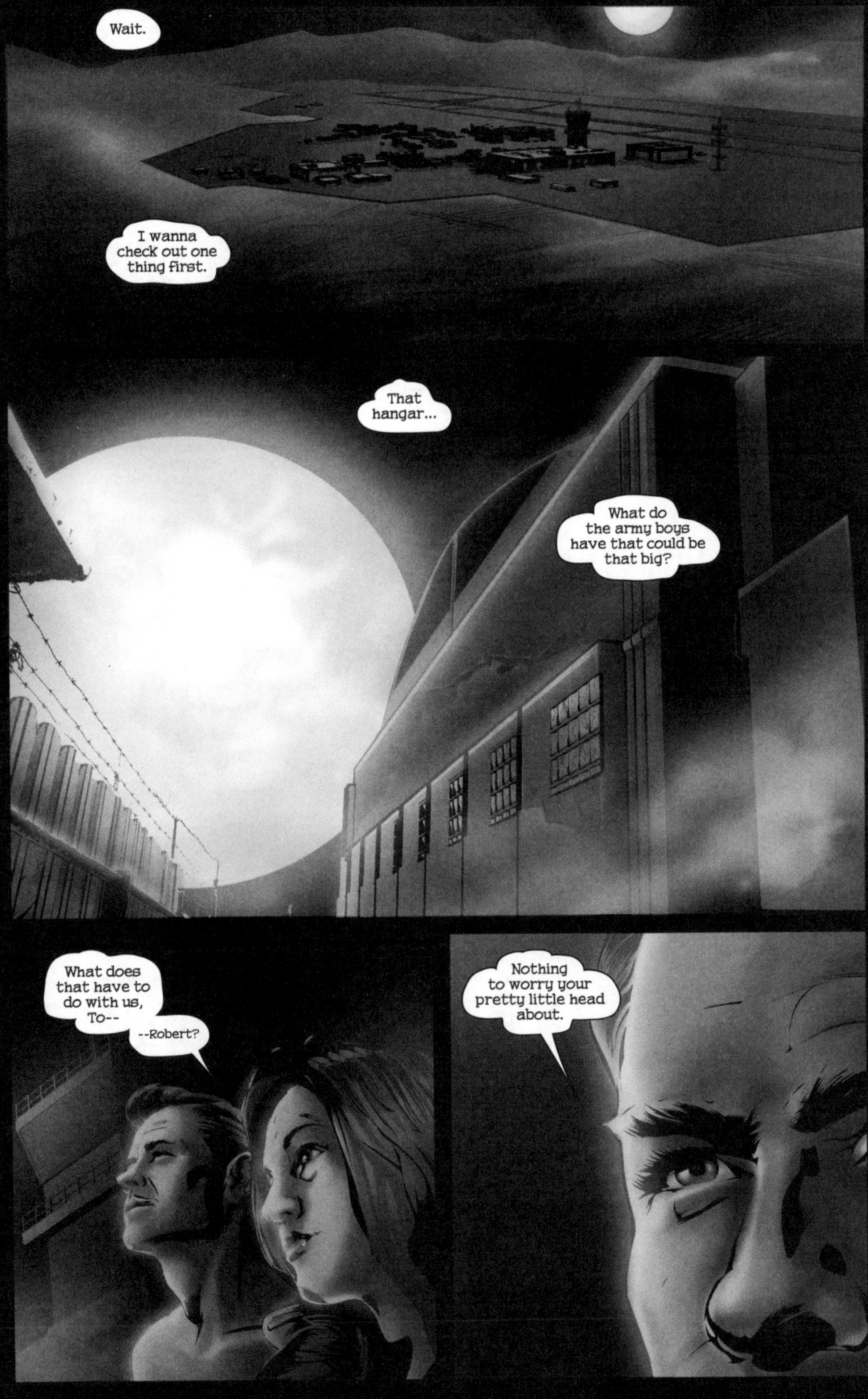
Wait.
I wanna check out one thing first.
That hangar...
What do the army boys have that could be that big?
What does that have to do with us, To--
--Robert?
Nothing to worry your pretty little head about.

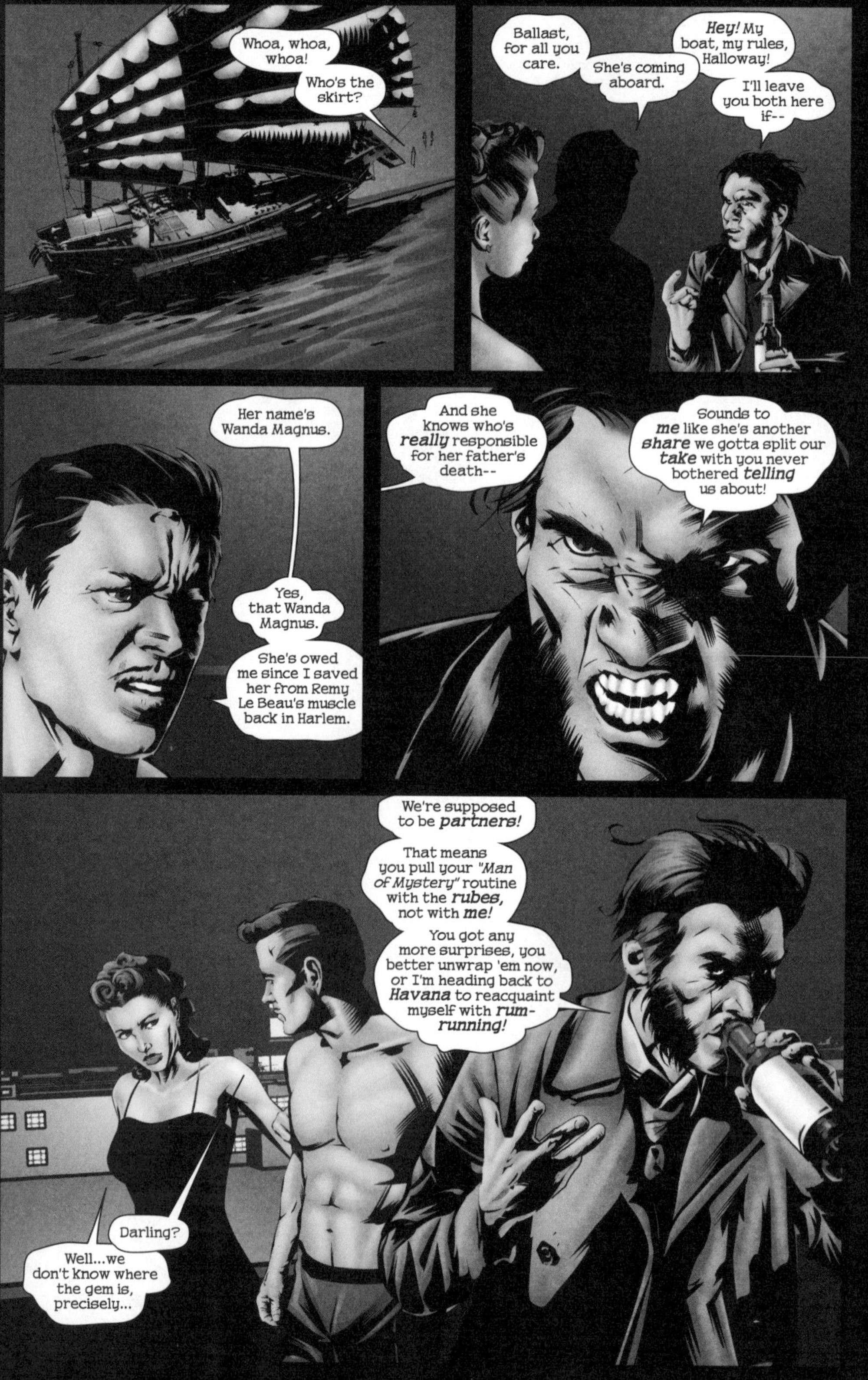

Whoa, whoa, whoa!
Who's the skirt?
Ballast, for all you care.
She's coming aboard.
Hey! My boat, my rules, Halloway!
I'll leave you both here if--
Her name's Wanda Magnus.
Yes, that Wanda Magnus.
She's owed me since I saved her from Remy Le Beau's muscle back in Harlem.
And she knows who's really responsible for her father's death--
Sounds to me like she's another share we gotta split our take with you never bothered telling us about!
We're supposed to be partners!
That means you pull your "Man of Mystery" routine with the rubes, not with me!
You got any more surprises, you better unwrap 'em now, or I'm heading back to Havana to reacquaint myself with rum-running!
Darling?
Well...we don't know where the gem is, precisely...

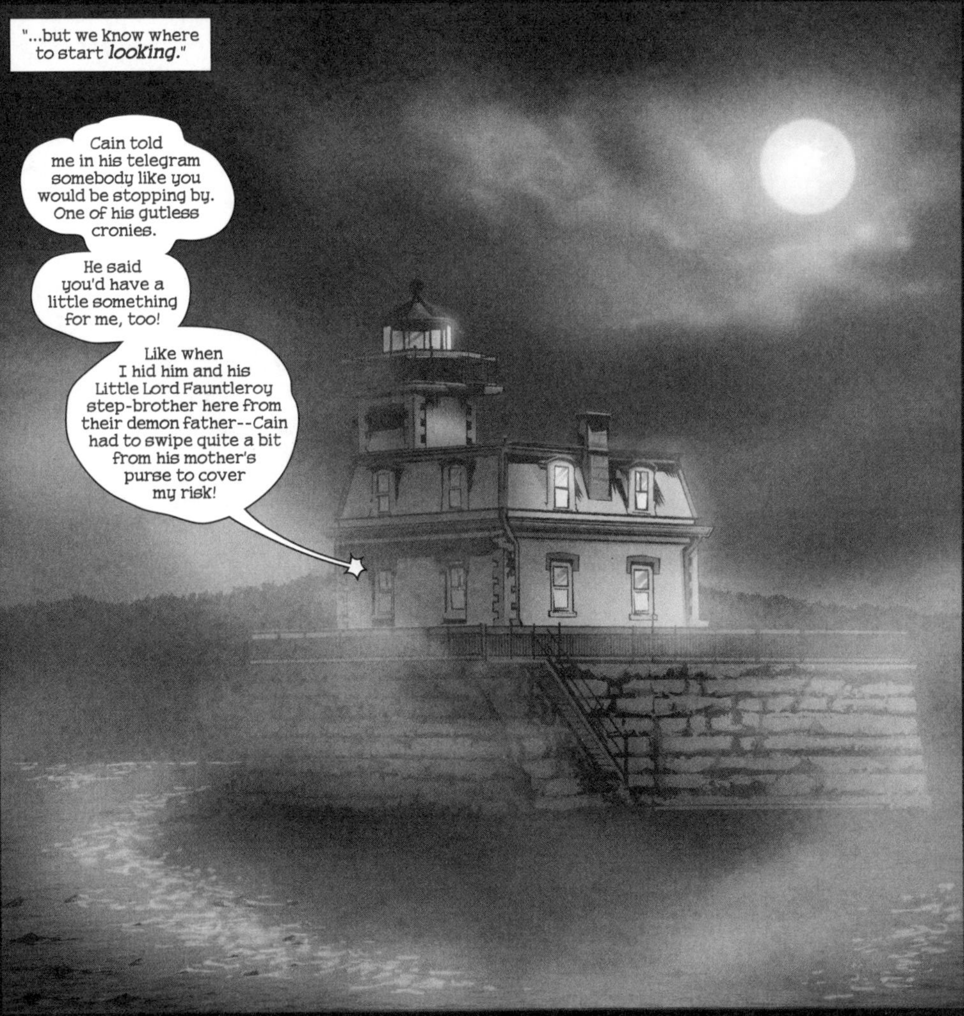
"...but we know where to start *looking*."
Cain told me in his telegram somebody like you would be stopping by. One of his gutless cronies.
He said you'd have a little something for me, too!
Like when I hid him and his Little Lord Fauntleroy step-brother here from their demon father--Cain had to swipe quite a bit from his mother's purse to cover my risk!

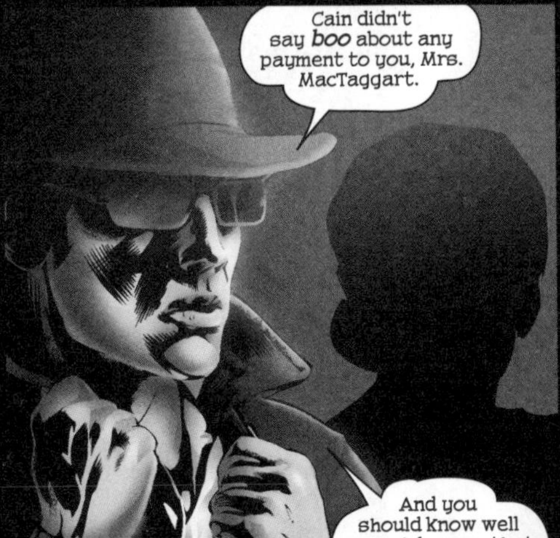
Cain didn't say *boo* about any payment to you, Mrs. MacTaggart.
And you should know well enough by now that he's not a man to be trifled with--

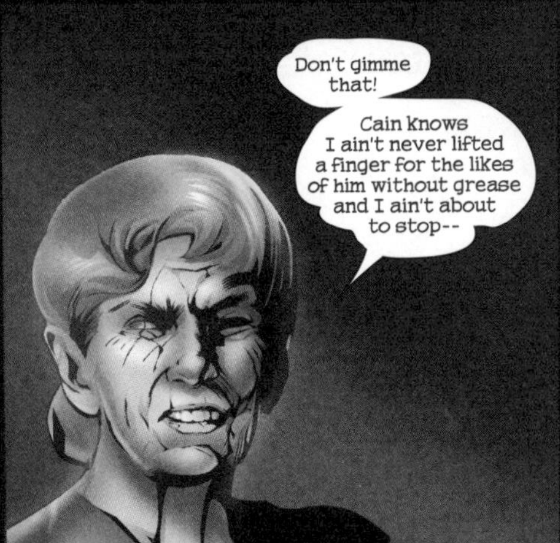
Don't gimme that!
Cain knows I ain't never lifted a finger for the likes of him without grease and I ain't about to stop--

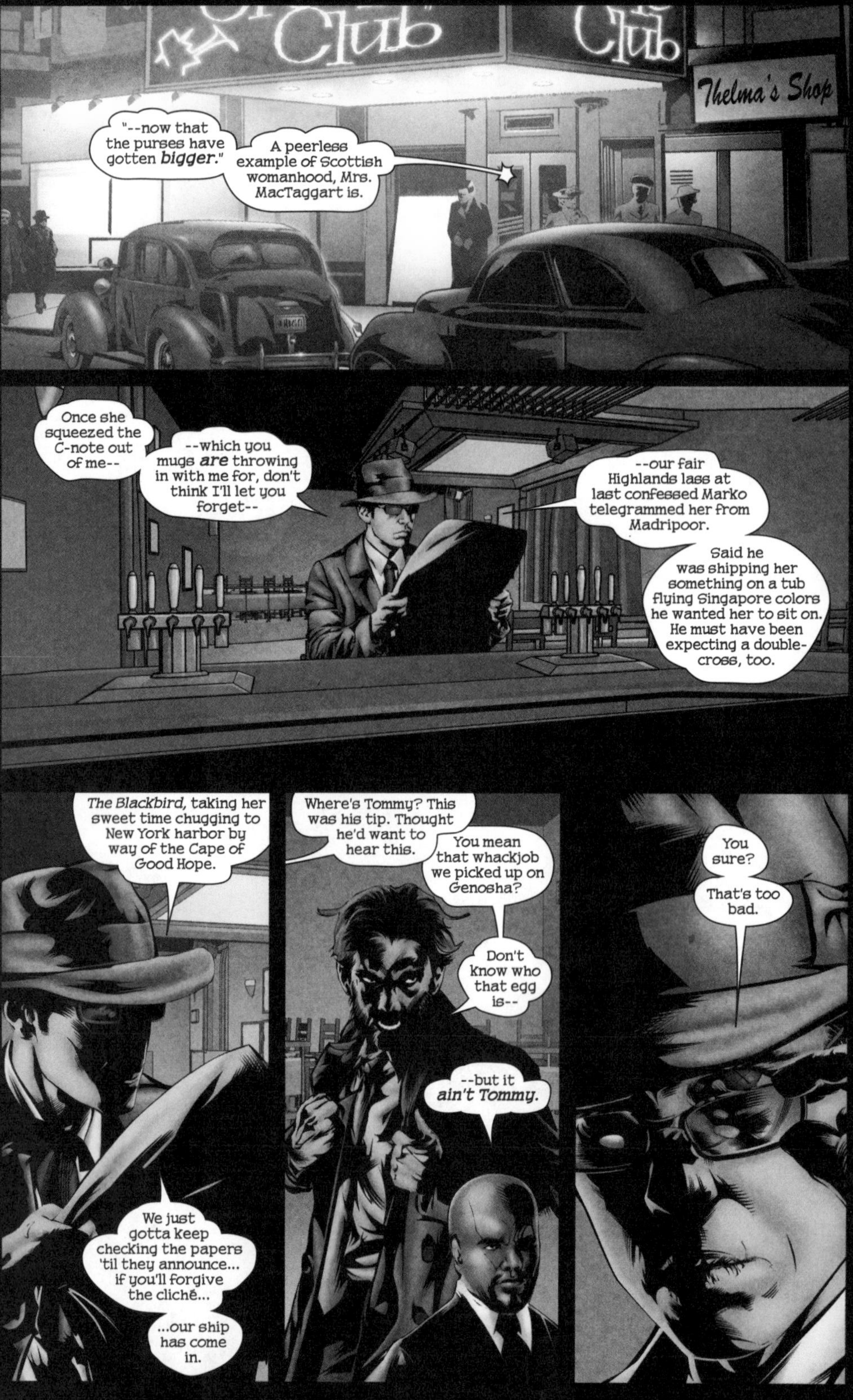

Club
Club
Thelma's Shop
"--now that the purses have gotten *bigger*."
A peerless example of Scottish womanhood, Mrs. MacTaggart is.
Once she squeezed the C-note out of me--
--which you mugs *are* throwing in with me for, don't think I'll let you forget--
--our fair Highlands lass at last confessed Marko telegrammed her from Madripoor.
Said he was shipping her something on a tub flying Singapore colors he wanted her to sit on. He must have been expecting a double-cross, too.
The Blackbird, taking her sweet time chugging to New York harbor by way of the Cape of Good Hope.
We just gotta keep checking the papers 'til they announce... if you'll forgive the cliché...
...our ship has come in.
Where's Tommy? This was his tip. Thought he'd want to hear this.
You mean that whackjob we picked up on Genosha?
Don't know who that egg is--
--but it *ain't Tommy.*
You sure?
That's too bad.

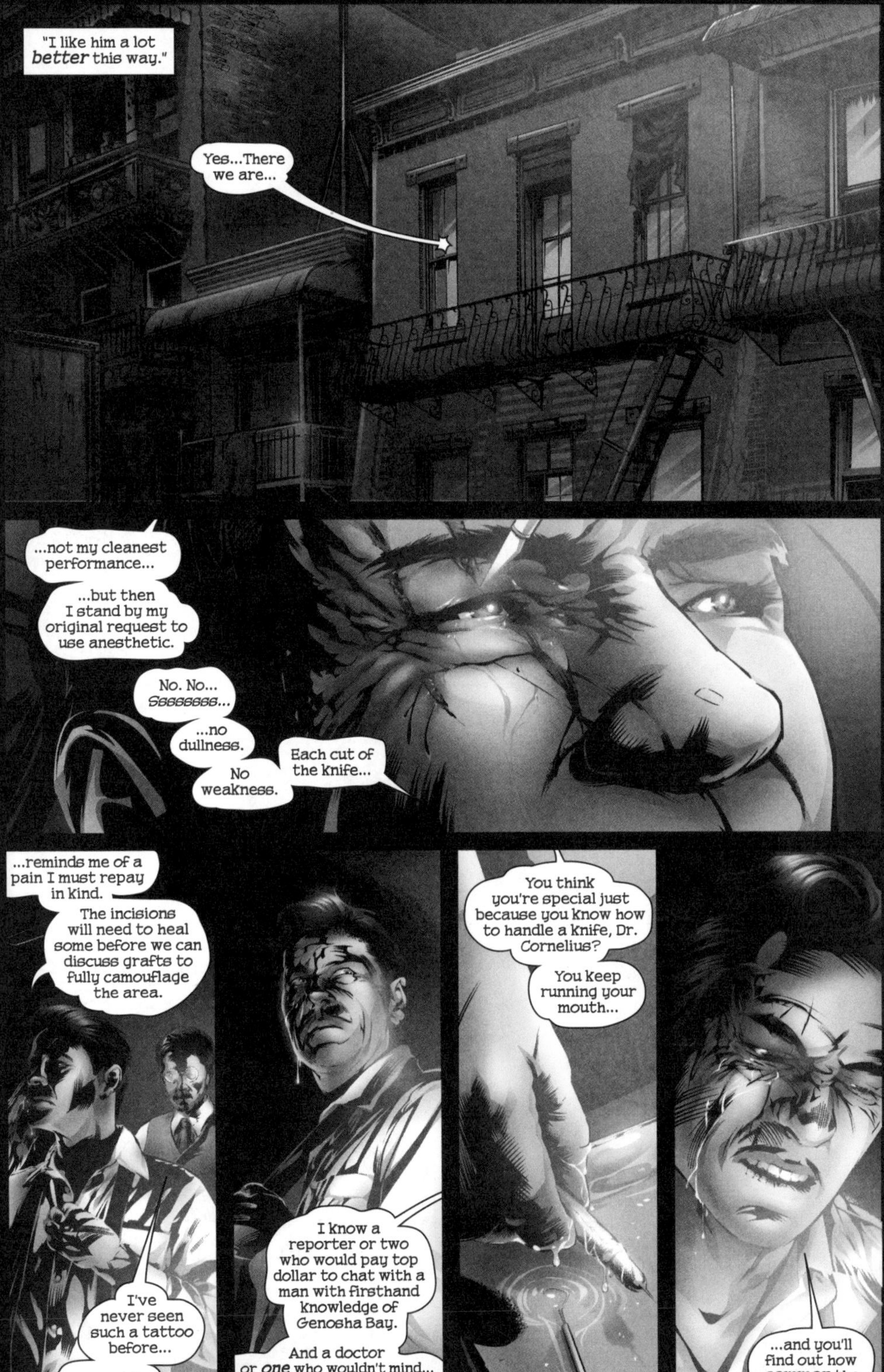
"I like him a lot *better* this way."
Yes...There we are...
...not my cleanest performance...
...but then I stand by my original request to use anesthetic.
No. No... *Sssssss...*
...no dullness.
No weakness.
Each cut of the knife...
...reminds me of a pain I must repay in kind.
The incisions will need to heal some before we can discuss grafts to fully camouflage the area.
I've never seen such a tattoo before...
...except in newsreels.
I know a reporter or two who would pay top dollar to chat with a man with firsthand knowledge of Genosha Bay.
And a doctor or *one* who wouldn't mind... extra consideration to keep that same information out of the hands of the FBI.
You think you're special just because you know how to handle a knife, Dr. Cornelius?
You keep running your mouth...
...and you'll find out how *common* the skill *is.*

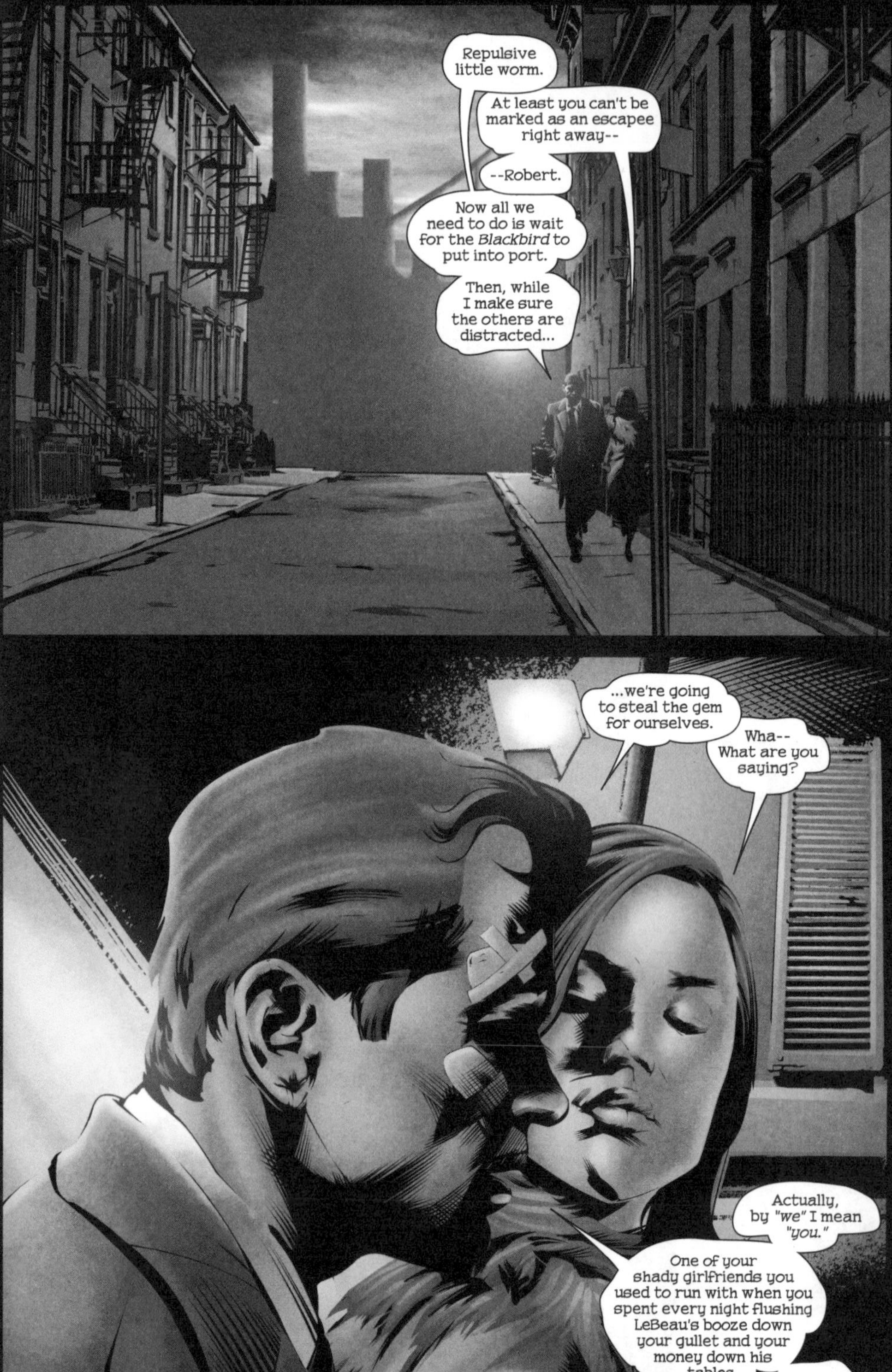

Repulsive little worm.
At least you can't be marked as an escapee right away--
--Robert.
Now all we need to do is wait for the *Blackbird* to put into port.
Then, while I make sure the others are distracted...
...we're going to steal the gem for ourselves.
Wha-- What are you saying?
Actually, by *"we"* I mean *"you."*
One of your shady girlfriends you used to run with when you spent every night flushing LeBeau's booze down your gullet and your money down his tables.
I'd do it myself--I'm the only one I really trust to...

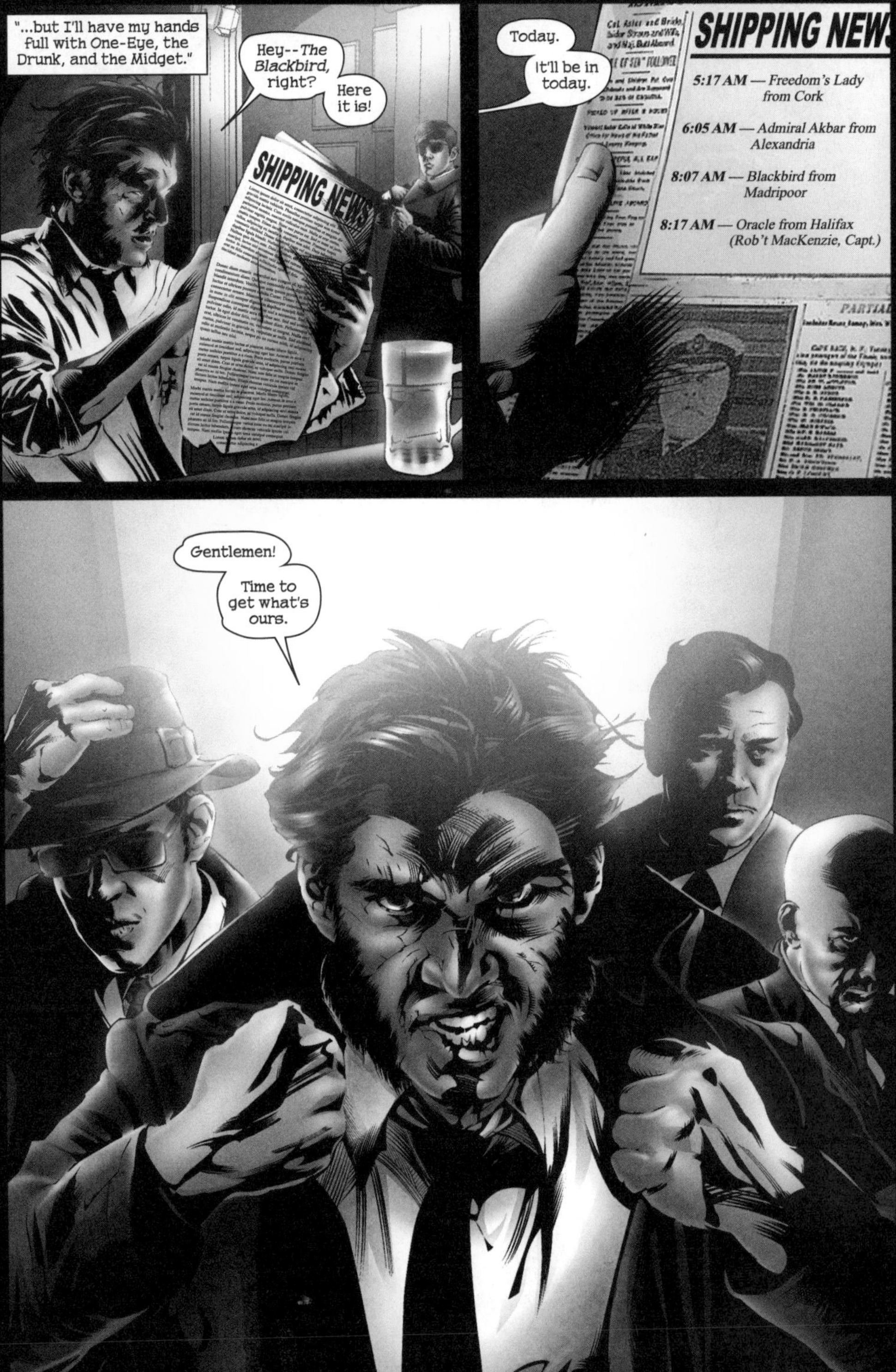
"...but I'll have my hands full with One-Eye, the Drunk, and the Midget."
Hey--*The Blackbird,* right?
Here it is!
SHIPPING NEWS
Today.
It'll be in today.
SHIPPING NEWS
5:17 AM — Freedom's Lady from Cork
6:05 AM — Admiral Akbar from Alexandria
8:07 AM — Blackbird from Madripoor
8:17 AM — Oracle from Halifax (Rob't MacKenzie, Capt.)
PARTIAL
Gentlemen!
Time to get what's ours.

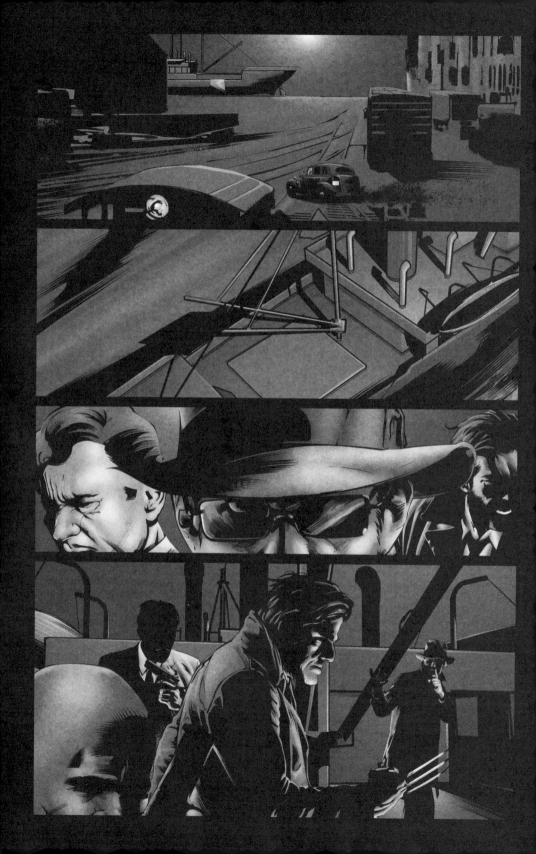

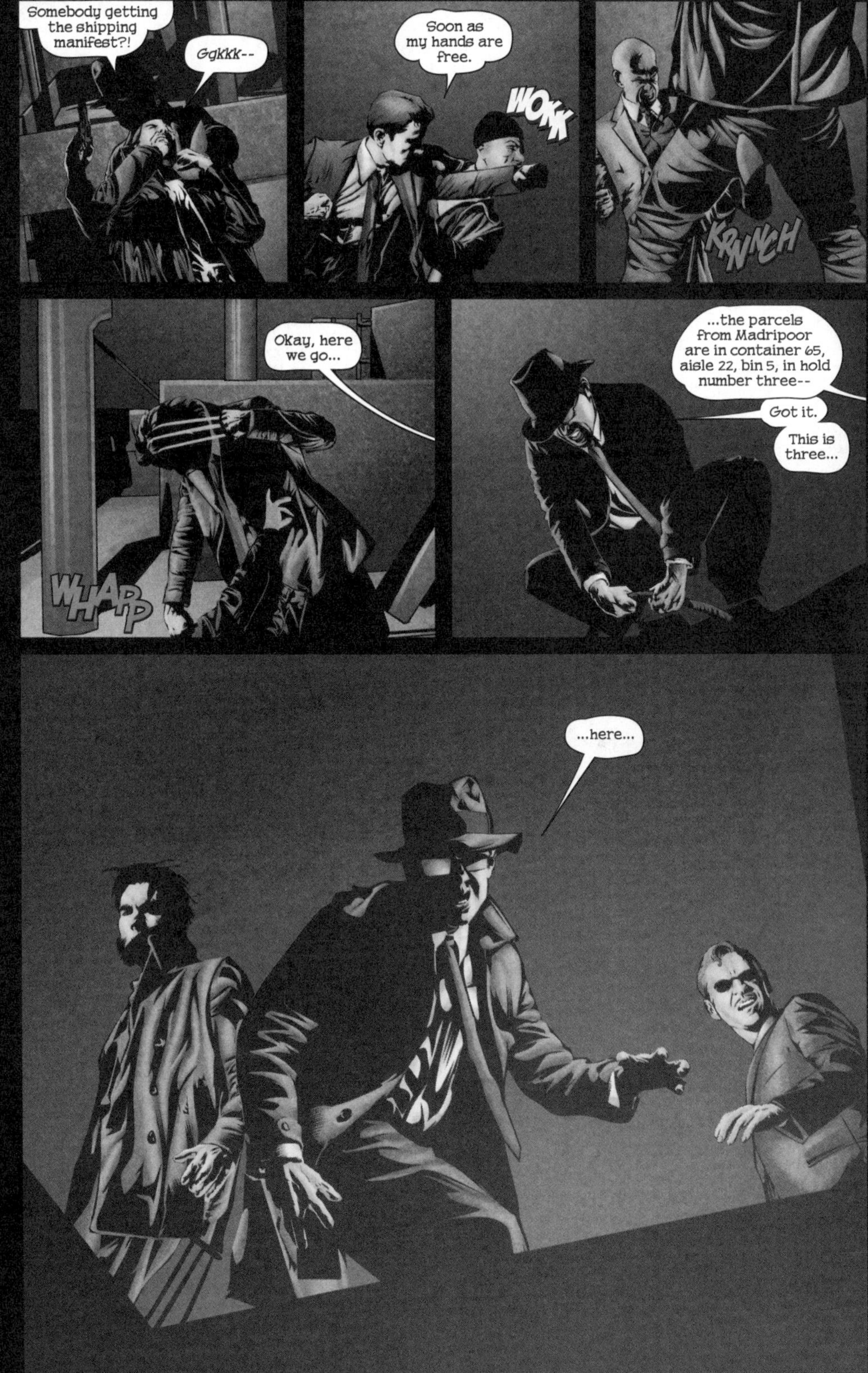

Somebody getting the shipping manifest?!
Ggkkk--
Soon as my hands are free.
WOKK
KRNNCH
Okay, here we go...
WHAPP
...the parcels from Madripoor are in container 65, aisle 22, bin 5, in hold number three--
Got it.
This is three...
...here...

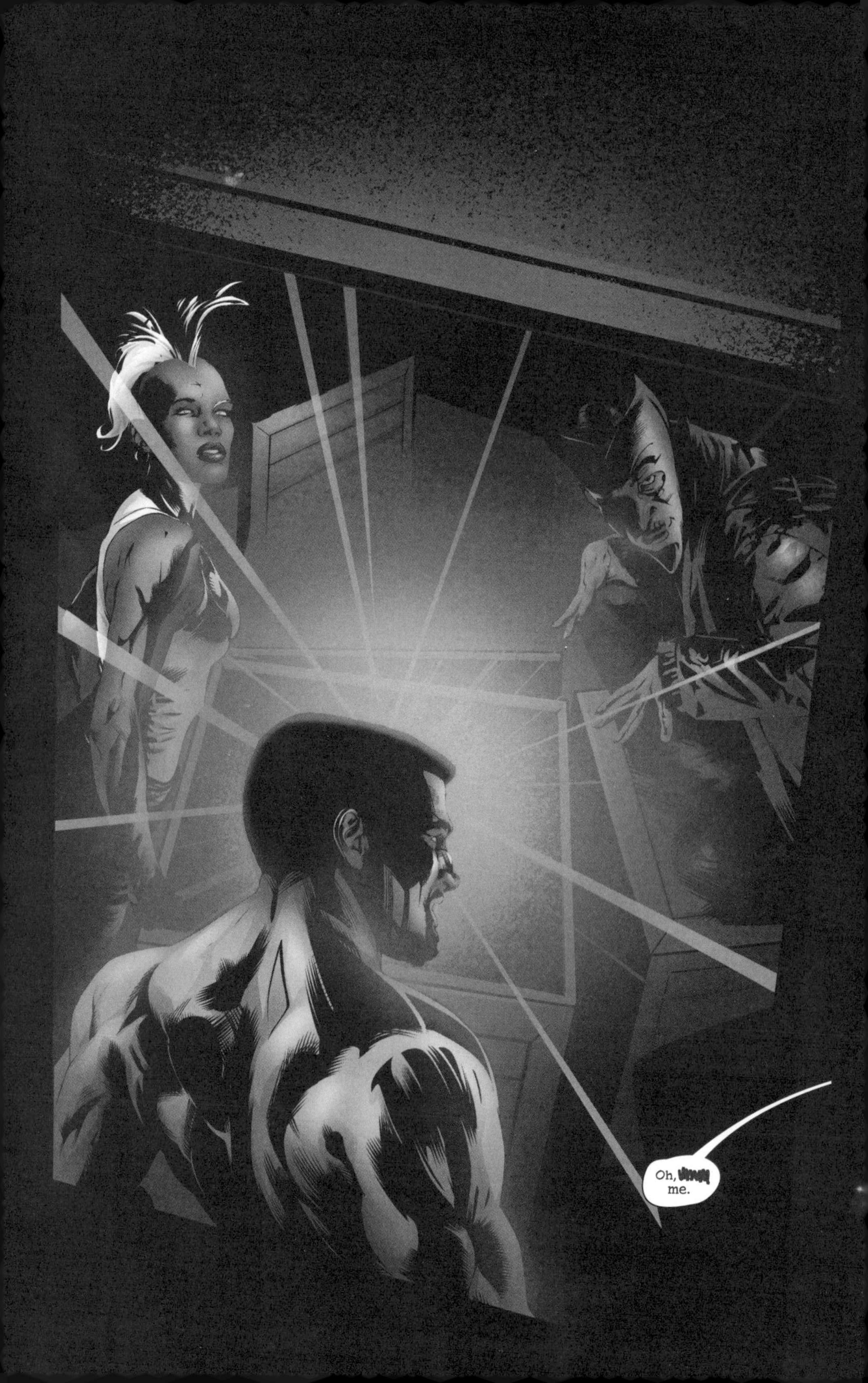
Oh, [redacted] me.

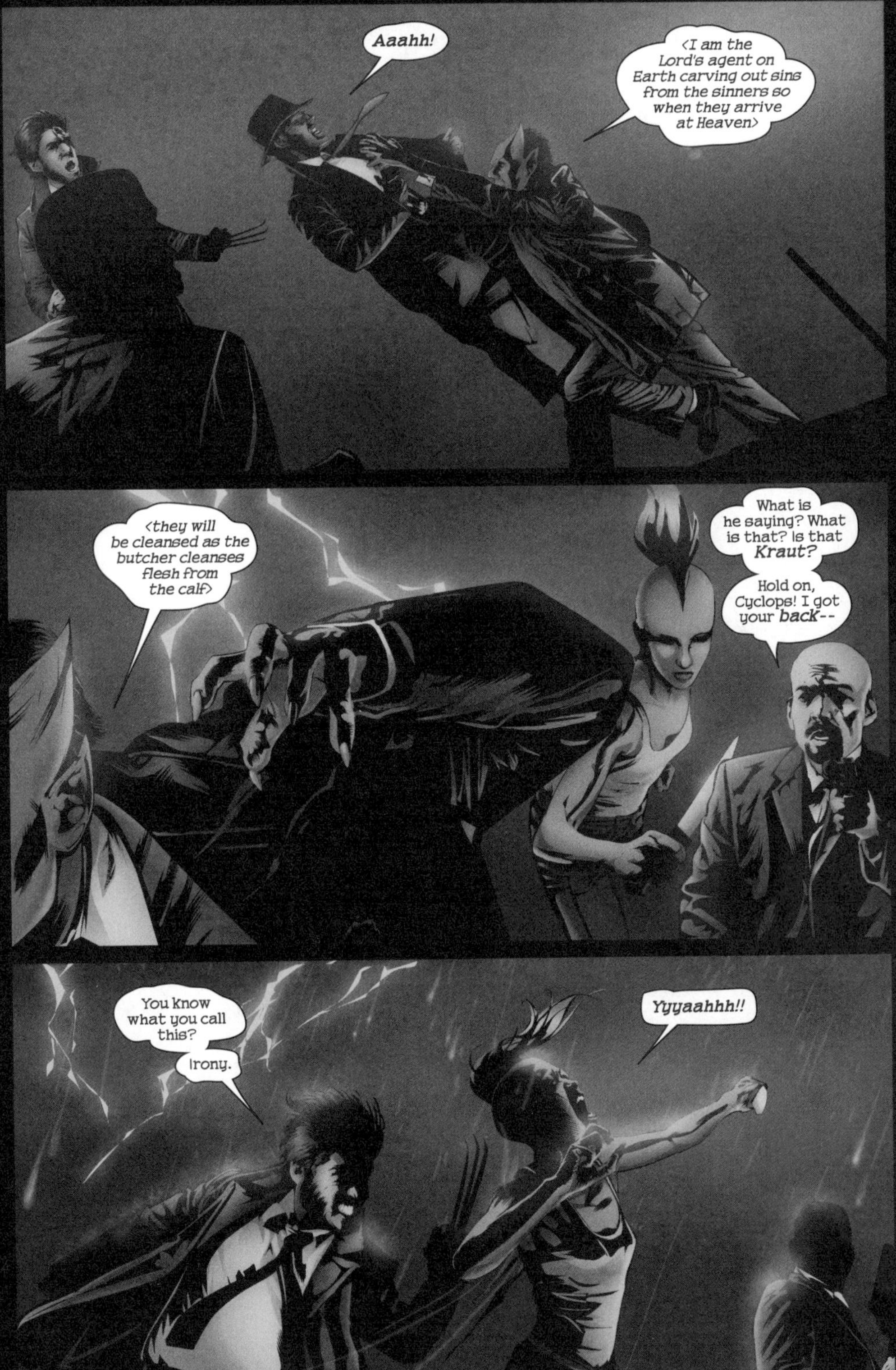
Aaahh!
<I am the Lord's agent on Earth carving out sins from the sinners so when they arrive at Heaven>
<they will be cleansed as the butcher cleanses flesh from the calf>
What is he saying? What is that? Is that Kraut?
Hold on, Cyclops! I got your back--
You know what you call this?
Irony.
Yyyaahhh!!

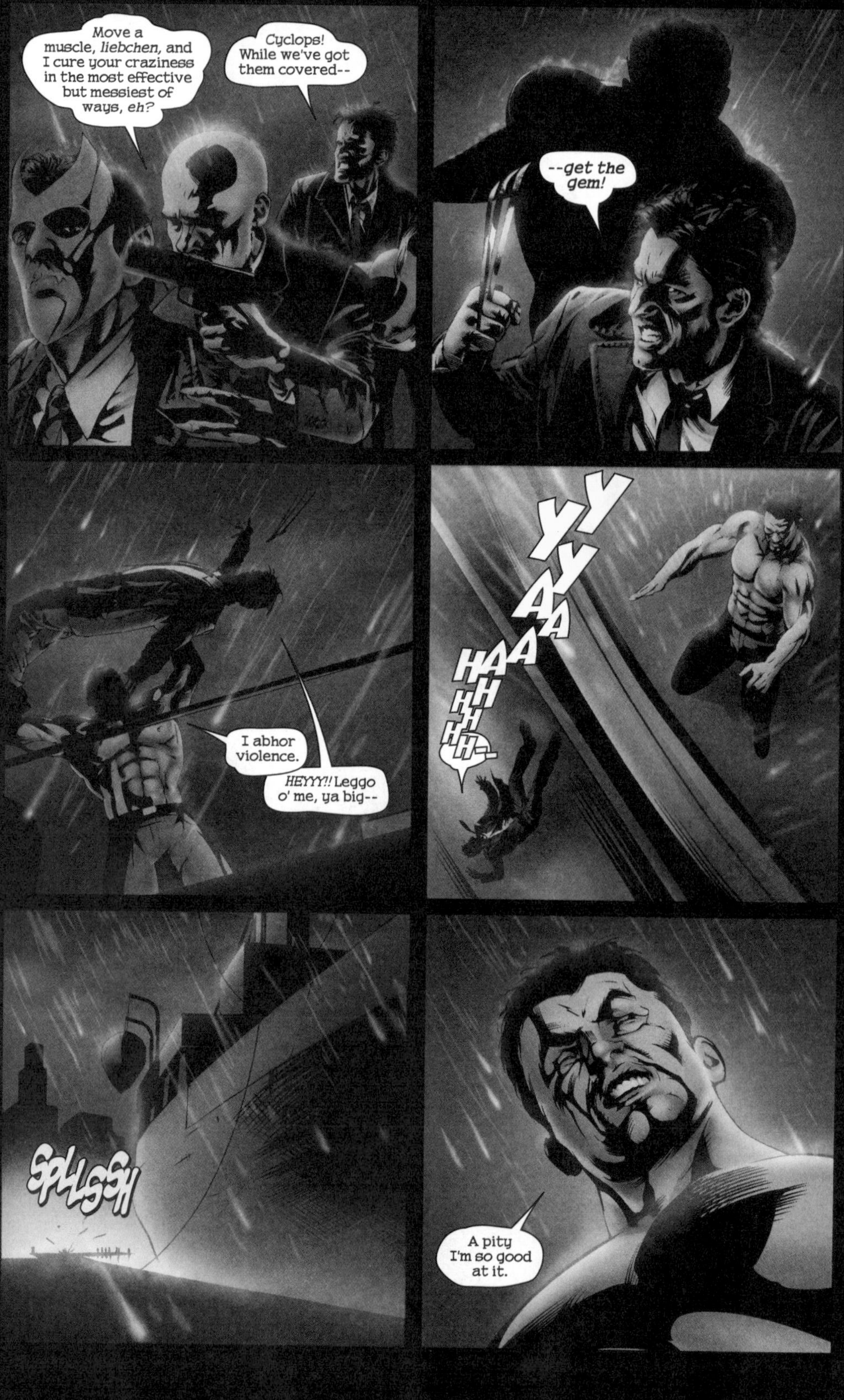

Move a muscle, liebchen, and I cure your craziness in the most effective but messiest of ways, eh?
Cyclops! While we've got them covered--
--get the gem!
I abhor violence.
HEYYY!! Leggo o' me, ya big--
YYYAAAAHHHHHH--
SPLLSSH
A pity I'm so good at it.

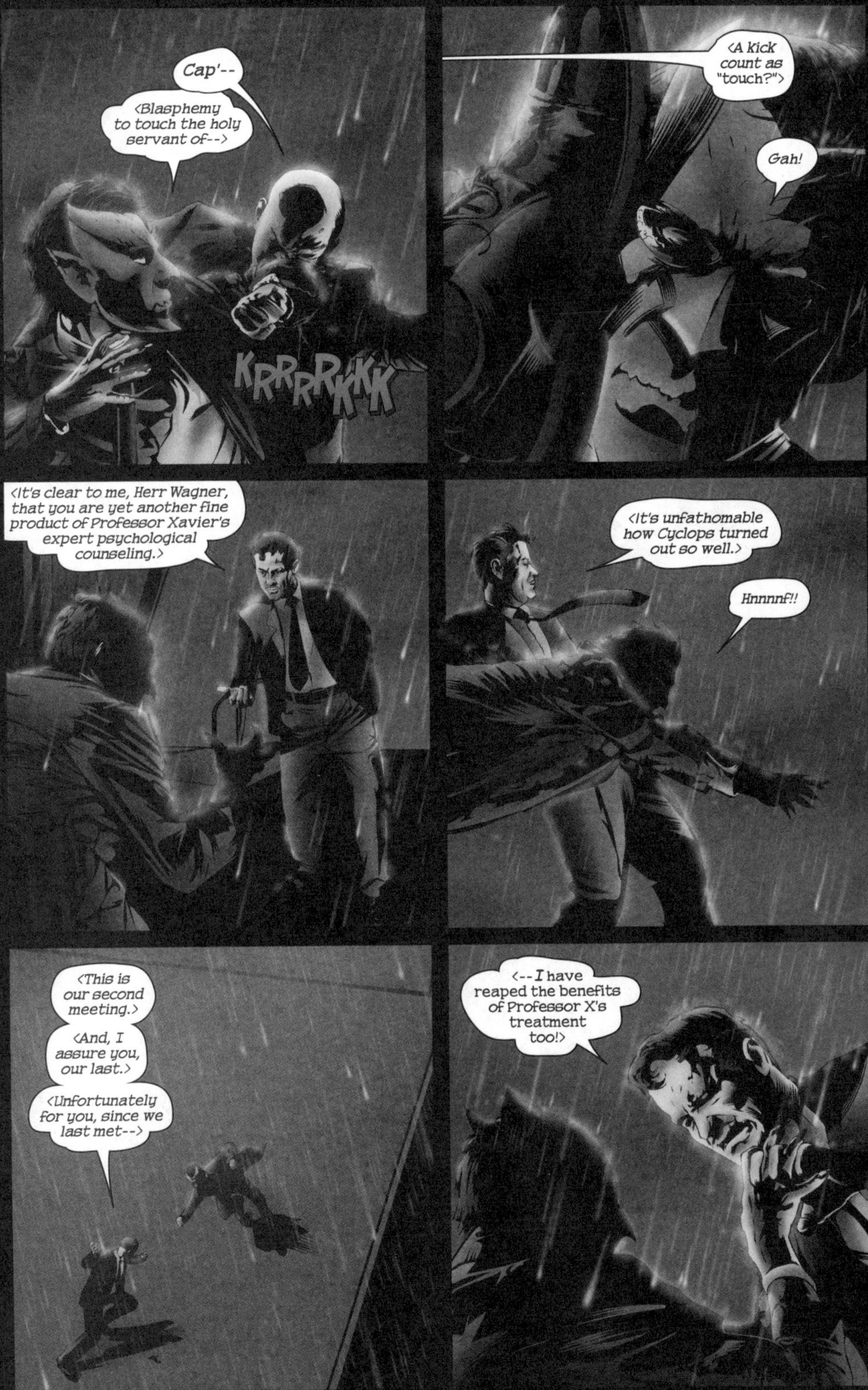
Cap'--
<Blasphemy to touch the holy servant of-->
KRRRRKKK
<A kick count as "touch?">
Gah!
<It's clear to me, Herr Wagner, that you are yet another fine product of Professor Xavier's expert psychological counseling.>
<It's unfathomable how Cyclops turned out so well.>
Hnnnnf!!
<This is our second meeting.>
<And, I assure you, our last.>
<Unfortunately for you, since we last met-->
<--I have reaped the benefits of Professor X's treatment too!>

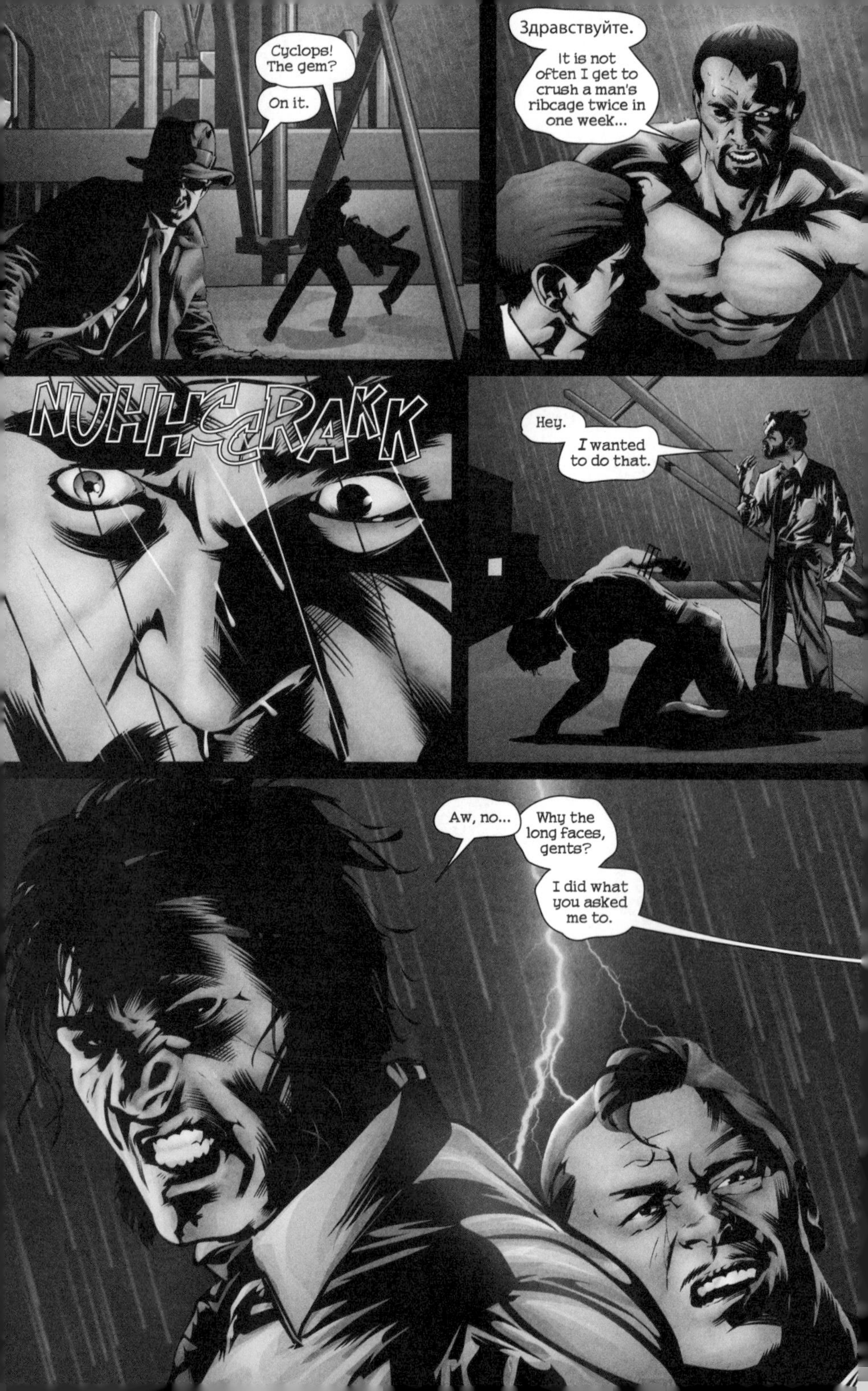
Cyclops! The gem?
On it.
Здравствуйте.
It is not often I get to crush a man's ribcage twice in one week...
NUHHCCRAKK
Hey.
I wanted to do that.
Aw, no...
Why the long faces, gents?
I did what you asked me to.

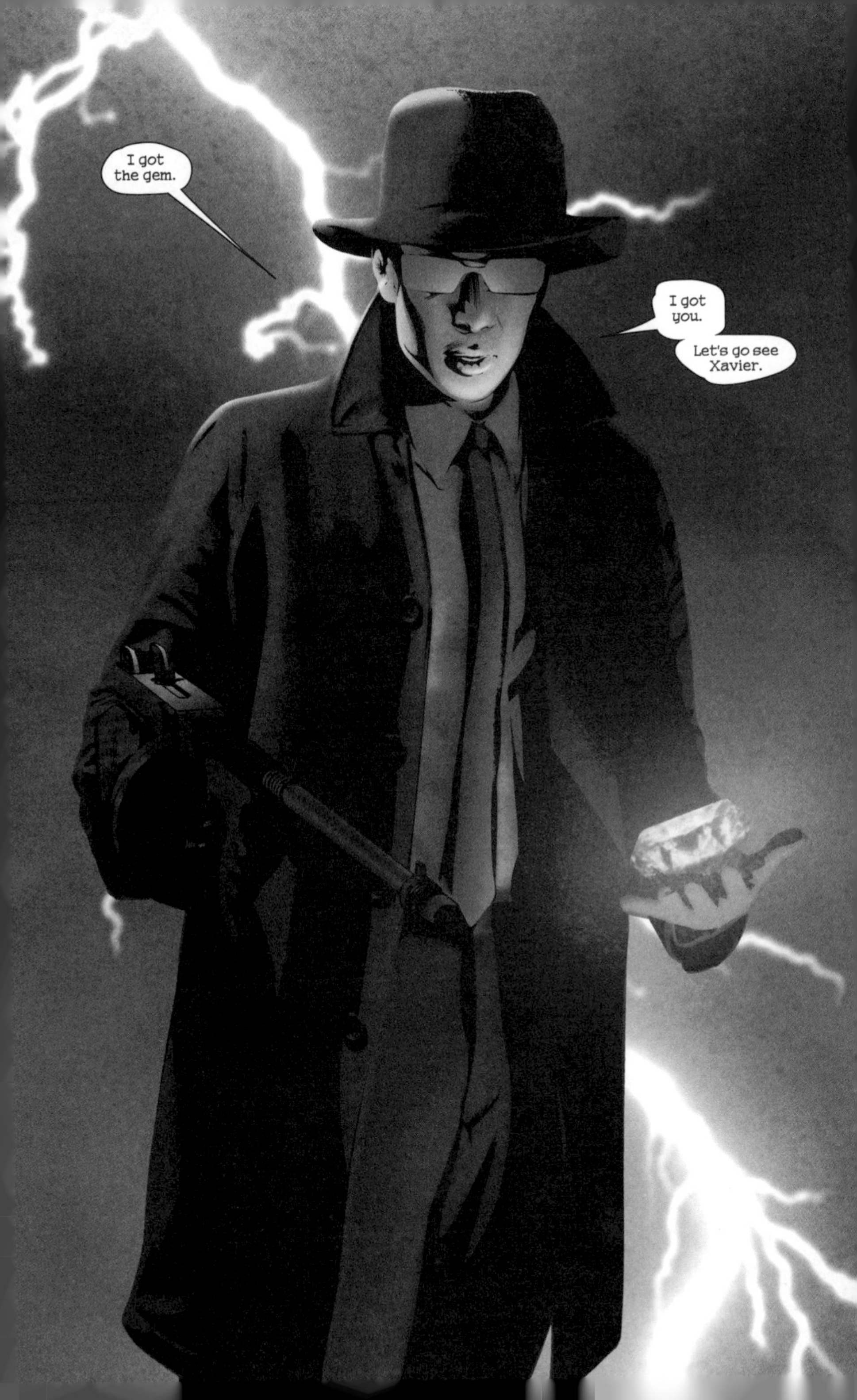
I got the gem.
I got you.
Let's go see Xavier.

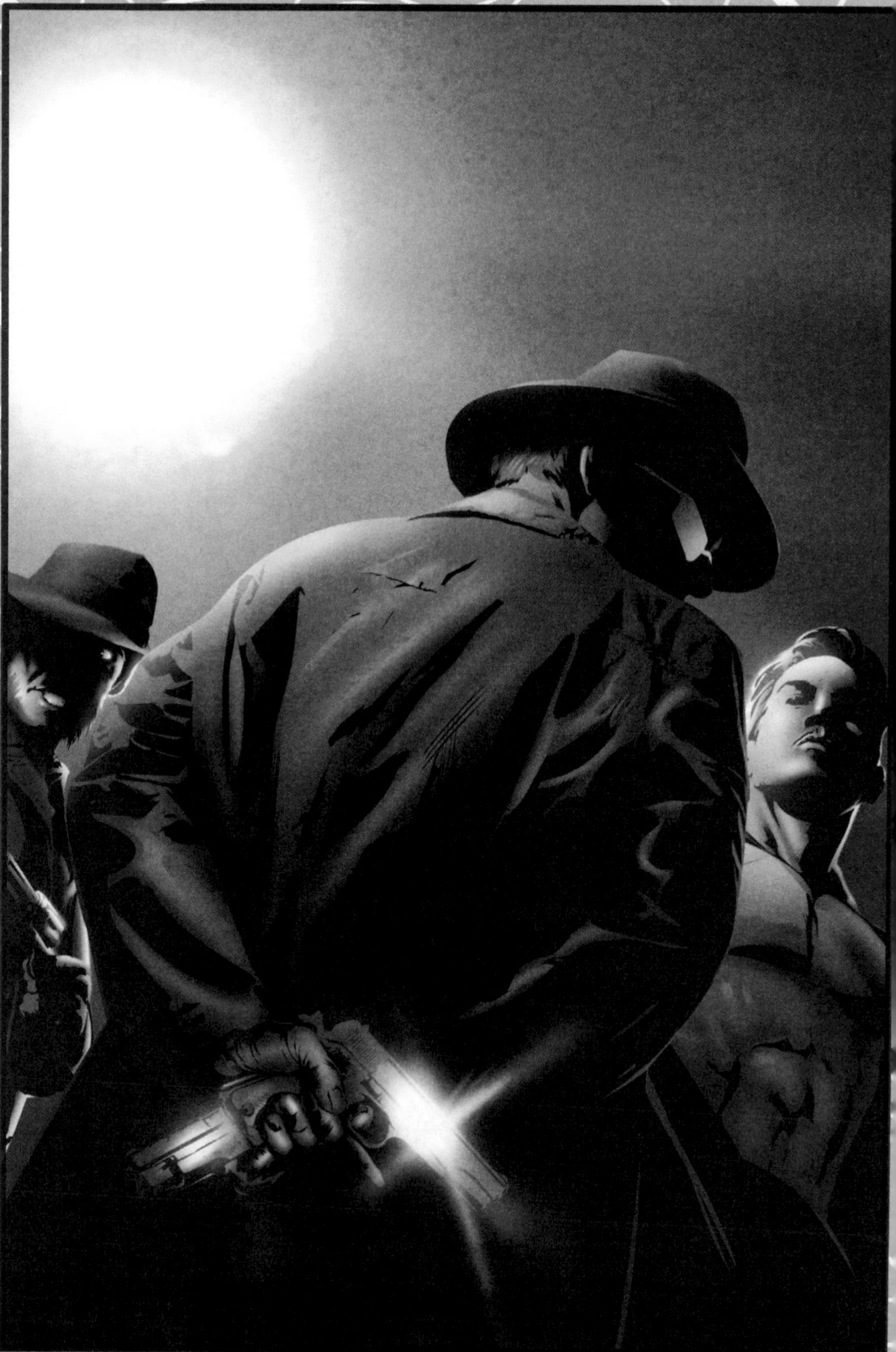

FOUR

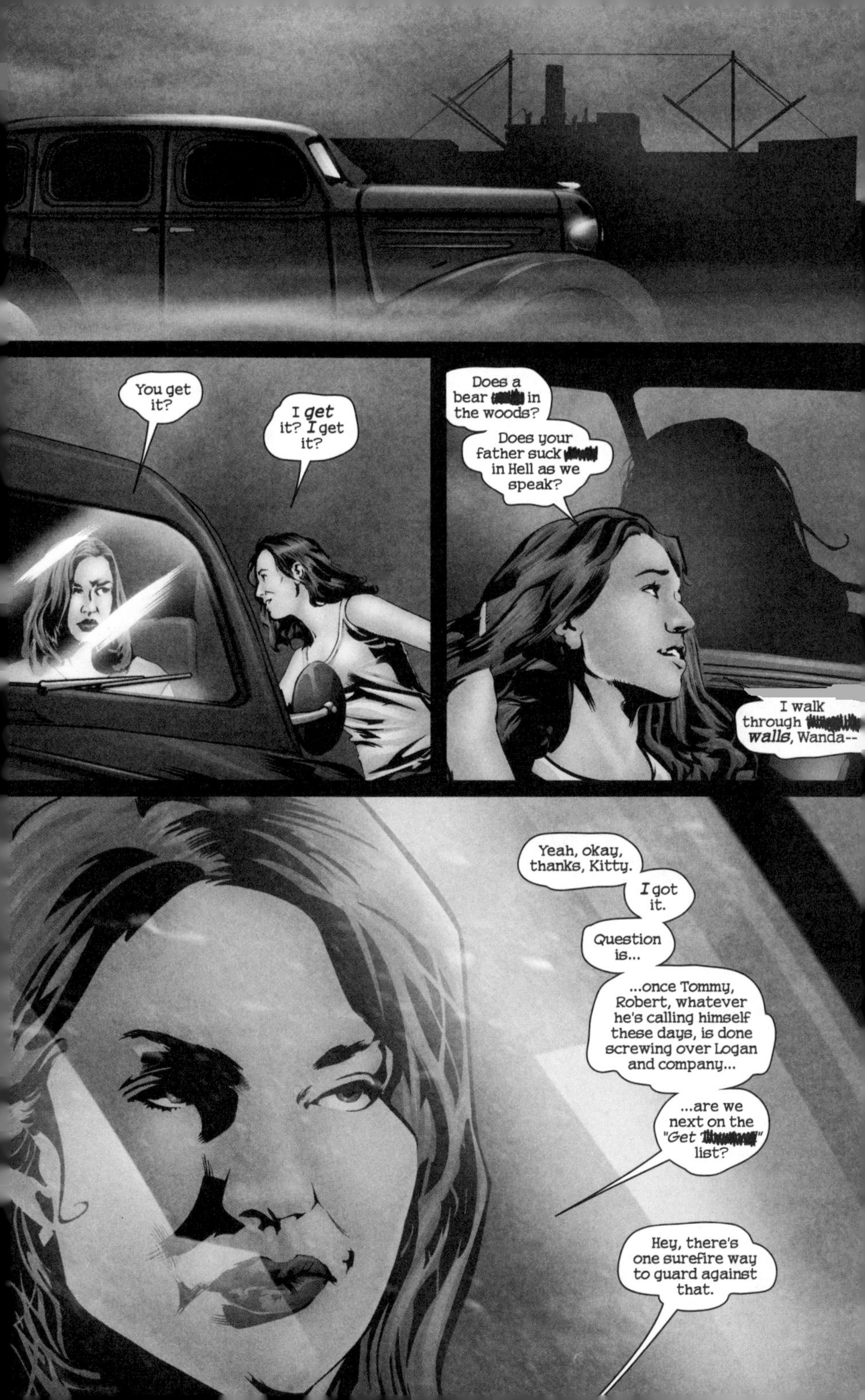
You get it?
I *get* it? *I* get it?
Does a bear [redacted] in the woods?
Does your father suck [redacted] in Hell as we speak?
I walk through [redacted] *walls*, Wanda--
Yeah, okay, thanks, Kitty.
I got it.
Question is...
...once Tommy, Robert, whatever he's calling himself these days, is done screwing over Logan and company...
...are we next on the *"Get [redacted]"* list?
Hey, there's one surefire way to guard against that.

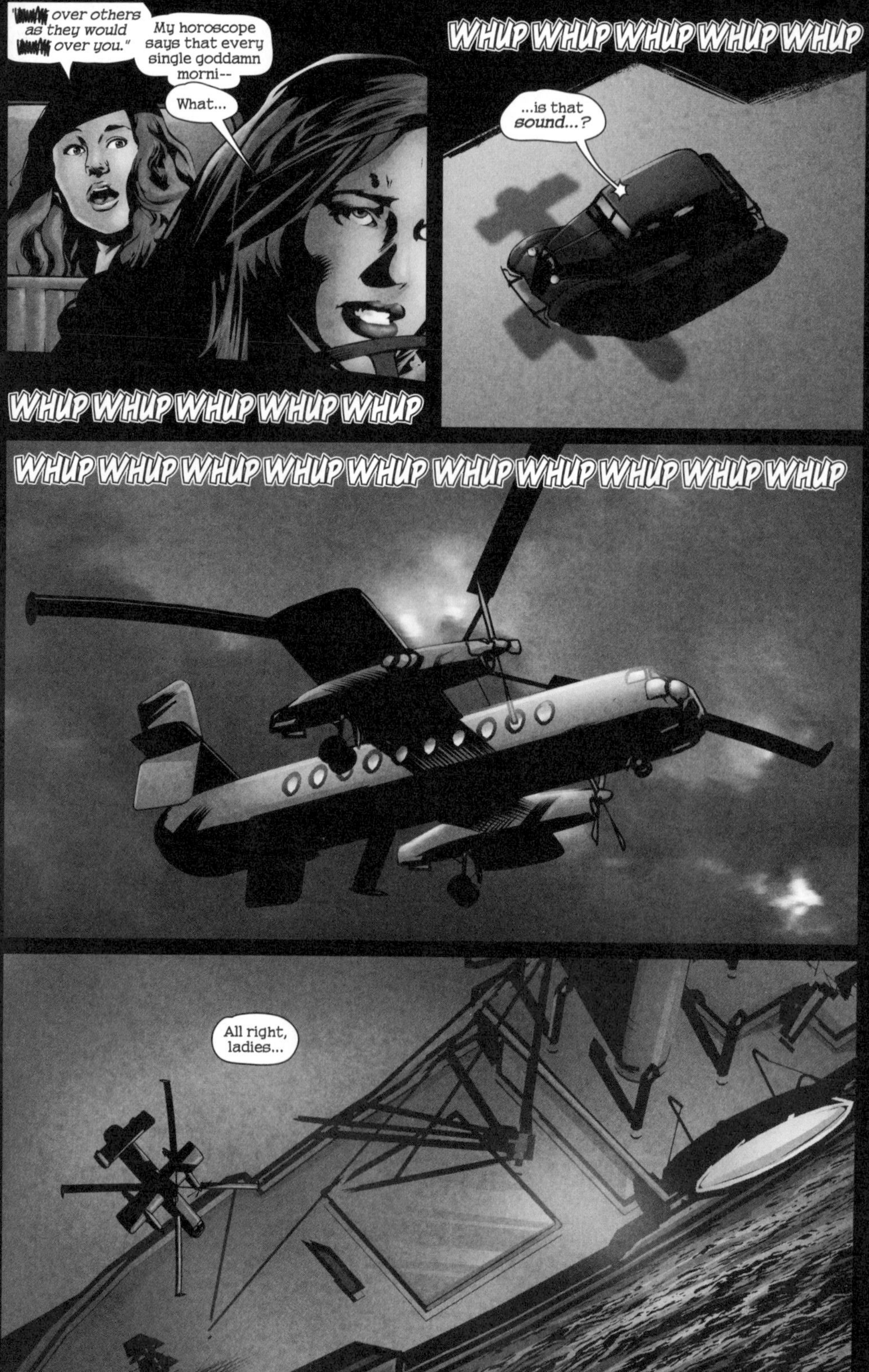
"[redacted] over others as they would [redacted] over you."
My horoscope says that every single goddamn morni--
What...
WHUP WHUP WHUP WHUP WHUP
WHUP WHUP WHUP WHUP WHUP
...is that sound...?
WHUP WHUP WHUP WHUP WHUP WHUP WHUP WHUP WHUP WHUP
All right, ladies...

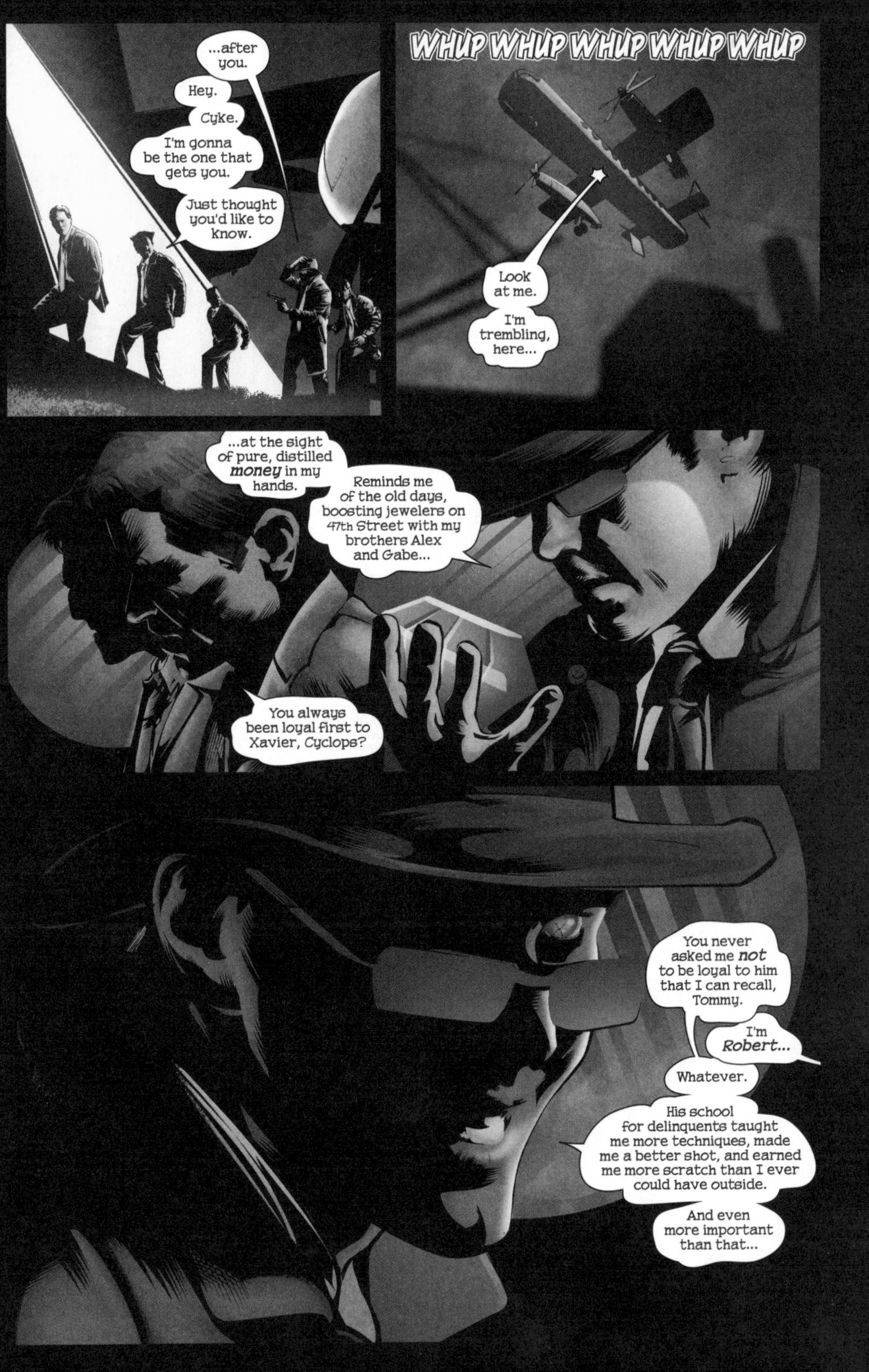
...after you.
Hey.
Cyke.
I'm gonna be the one that gets you.
Just thought you'd like to know.
WHUP WHUP WHUP WHUP WHUP
Look at me.
I'm trembling, here...
...at the sight of pure, distilled *money* in my hands.
Reminds me of the old days, boosting jewelers on 47th Street with my brothers Alex and Gabe...
You always been loyal first to Xavier, Cyclops?
You never asked me *not* to be loyal to him that I can recall, Tommy.
I'm *Robert...*
Whatever.
His school for delinquents taught me more techniques, made me a better shot, and earned me more scratch than I ever could have outside.
And even more important than that...

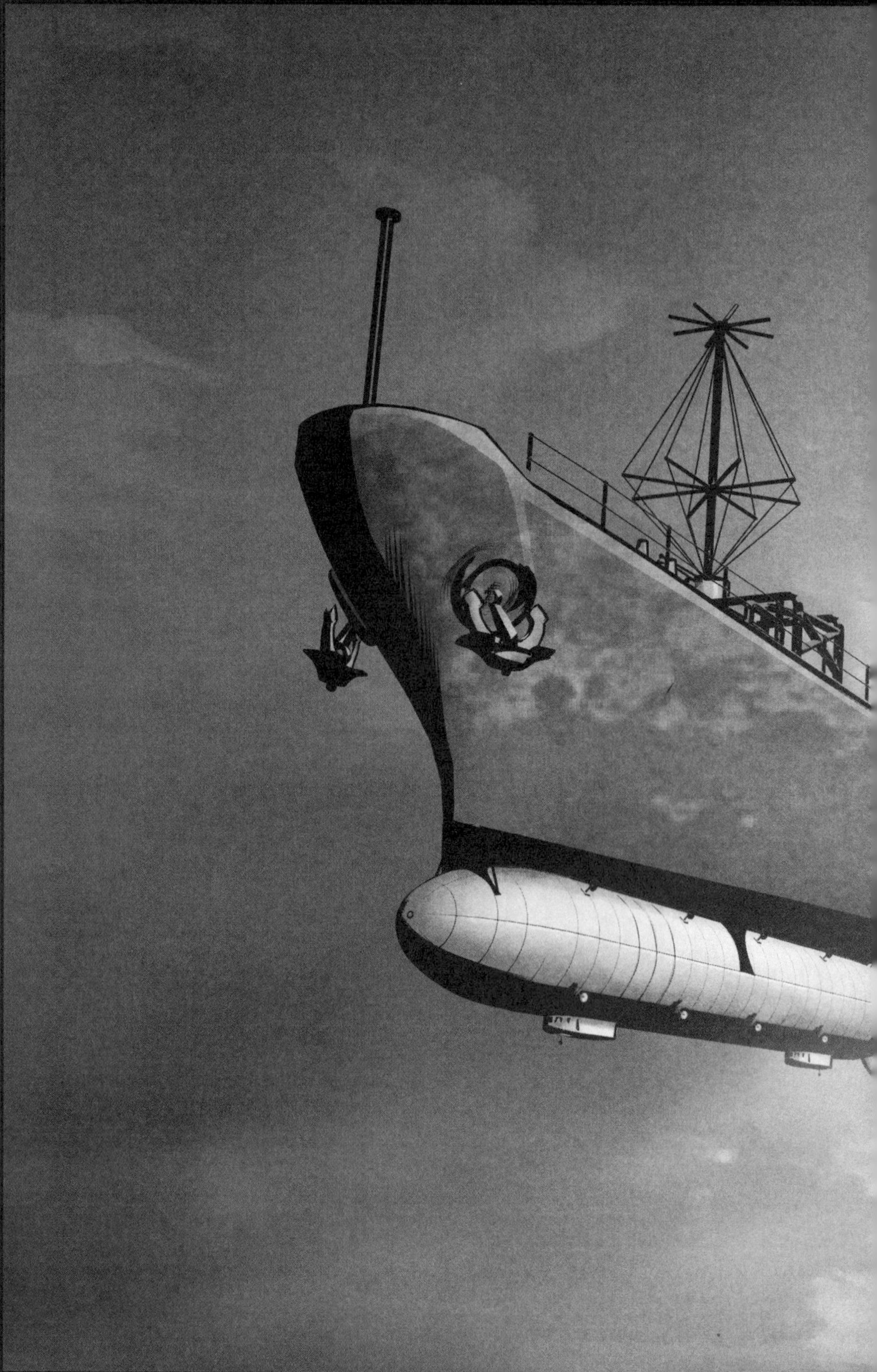

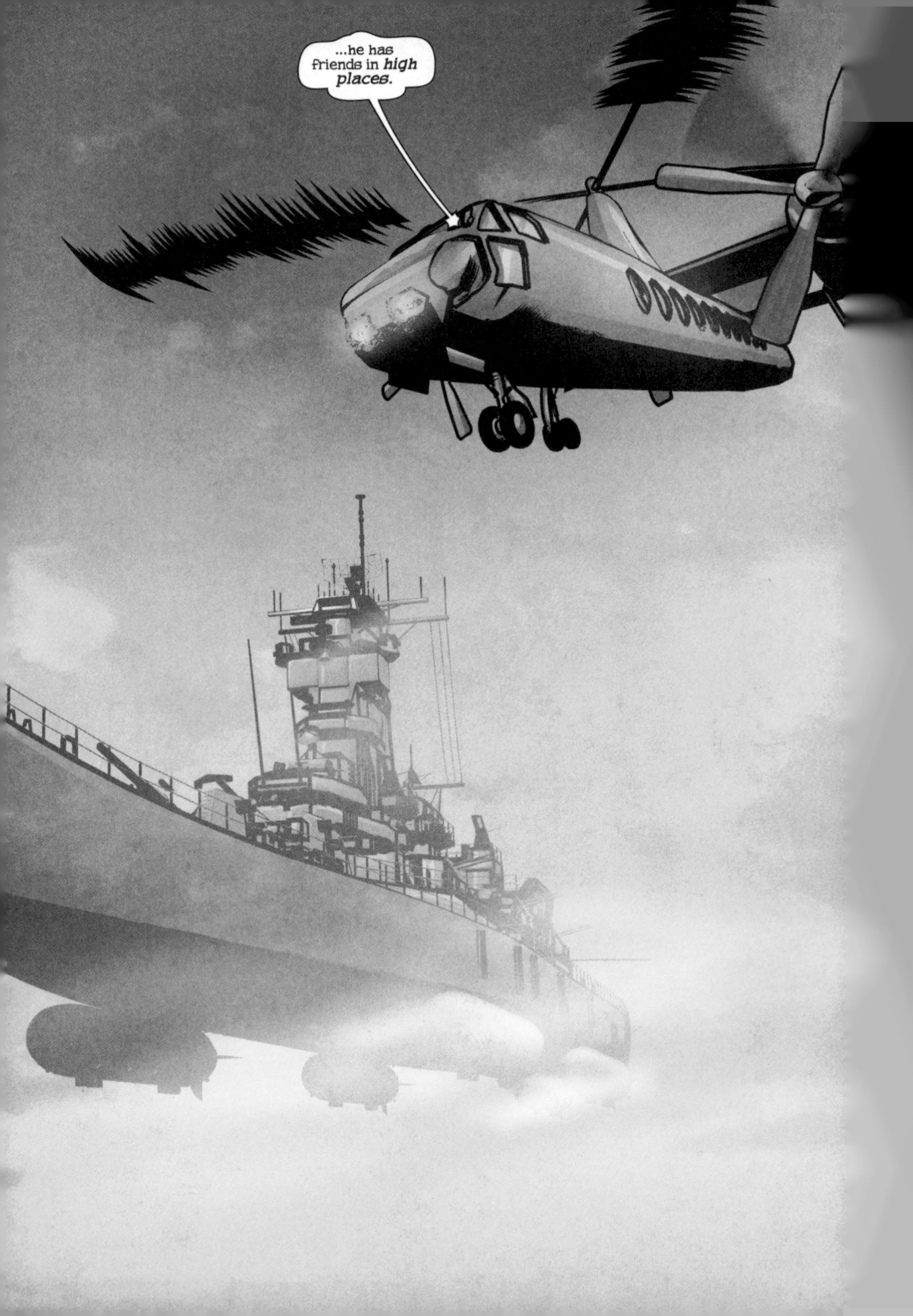
...he has friends in *high places.*

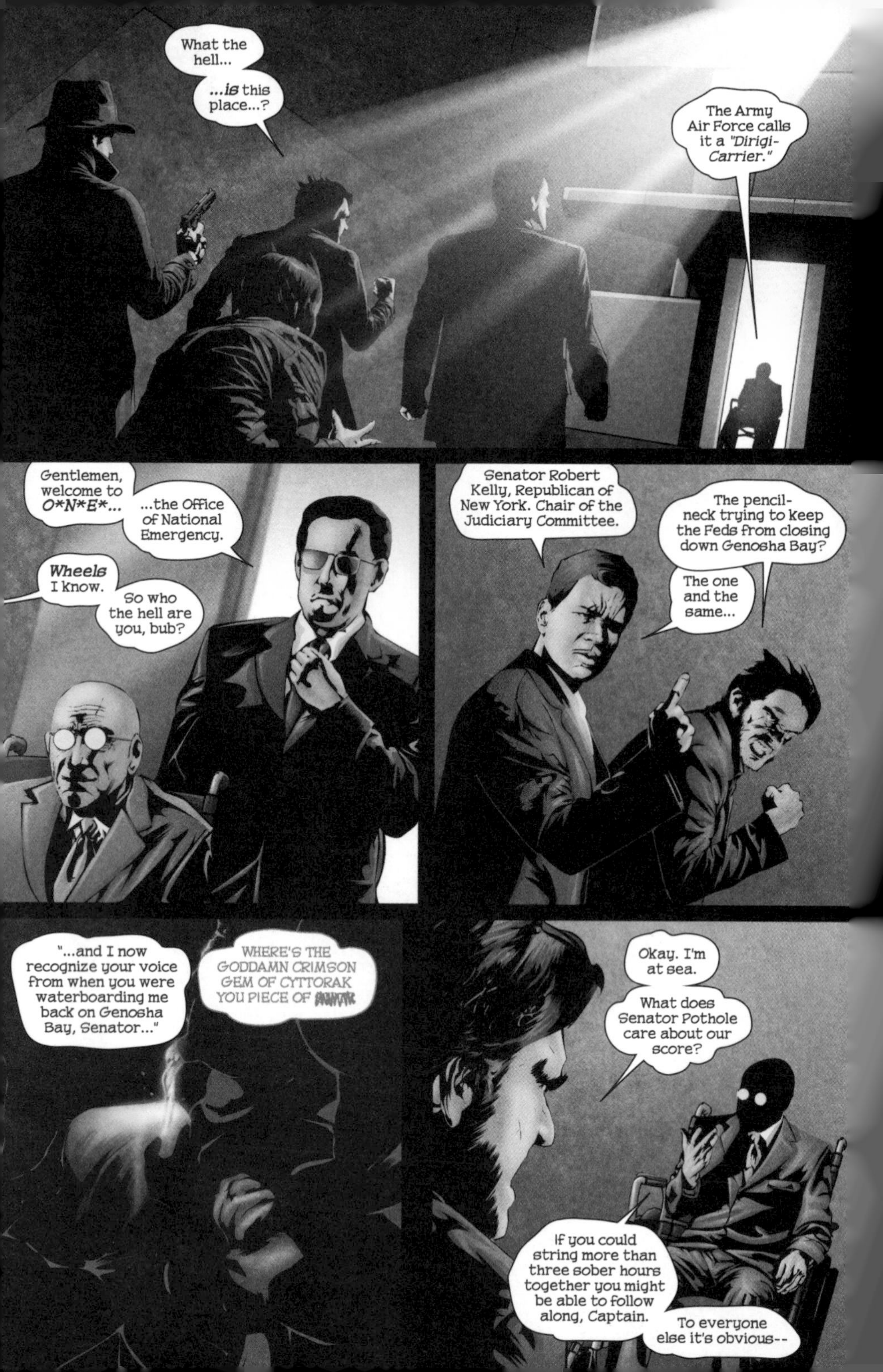
What the hell...
...is this place...?
The Army Air Force calls it a "Dirigi-Carrier."
Gentlemen, welcome to O*N*E*...
...the Office of National Emergency.
Wheels I know.
So who the hell are you, bub?
Senator Robert Kelly, Republican of New York. Chair of the Judiciary Committee.
The pencil-neck trying to keep the Feds from closing down Genosha Bay?
The one and the same...
"...and I now recognize your voice from when you were waterboarding me back on Genosha Bay, Senator..."
WHERE'S THE GODDAMN CRIMSON GEM OF CYTTORAK YOU PIECE OF
Okay. I'm at sea.
What does Senator Pothole care about our score?
If you could string more than three sober hours together you might be able to follow along, Captain.
To everyone else it's obvious--

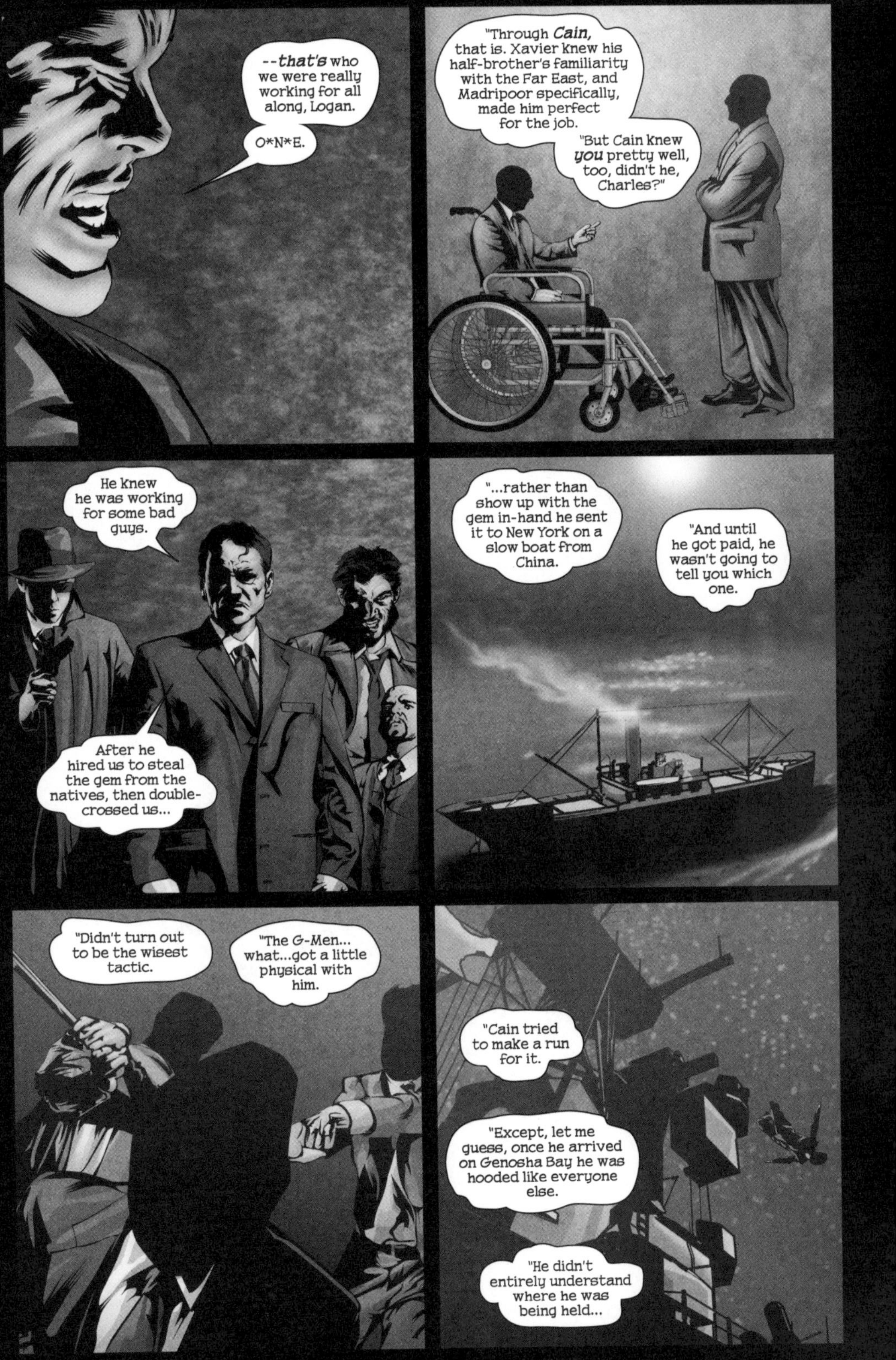
--*that's* who we were really working for all along, Logan.
O*N*E.
"Through *Cain,* that is. Xavier knew his half-brother's familiarity with the Far East, and Madripoor specifically, made him perfect for the job.
"But Cain knew *you* pretty well, too, didn't he, Charles?"
He knew he was working for some bad guys.
After he hired us to steal the gem from the natives, then double-crossed us...
"...rather than show up with the gem in-hand he sent it to New York on a slow boat from China.
"And until he got paid, he wasn't going to tell you which one.
"Didn't turn out to be the wisest tactic.
"The G-Men... what...got a little physical with him.
"Cain tried to make a run for it.
"Except, let me guess, once he arrived on Genosha Bay he was hooded like everyone else.
"He didn't entirely understand where he was being held...

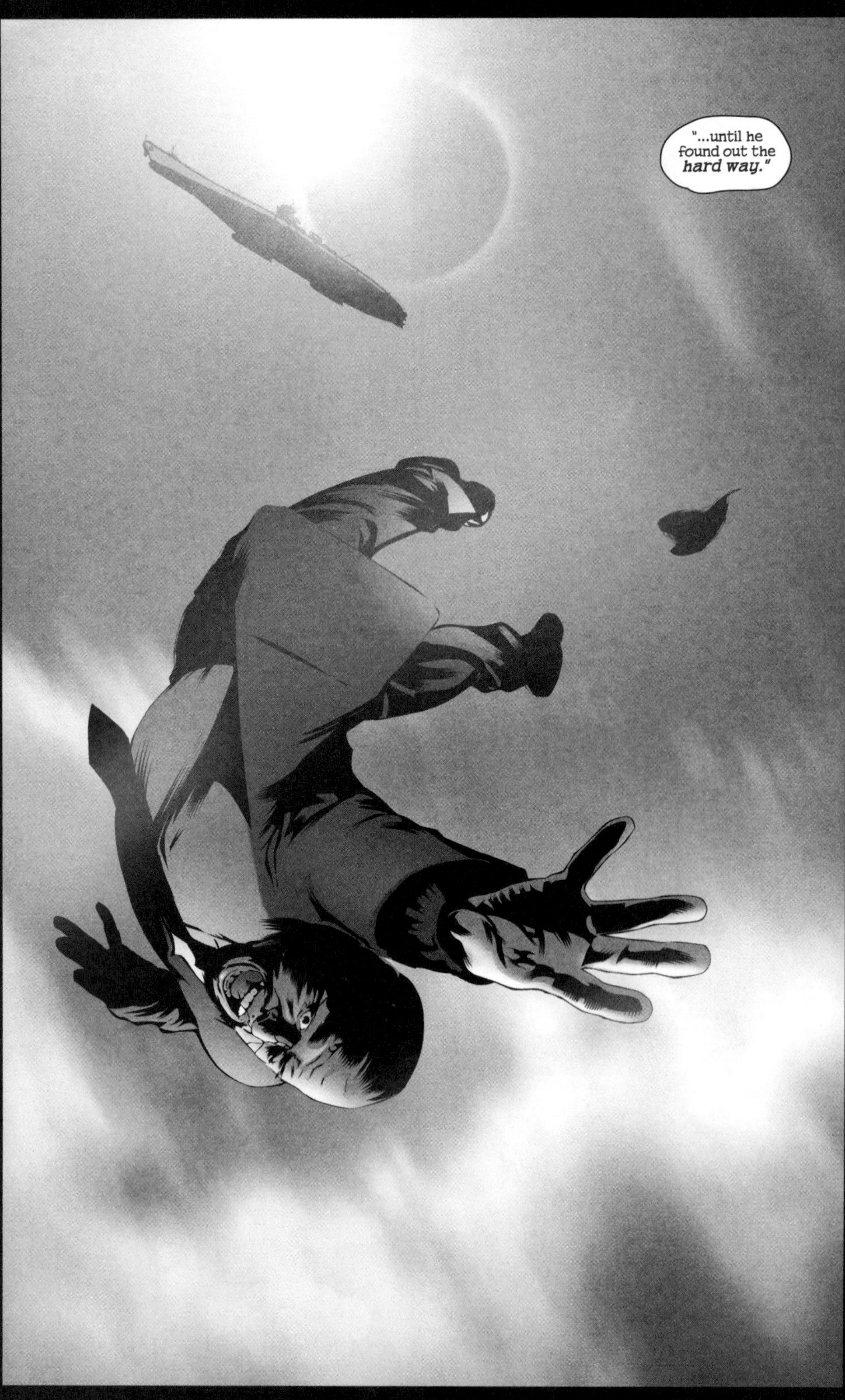
"...until he found out the *hard way.*"

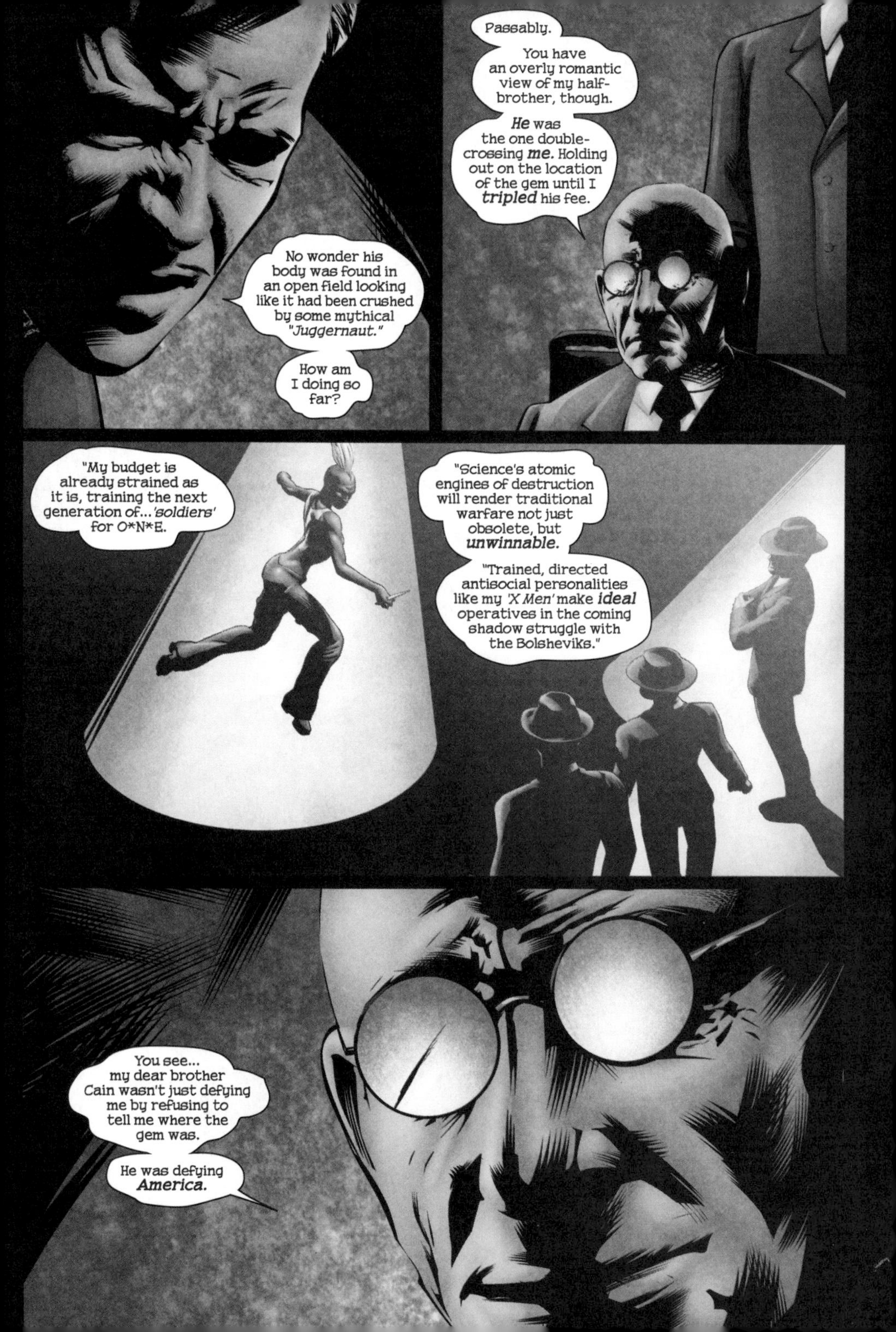
No wonder his body was found in an open field looking like it had been crushed by some mythical "Juggernaut."
How am I doing so far?
Passably.
You have an overly romantic view of my half-brother, though.
He was the one double-crossing me. Holding out on the location of the gem until I tripled his fee.
"My budget is already strained as it is, training the next generation of... 'soldiers' for O*N*E.
"Science's atomic engines of destruction will render traditional warfare not just obsolete, but unwinnable.
"Trained, directed antisocial personalities like my 'X Men' make ideal operatives in the coming shadow struggle with the Bolsheviks."
You see... my dear brother Cain wasn't just defying me by refusing to tell me where the gem was.
He was defying America.

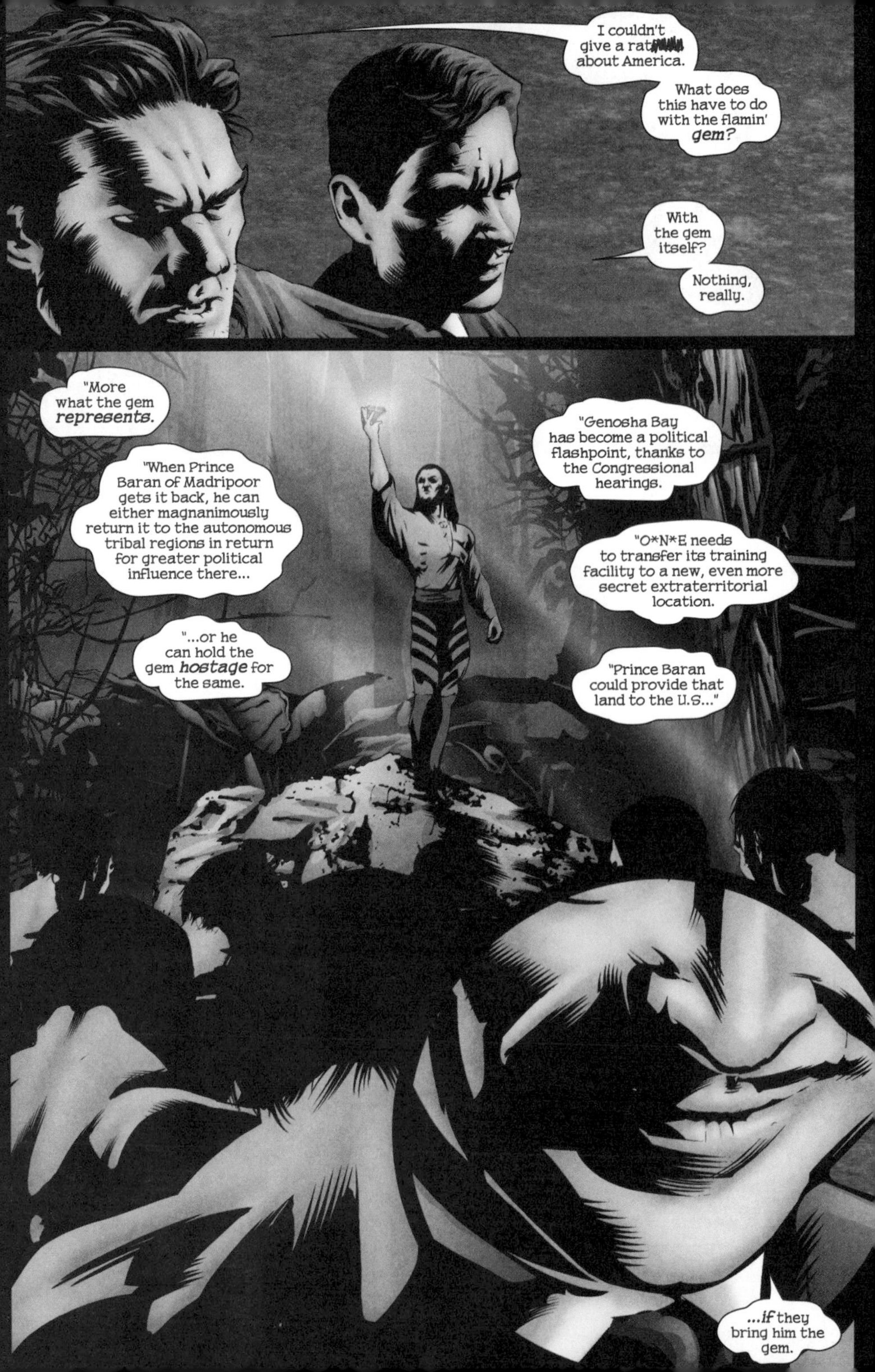
I couldn't give a rat[redacted] about America.
What does this have to do with the flamin' *gem*?
With the gem itself?
Nothing, really.
"More what the gem *represents*.
"When Prince Baran of Madripoor gets it back, he can either magnanimously return it to the autonomous tribal regions in return for greater political influence there...
"...or he can hold the gem *hostage* for the same.
"Genosha Bay has become a political flashpoint, thanks to the Congressional hearings.
"O*N*E needs to transfer its training facility to a new, even more secret extraterritorial location.
"Prince Baran could provide that land to the U.S..."
...*if* they bring him the gem.

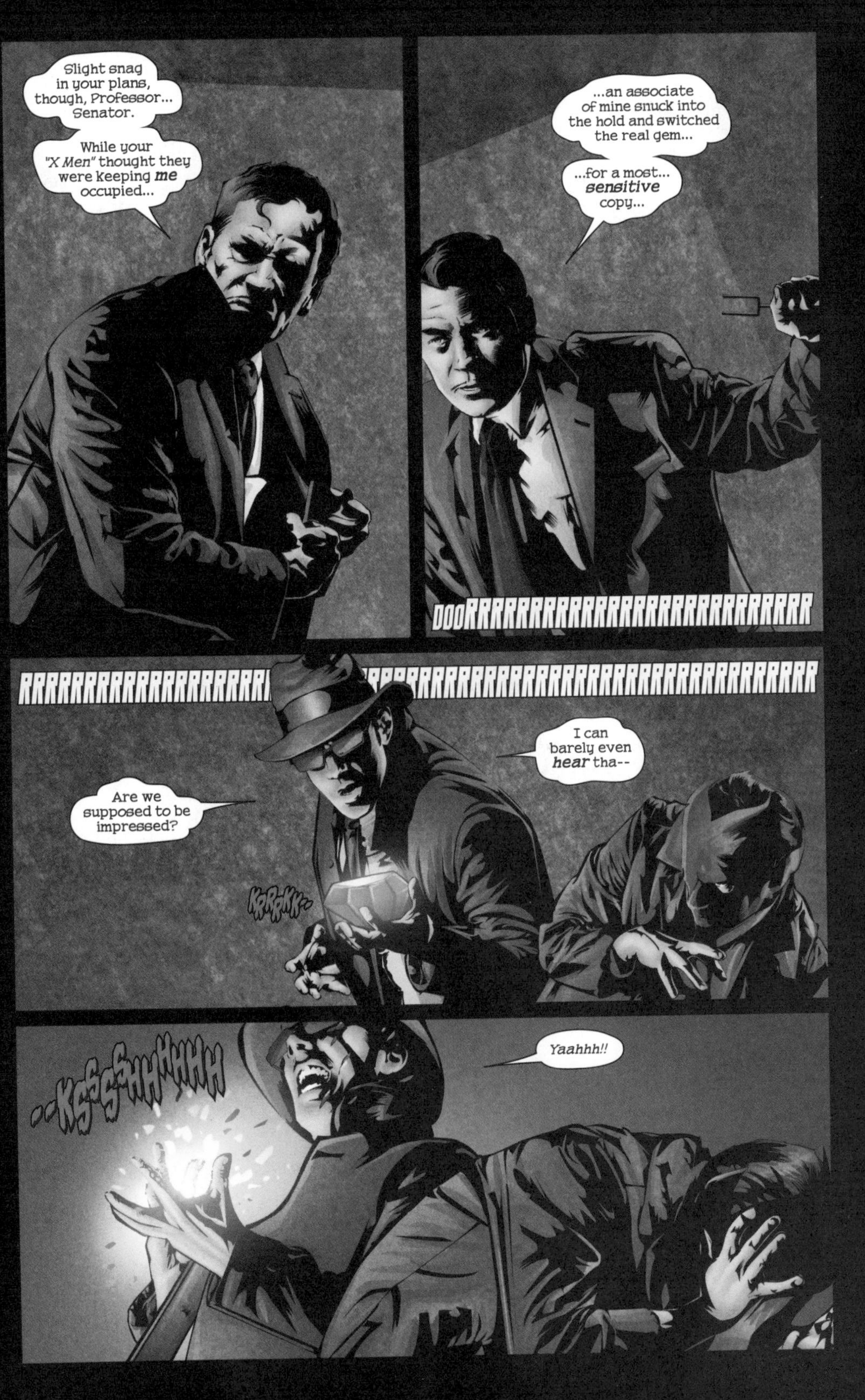
Slight snag in your plans, though, Professor... Senator.
While your "X Men" thought they were keeping *me* occupied...
...an associate of mine snuck into the hold and switched the real gem...
...for a most... ***sensitive*** copy...
DOORRRRRRRRRRRRRRRRRRRRRRRRRRR
RRRRRRRRRRRRRRRRR
RRRRRRRRRRRRRRRRRRRRRRRRRRRRRRRR
I can barely even ***hear*** tha--
Are we supposed to be impressed?
KRRRKK--
Yaahhh!!
--KSSSHHHHHH

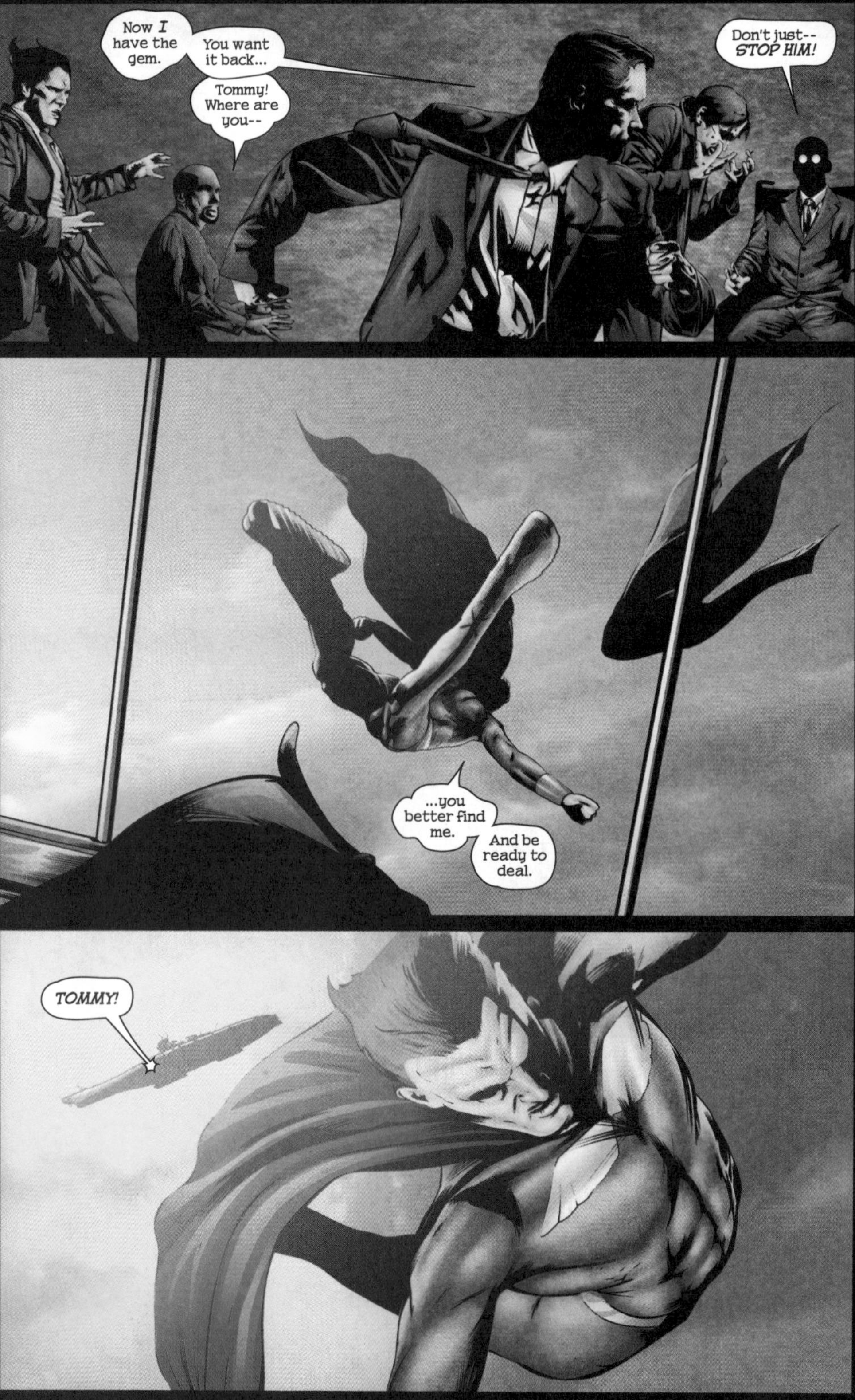
Now I have the gem.
You want it back...
Tommy! Where are you--
Don't just-- STOP HIM!
...you better find me.
And be ready to deal.
TOMMY!

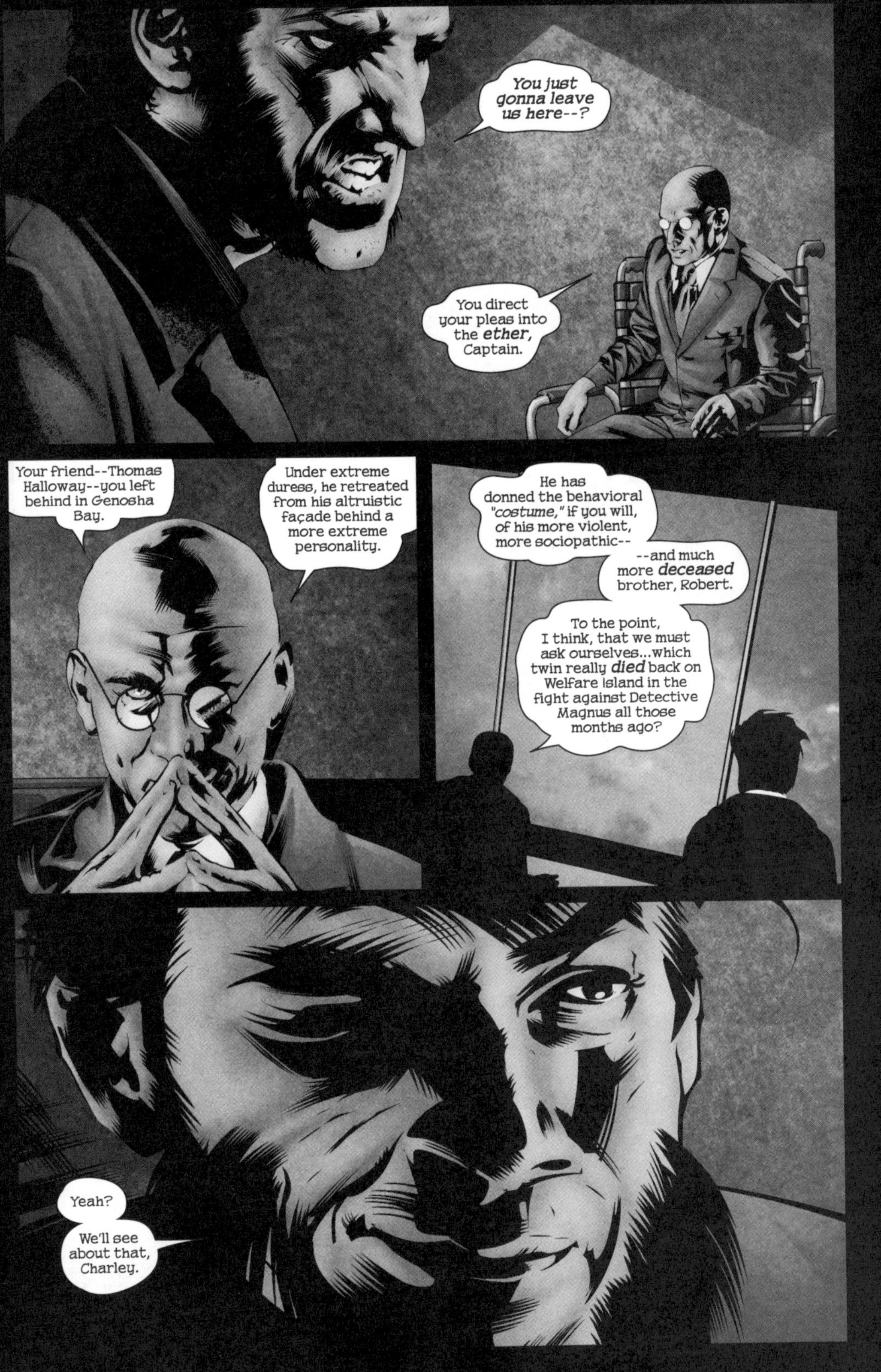
You just gonna leave us here--?
You direct your pleas into the *ether,* Captain.
Your friend--Thomas Halloway--you left behind in Genosha Bay.
Under extreme duress, he retreated from his altruistic façade behind a more extreme personality.
He has donned the behavioral *"costume,"* if you will, of his more violent, more sociopathic--
--and much more *deceased* brother, Robert.
To the point, I think, that we must ask ourselves...which twin really *died* back on Welfare Island in the fight against Detective Magnus all those months ago?
Yeah?
We'll see about that, Charley.

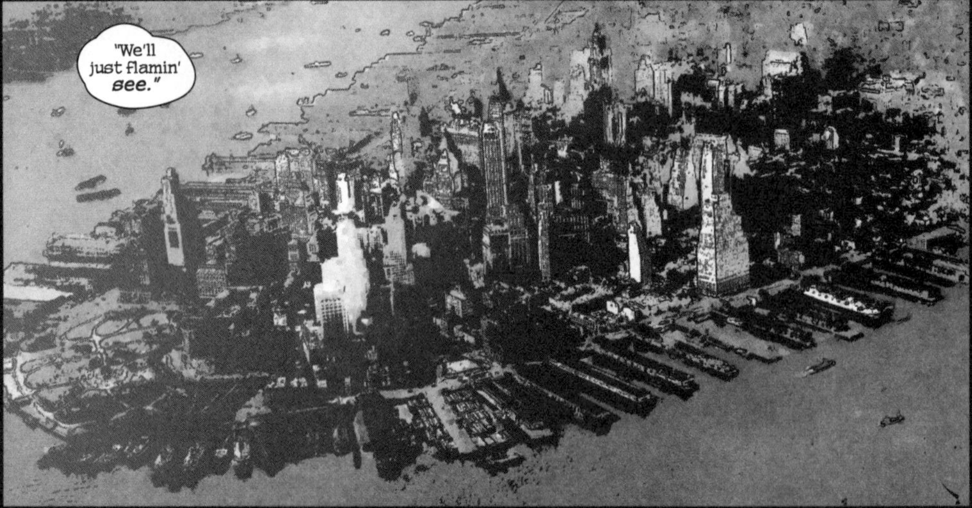
"We'll just flamin' *see.*"

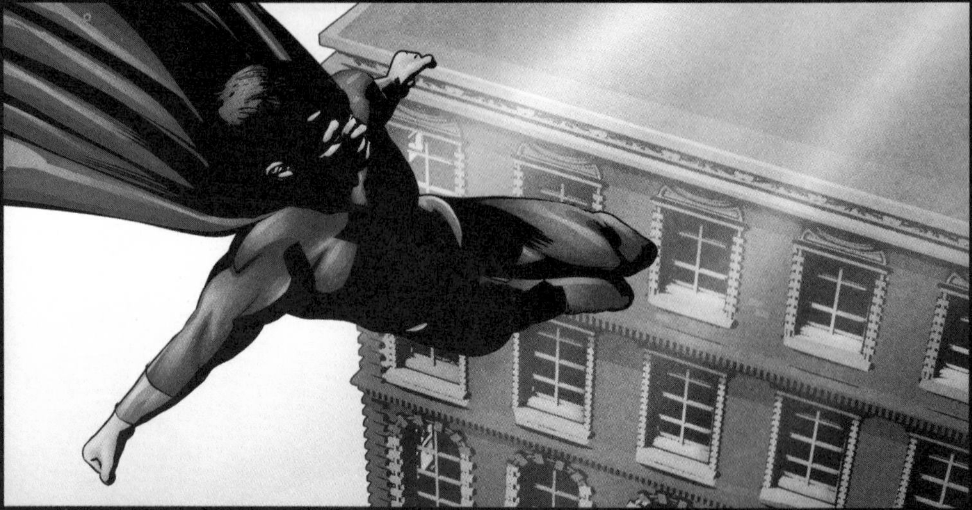

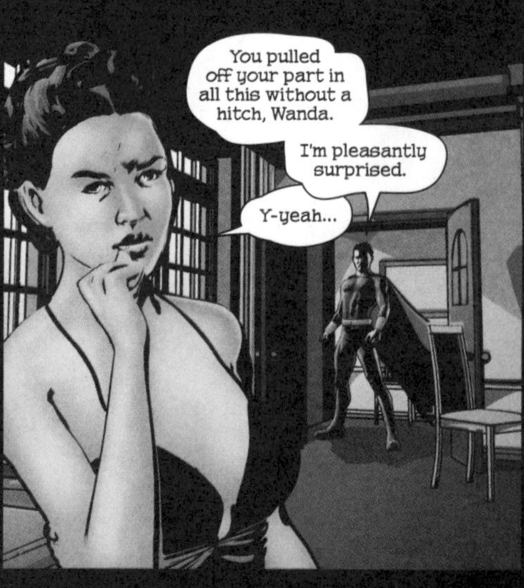
You pulled off your part in all this without a hitch, Wanda.
I'm pleasantly surprised.
Y-yeah...

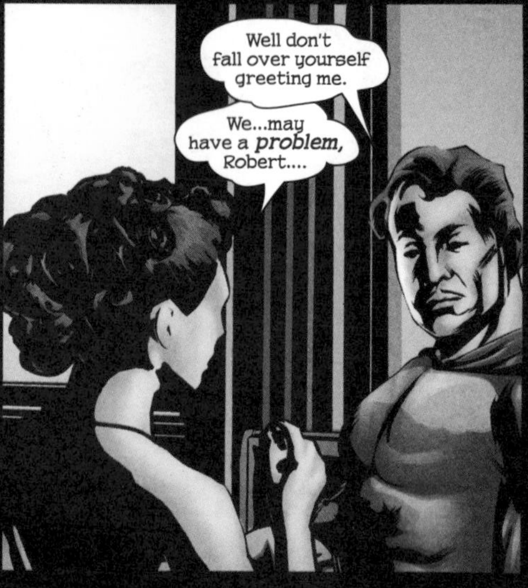
Well don't fall over yourself greeting me.
We...may have a *problem,* Robert....

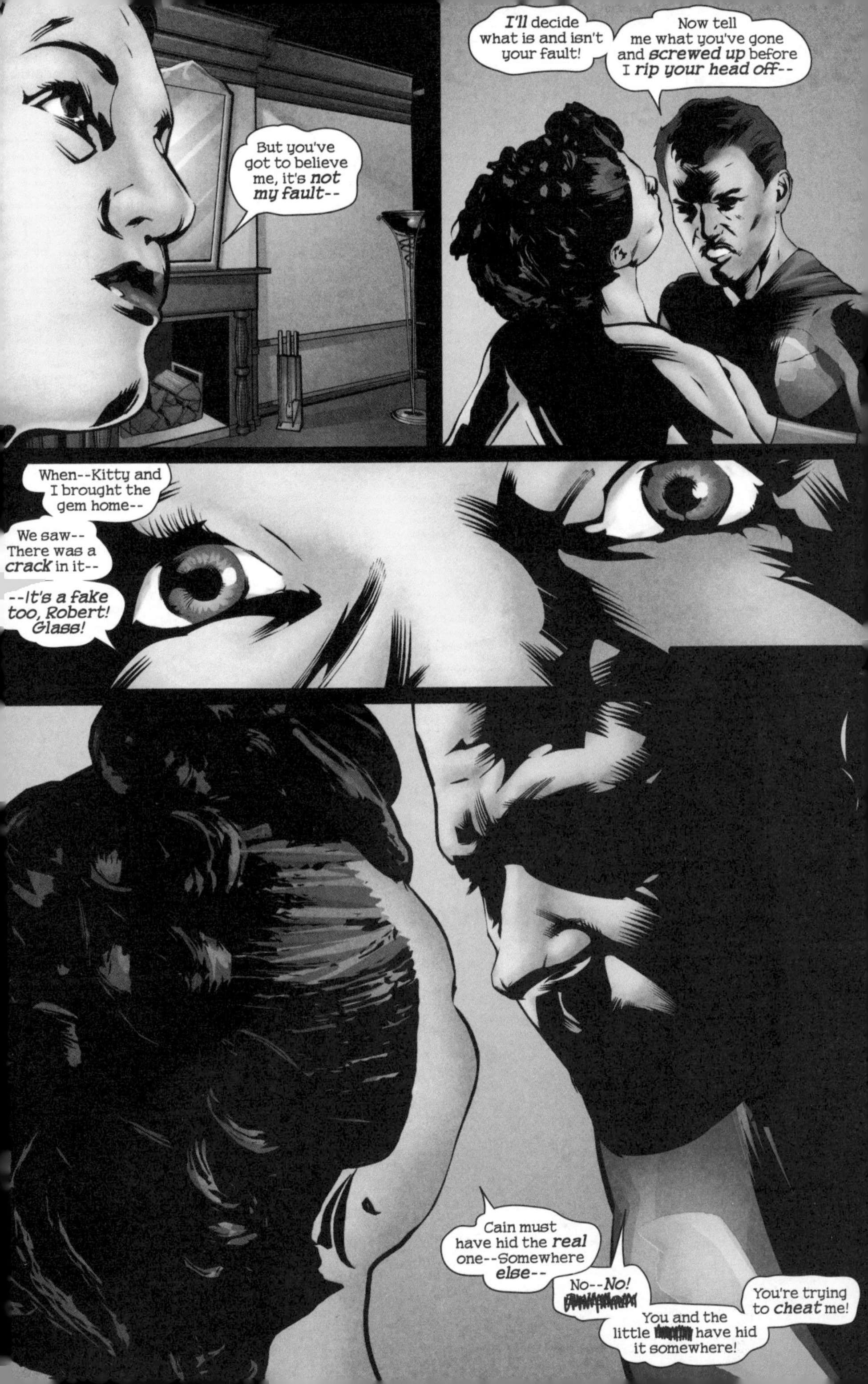
But you've got to believe me, it's **not my fault**--
I'll decide what is and isn't your fault!
Now tell me what you've gone and ***screwed up*** before I ***rip your head off***--
When--Kitty and I brought the gem home--
We saw-- There was a ***crack*** in it--
--It's a fake too, Robert! Glass!
Cain must have hid the ***real*** one--Somewhere ***else***--
No--***No!*** [redacted]
You and the little [redacted] have hid it somewhere!
You're trying to ***cheat*** me!

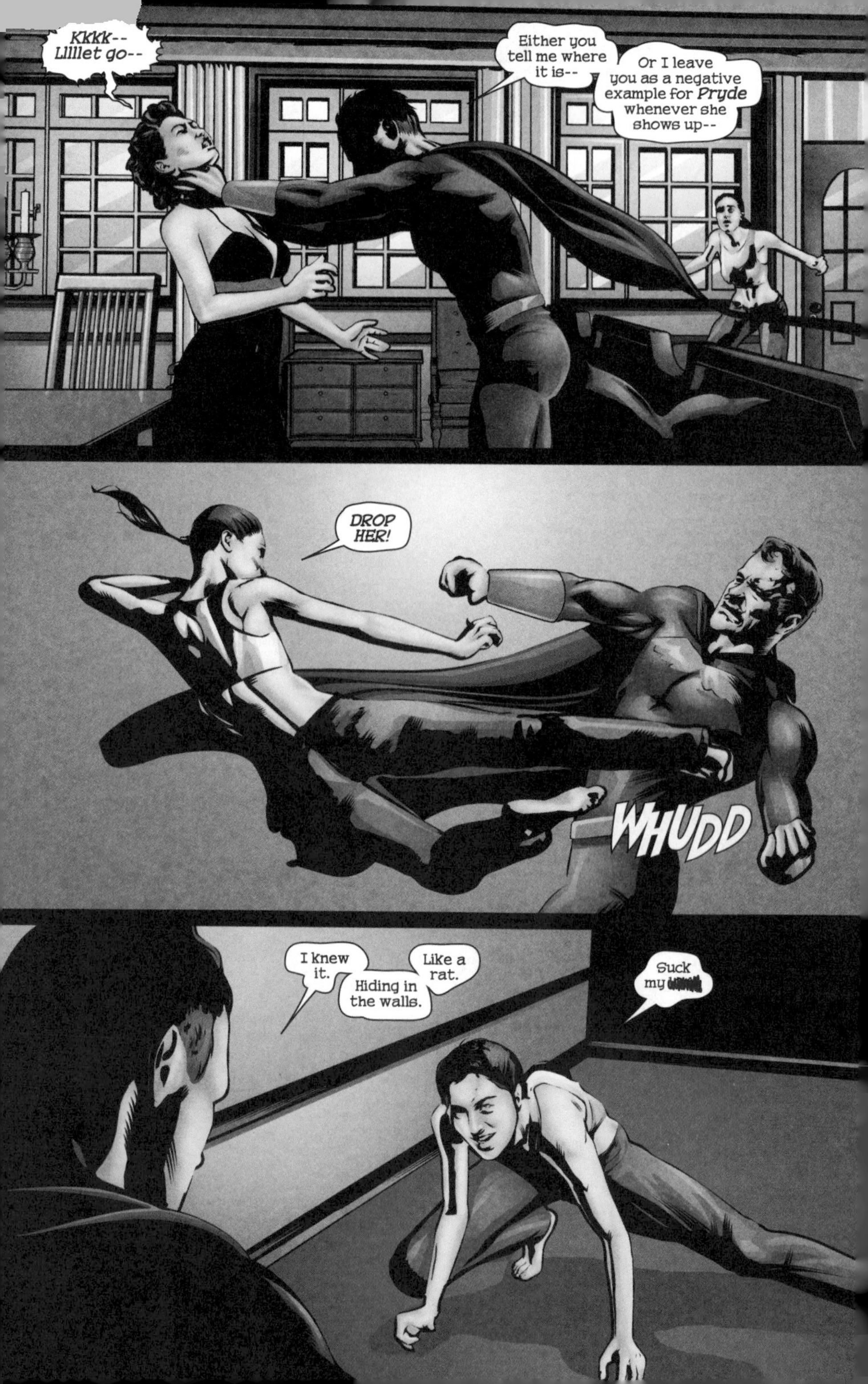
KKKK-- Lllllet go--
Either you tell me where it is--
Or I leave you as a negative example for Pryde whenever she shows up--
DROP HER!
WHUDD
I knew it.
Hiding in the walls.
Like a rat.
Suck my [redacted]

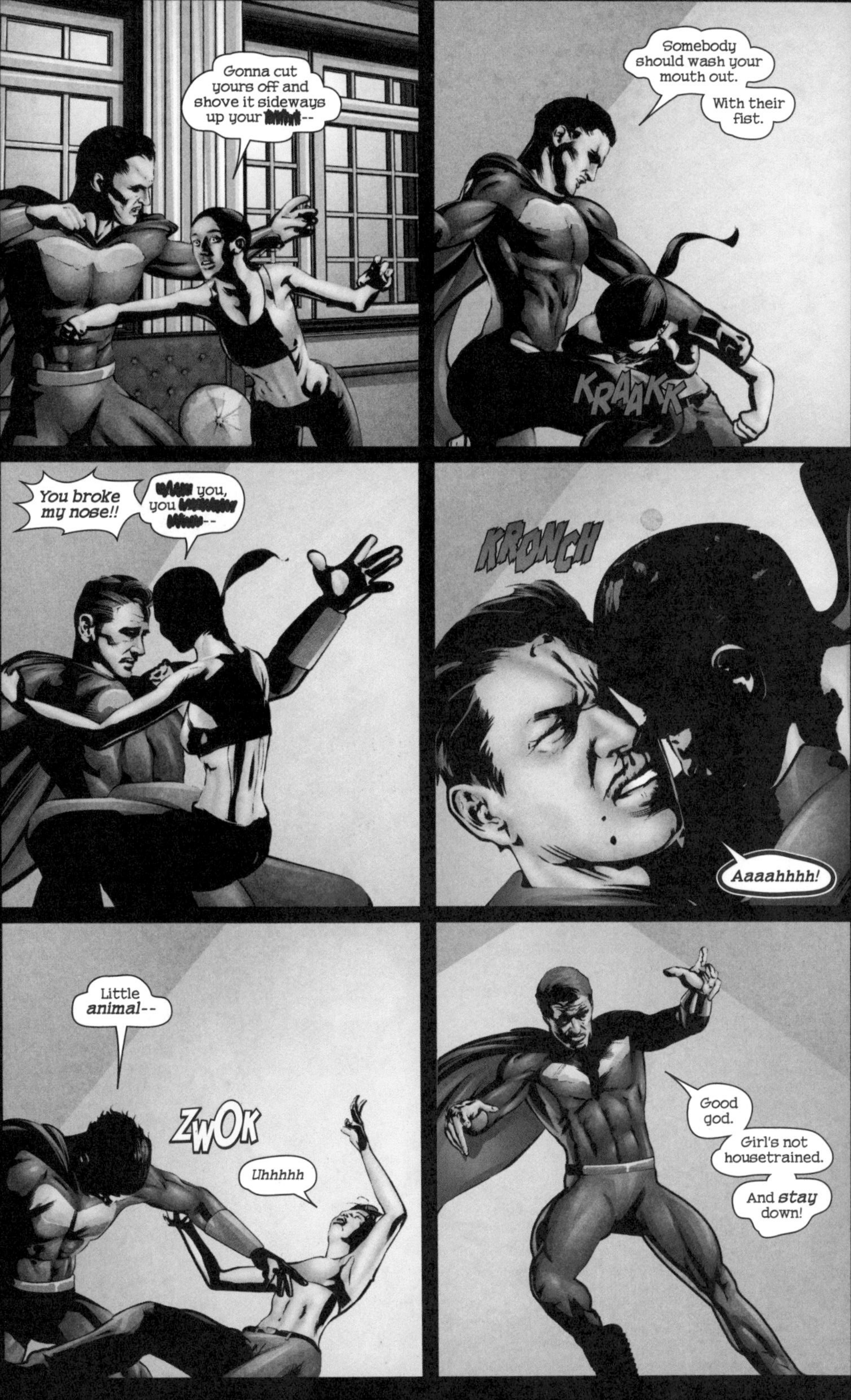
Gonna cut yours off and shove it sideways up your [redacted]--
Somebody should wash your mouth out.
With their fist.
KRAAKK
You broke my nose!!
[redacted] you, you [redacted]--
KRONCH
Aaaahhhh!
Little animal--
ZWOK
Uhhhhh
Good god.
Girl's not housetrained.
And stay down!

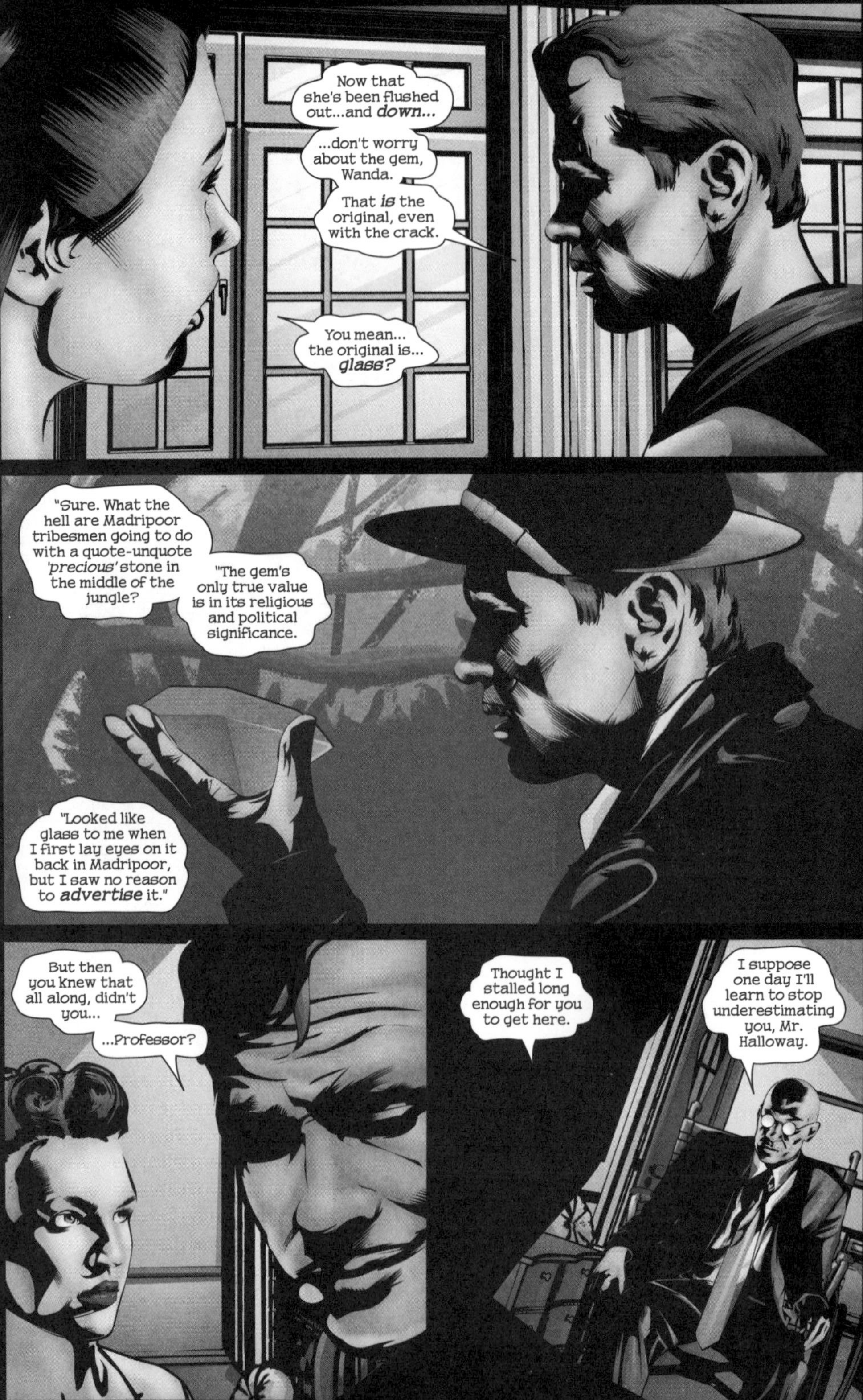
Now that she's been flushed out...and *down*...
...don't worry about the gem, Wanda.
That *is* the original, even with the crack.
You mean... the original is... *glass?*
"Sure. What the hell are Madripoor tribesmen going to do with a quote-unquote *'precious'* stone in the middle of the jungle?
"The gem's only true value is in its religious and political significance.
"Looked like glass to me when I first lay eyes on it back in Madripoor, but I saw no reason to *advertise* it."
But then you knew that all along, didn't you...
...Professor?
Thought I stalled long enough for you to get here.
I suppose one day I'll learn to stop underestimating you, Mr. Halloway.

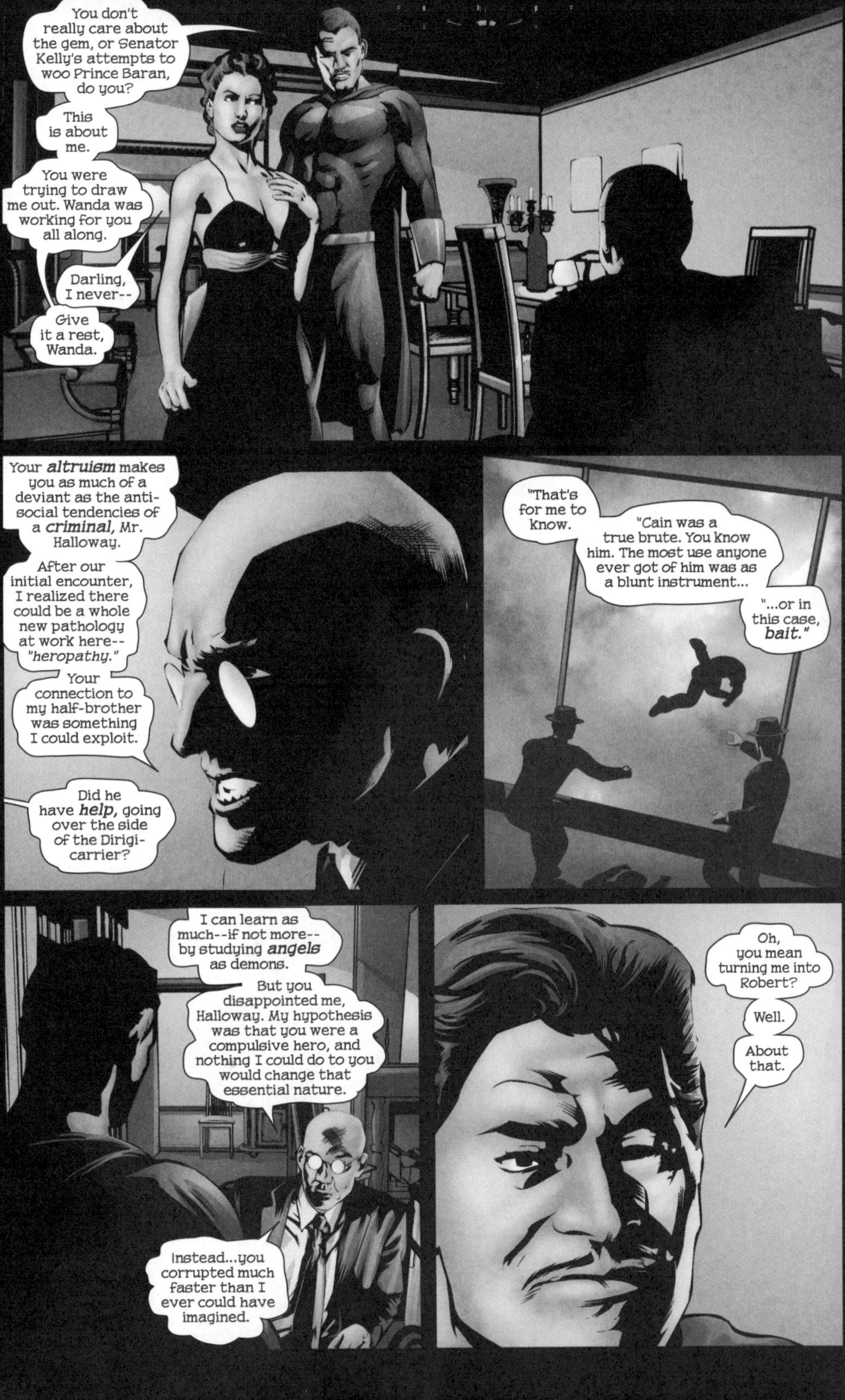

You don't really care about the gem, or Senator Kelly's attempts to woo Prince Baran, do you?
This is about me.
You were trying to draw me out. Wanda was working for you all along.
Darling, I never--
Give it a rest, Wanda.
Your ***altruism*** makes you as much of a deviant as the anti-social tendencies of a ***criminal***, Mr. Halloway.
After our initial encounter, I realized there could be a whole new pathology at work here-- *"heropathy."*
Your connection to my half-brother was something I could exploit.
Did he have ***help***, going over the side of the Dirigi-carrier?
"That's for me to know.
"Cain was a true brute. You know him. The most use anyone ever got of him was as a blunt instrument...
"...or in this case, ***bait.***"
I can learn as much--if not more--by studying ***angels*** as demons.
But you disappointed me, Halloway. My hypothesis was that you were a compulsive hero, and nothing I could do to you would change that essential nature.
Instead...you corrupted much faster than I ever could have imagined.
Oh, you mean turning me into Robert?
Well.
About that.

I was faking.
You heard that man confess to the murder of *Cain Marko,* formerly of Madripoor.
F.B.I.! Don't move!
That woman, Wanda Magnus, is his accomplice.
Miss Pryde, over there on the floor, has six outstanding warrants in three jurisdictions.

In order to reduce his parole violation, I imagine Professor X will want to sing to Director Duncan about a secret illegal Federal agency competing with the Bureau.
But now, if you'll excuse me...

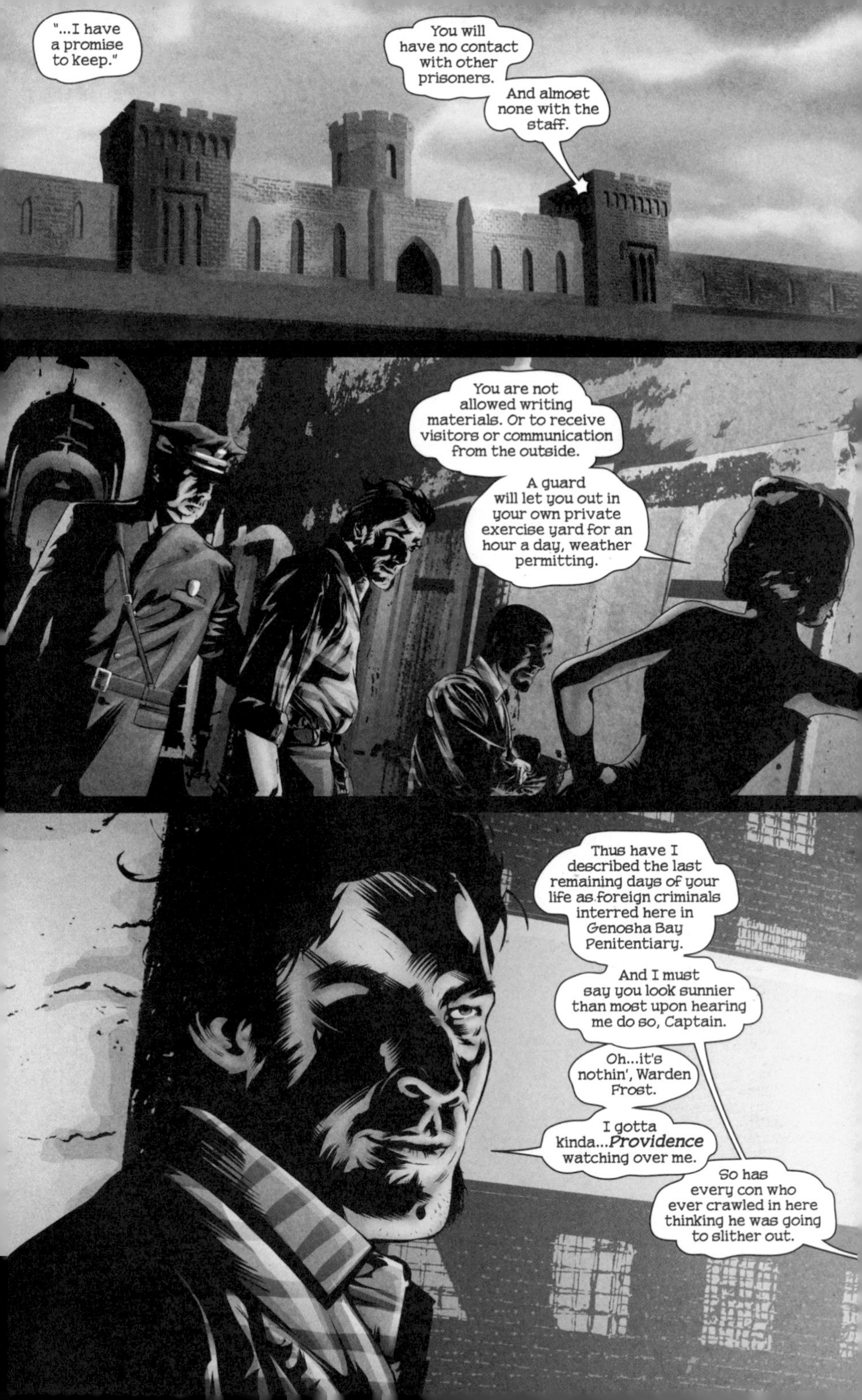
"...I have a promise to keep."
You will have no contact with other prisoners.
And almost none with the staff.
You are not allowed writing materials. Or to receive visitors or communication from the outside.
A guard will let you out in your own private exercise yard for an hour a day, weather permitting.
Thus have I described the last remaining days of your life as foreign criminals interred here in Genosha Bay Penitentiary.
And I must say you look sunnier than most upon hearing me do so, Captain.
Oh...it's nothin', Warden Frost.
I gotta kinda...*Providence* watching over me.
So has every con who ever crawled in here thinking he was going to slither out.

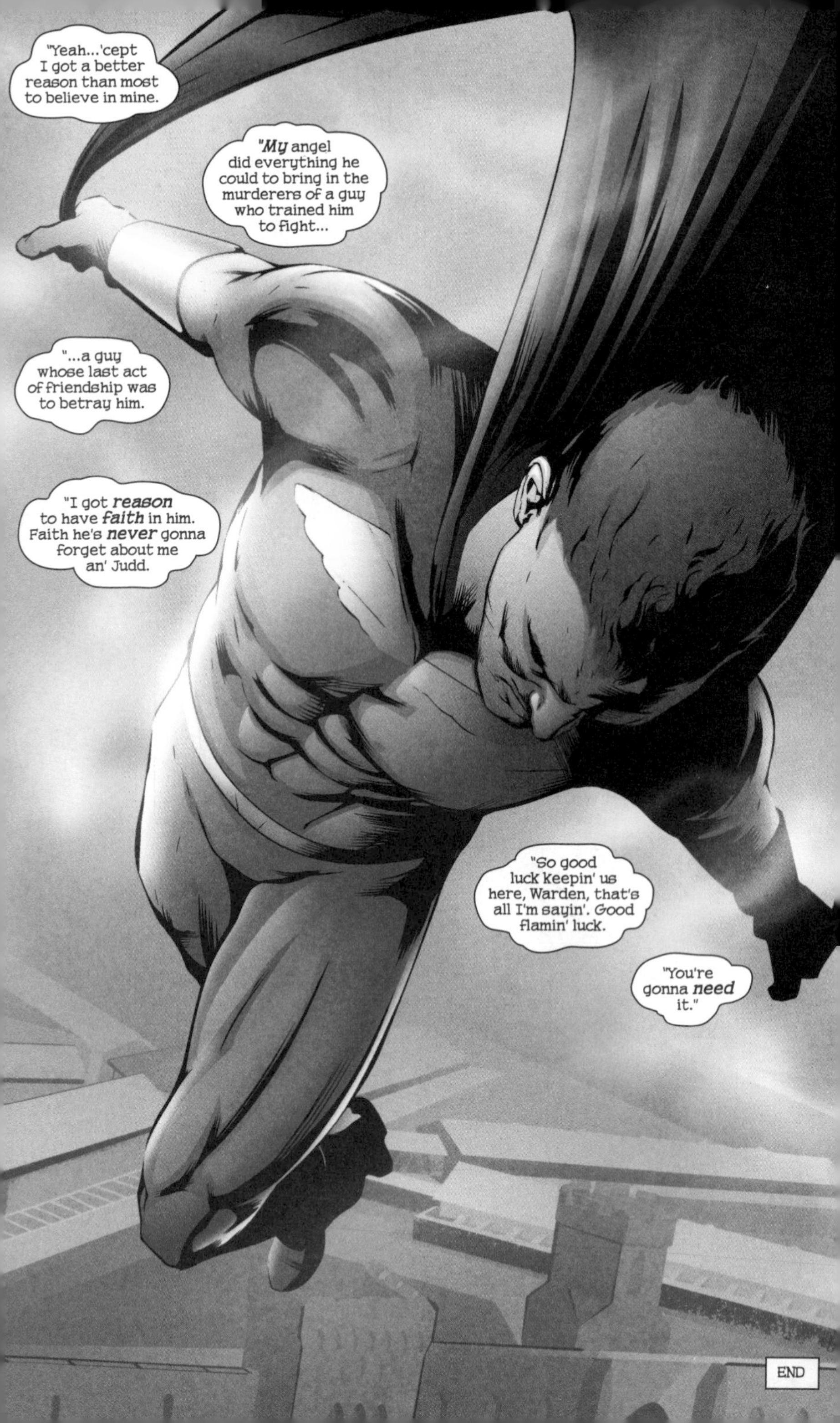
"Yeah...'cept I got a better reason than most to believe in mine.
"My angel did everything he could to bring in the murderers of a guy who trained him to fight...
"...a guy whose last act of friendship was to betray him.
"I got reason to have faith in him. Faith he's never gonna forget about me an' Judd.
"So good luck keepin' us here, Warden, that's all I'm sayin'. Good flamin' luck.
"You're gonna need it."
END

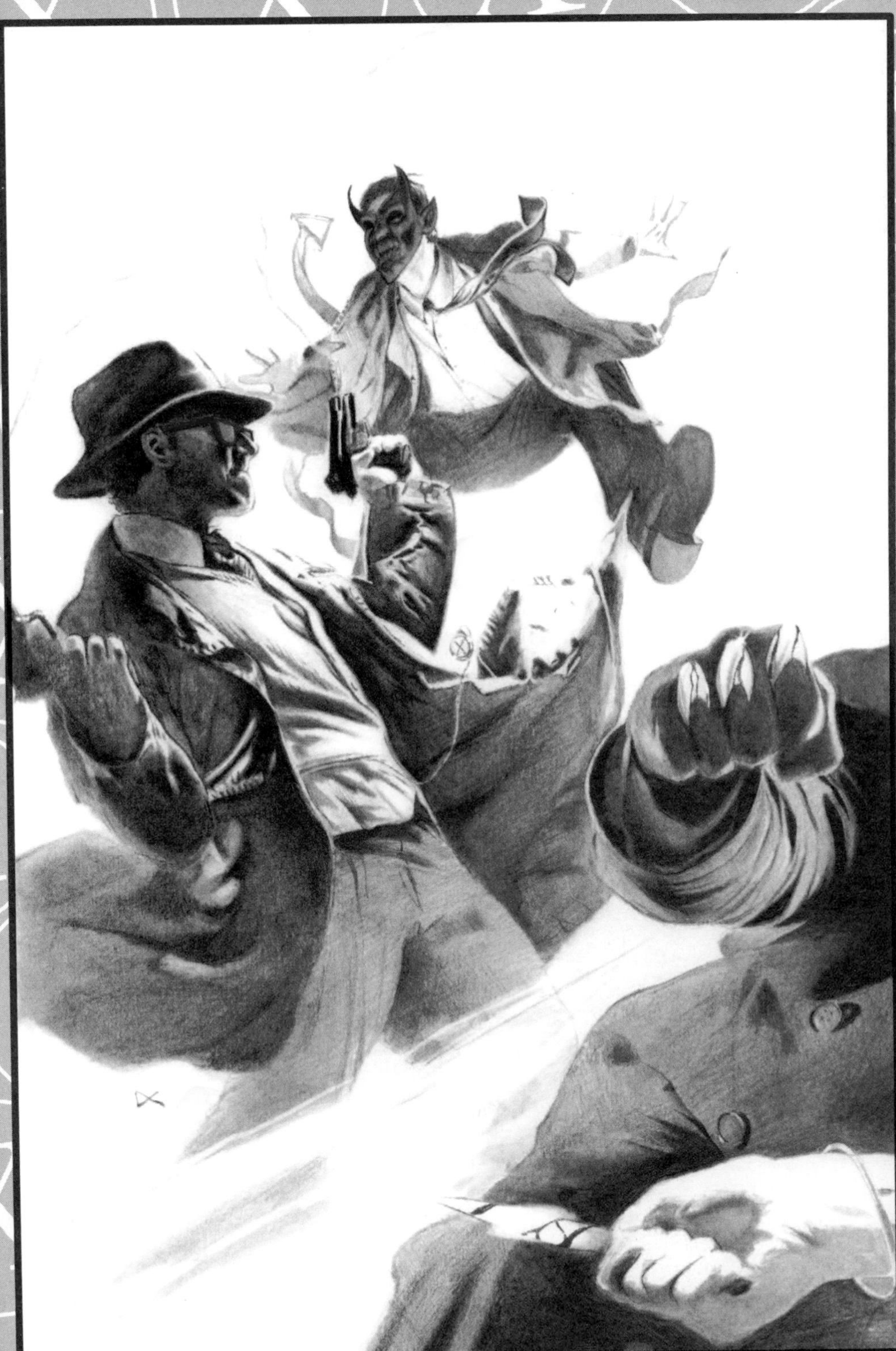

#1 VARIANT BY DENNIS CALERO

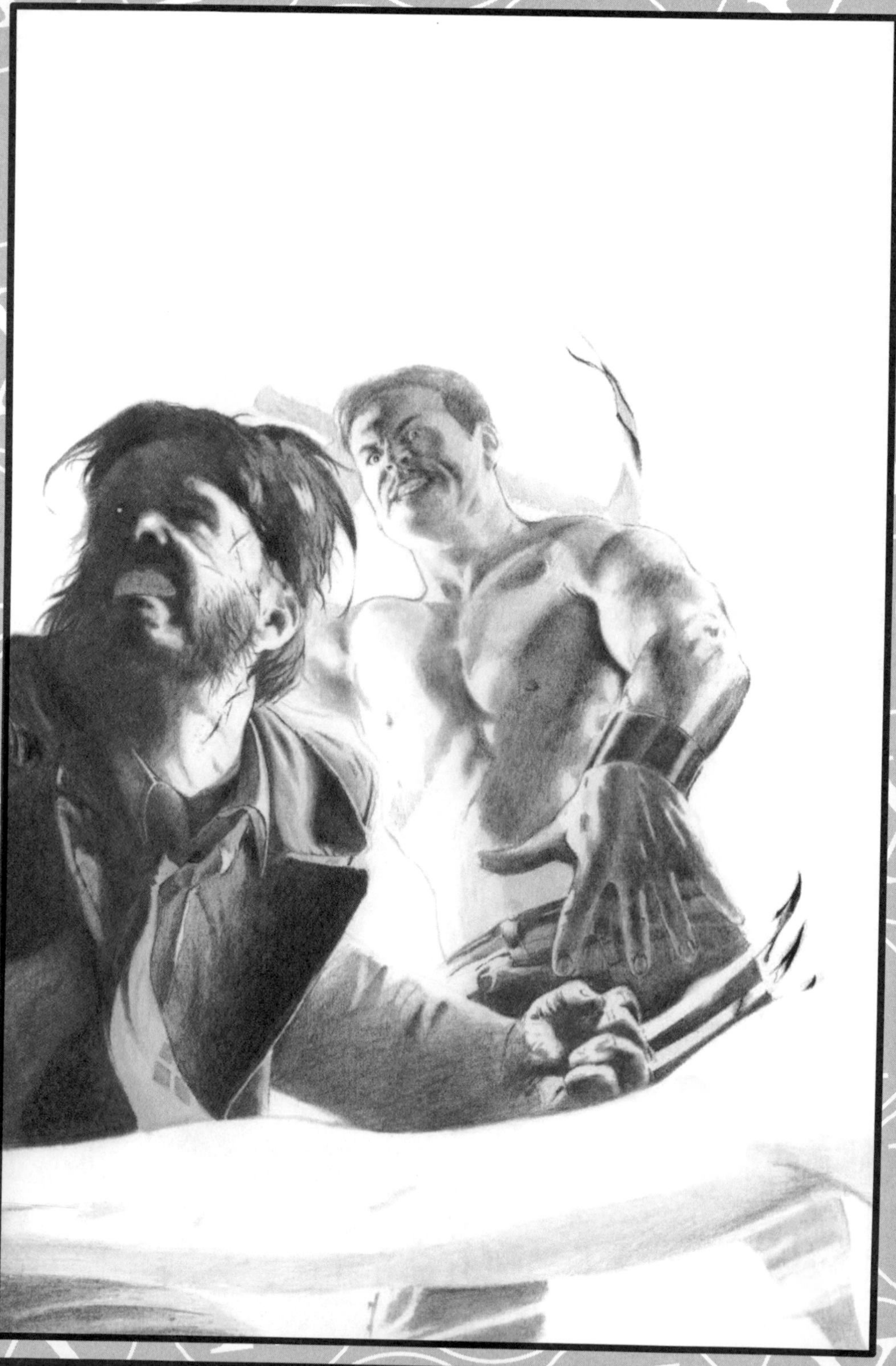

#2 VARIANT BY DENNIS CALERO

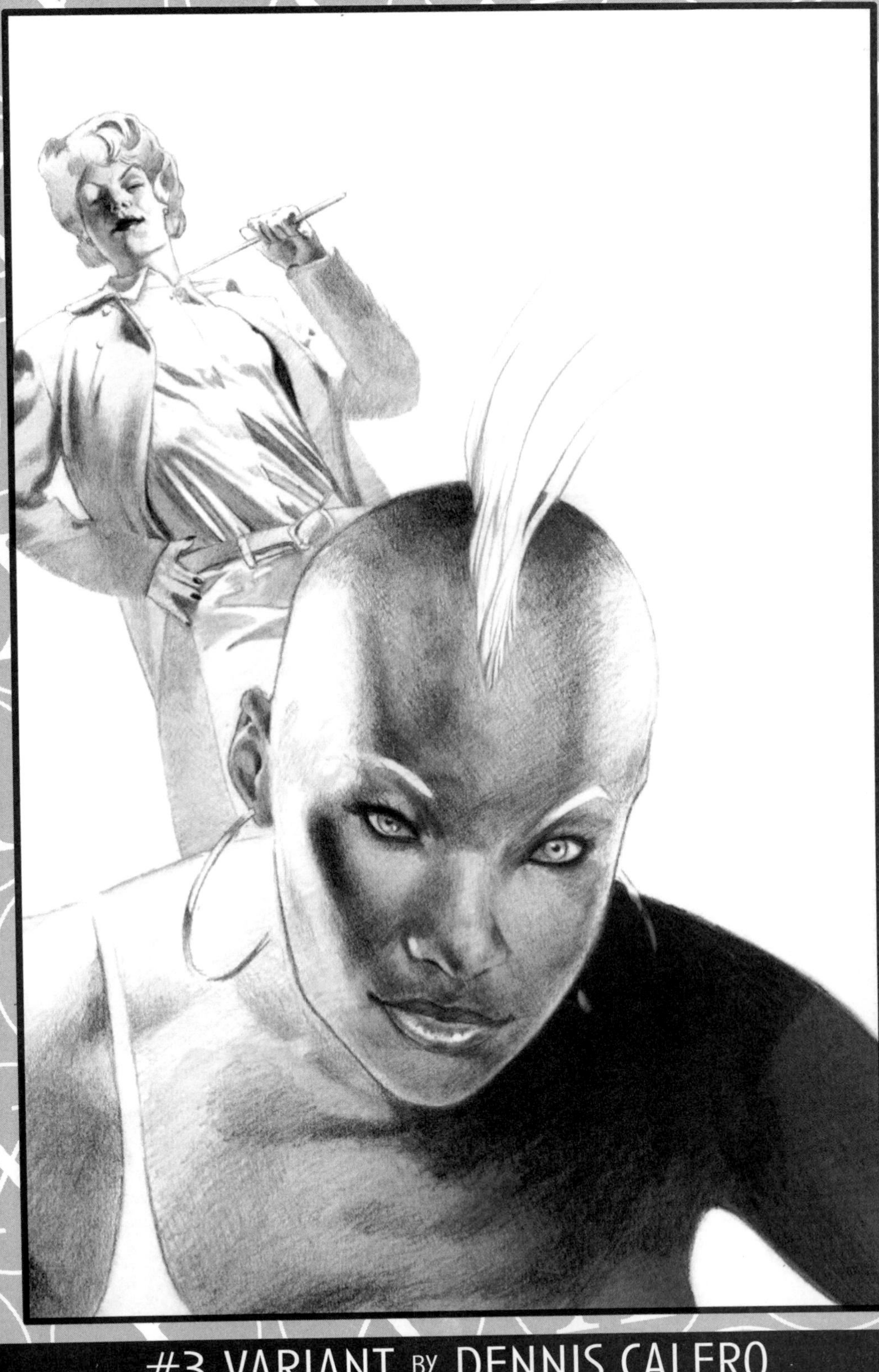

#3 VARIANT BY DENNIS CALERO

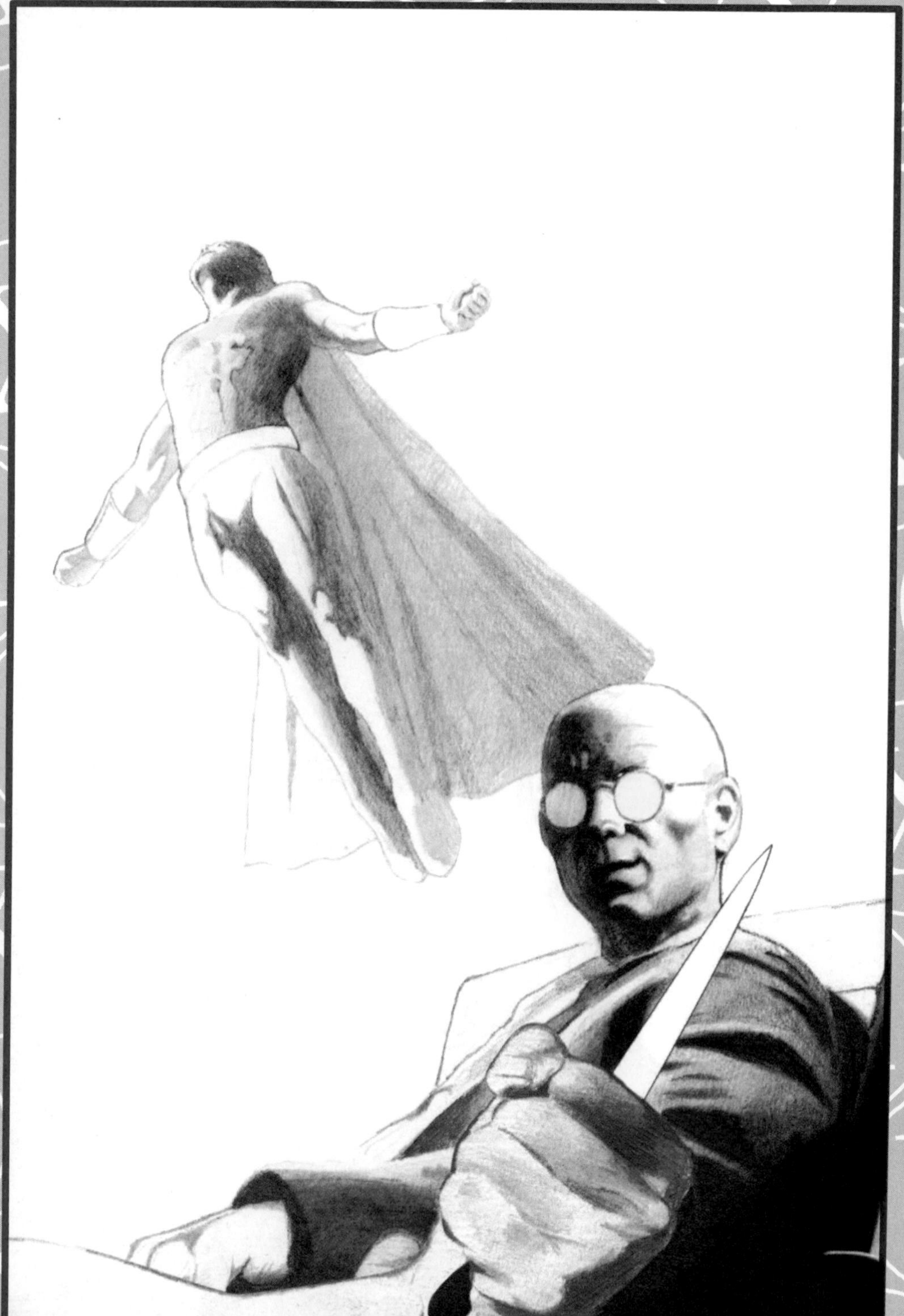

#4 VARIANT BY DENNIS CALERO

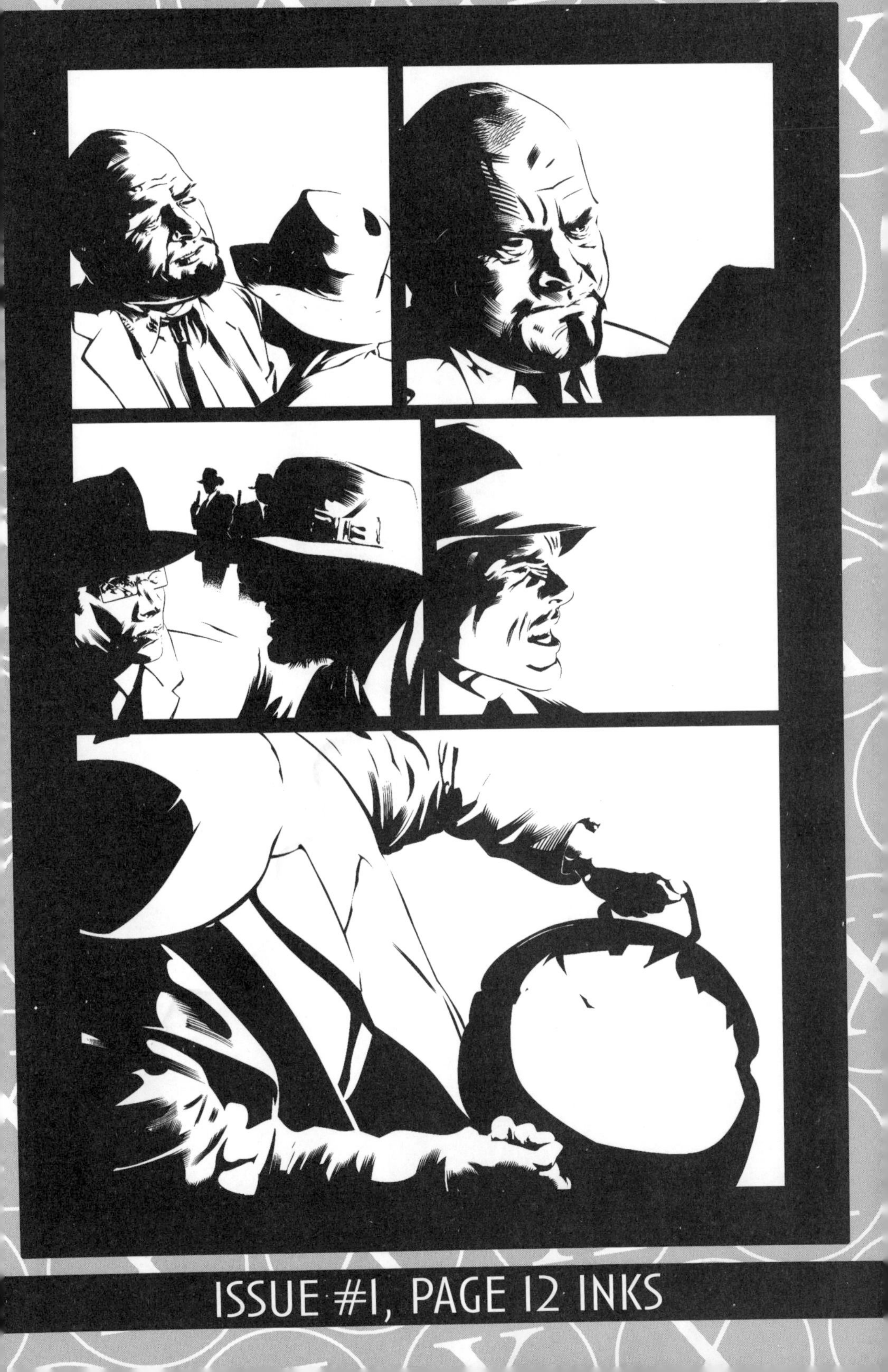

ISSUE #1, PAGE 12 INKS

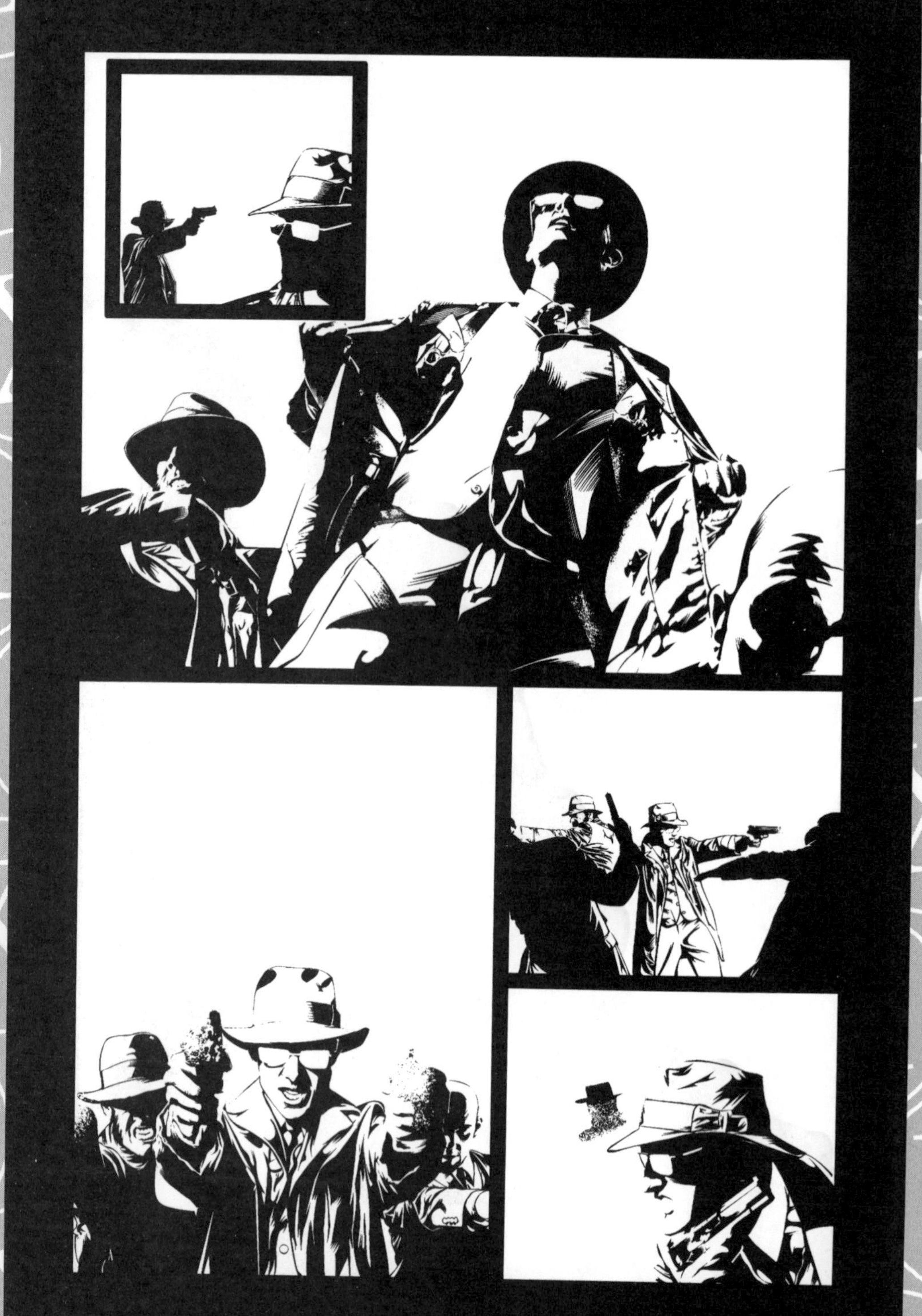

ISSUE #1, PAGE 13 INKS

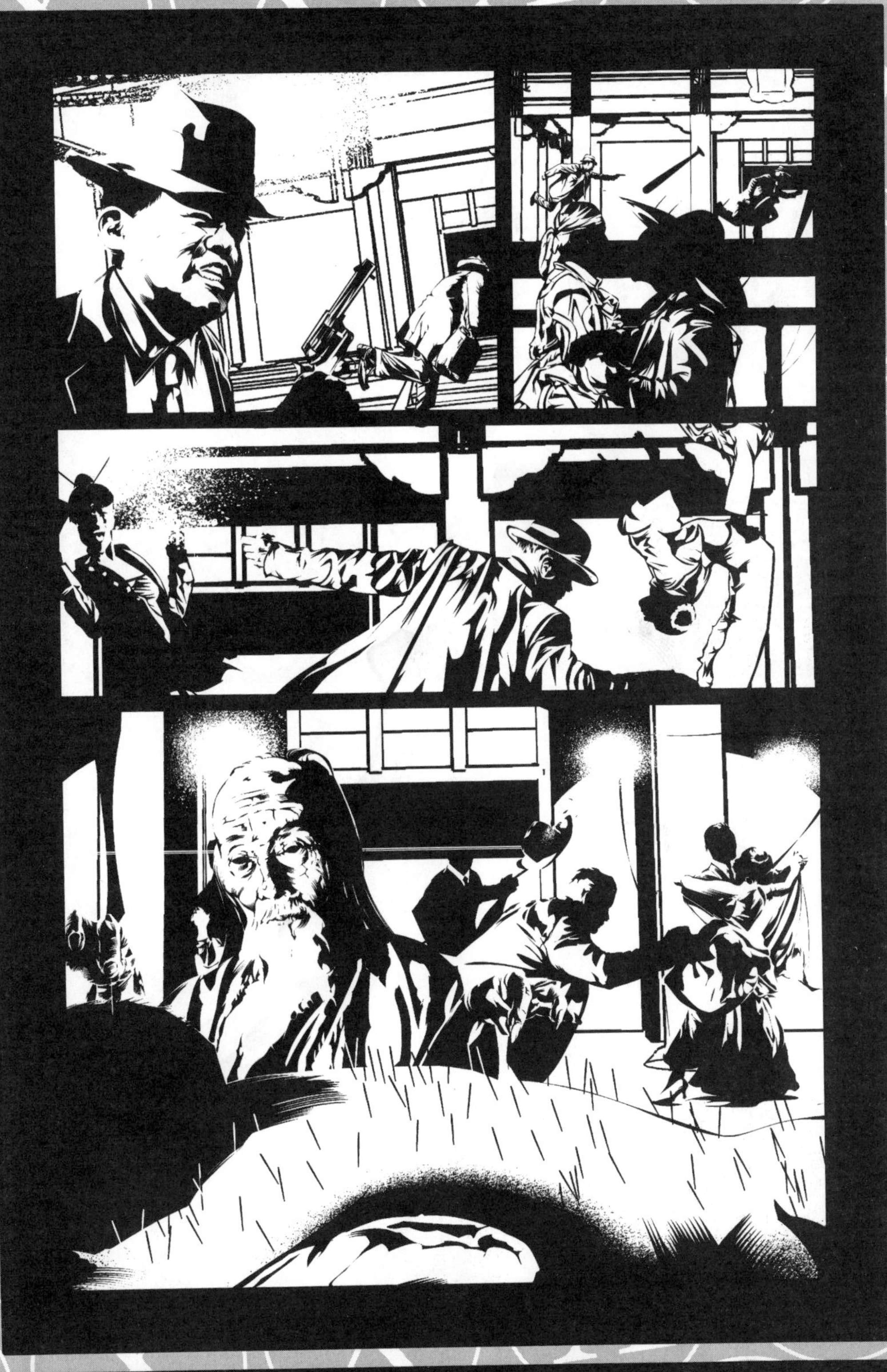

ISSUE #1, PAGE 14 INKS

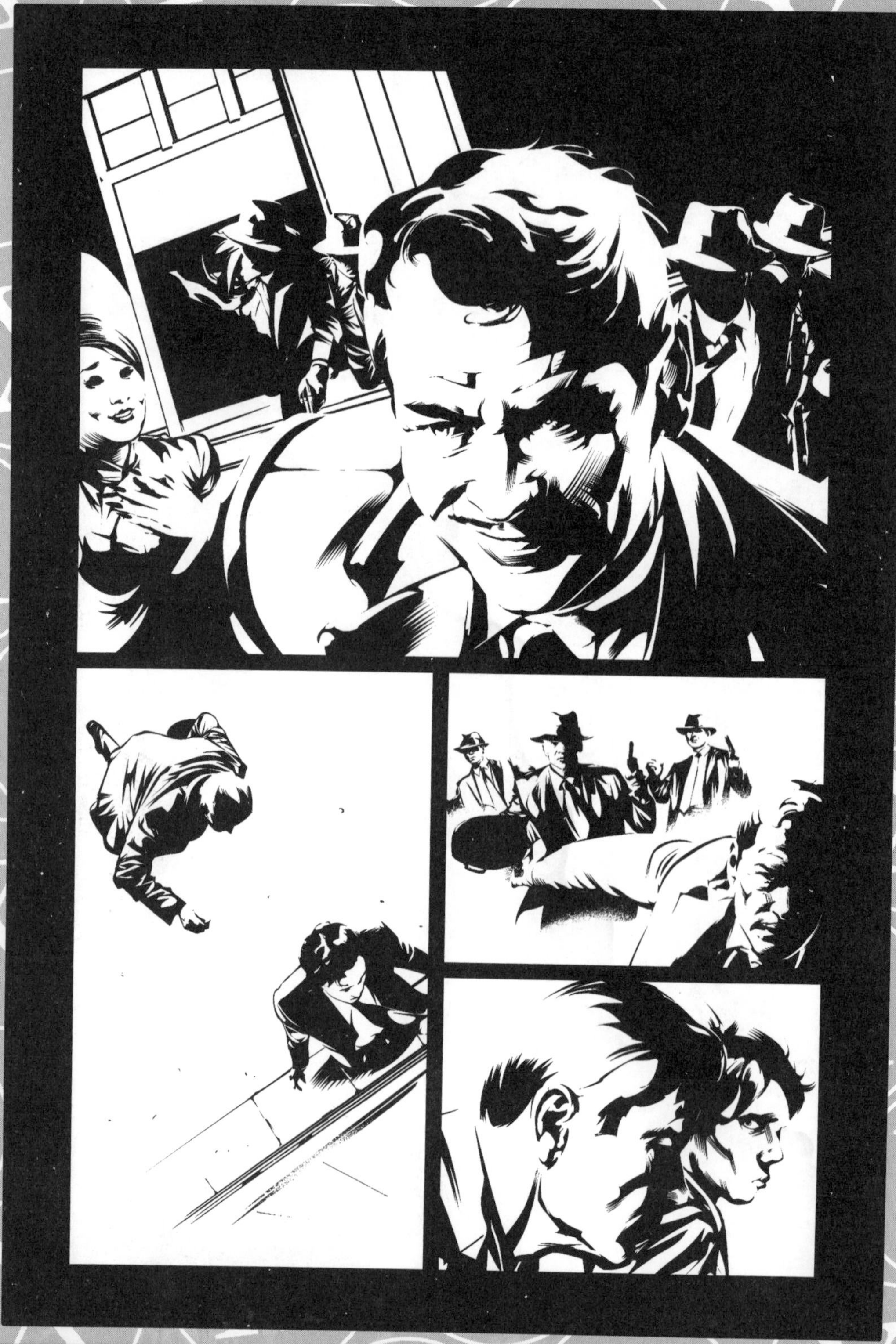

ISSUE #1, PAGE 15 INKS

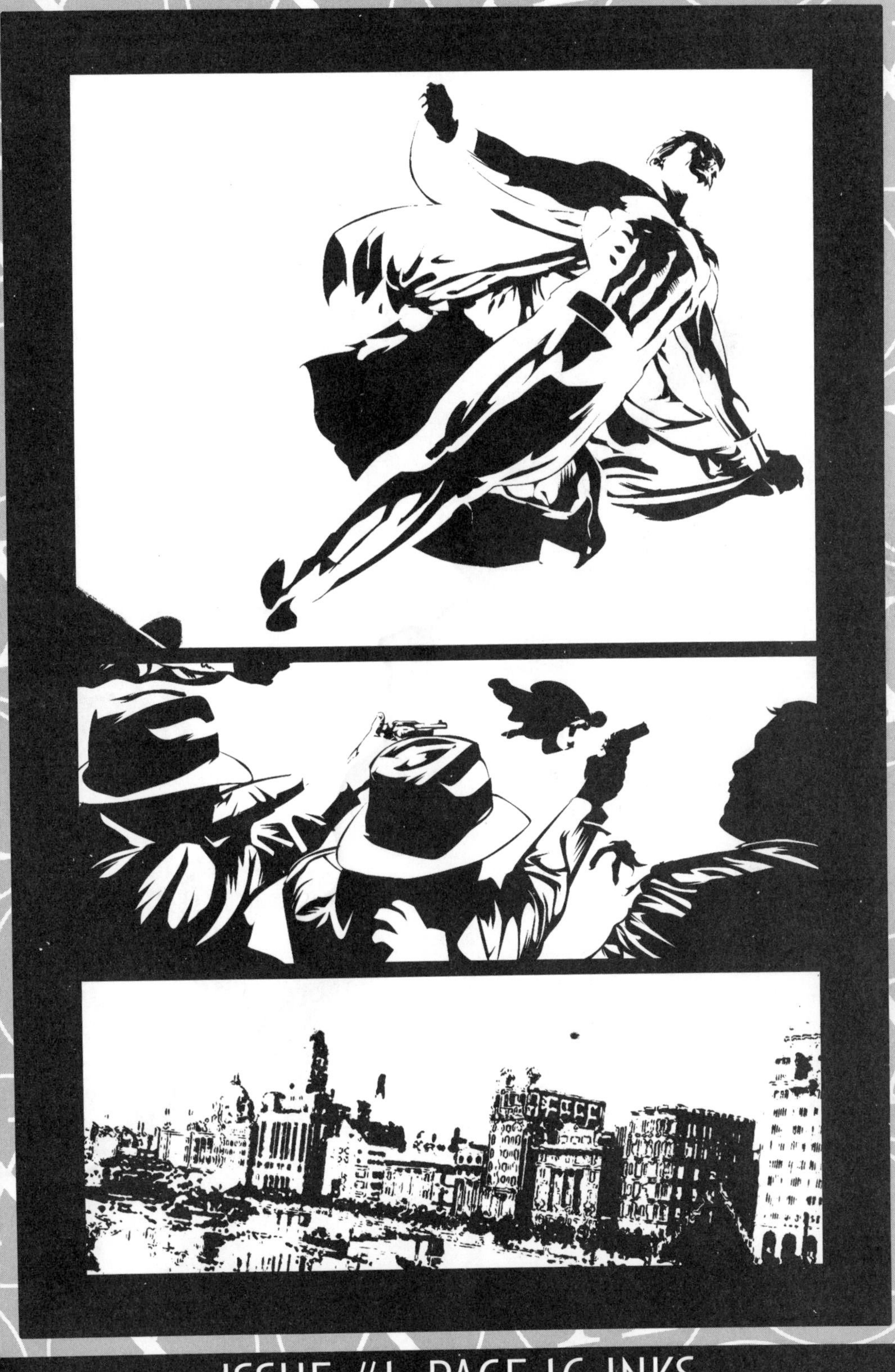

ISSUE #1, PAGE 16 INKS

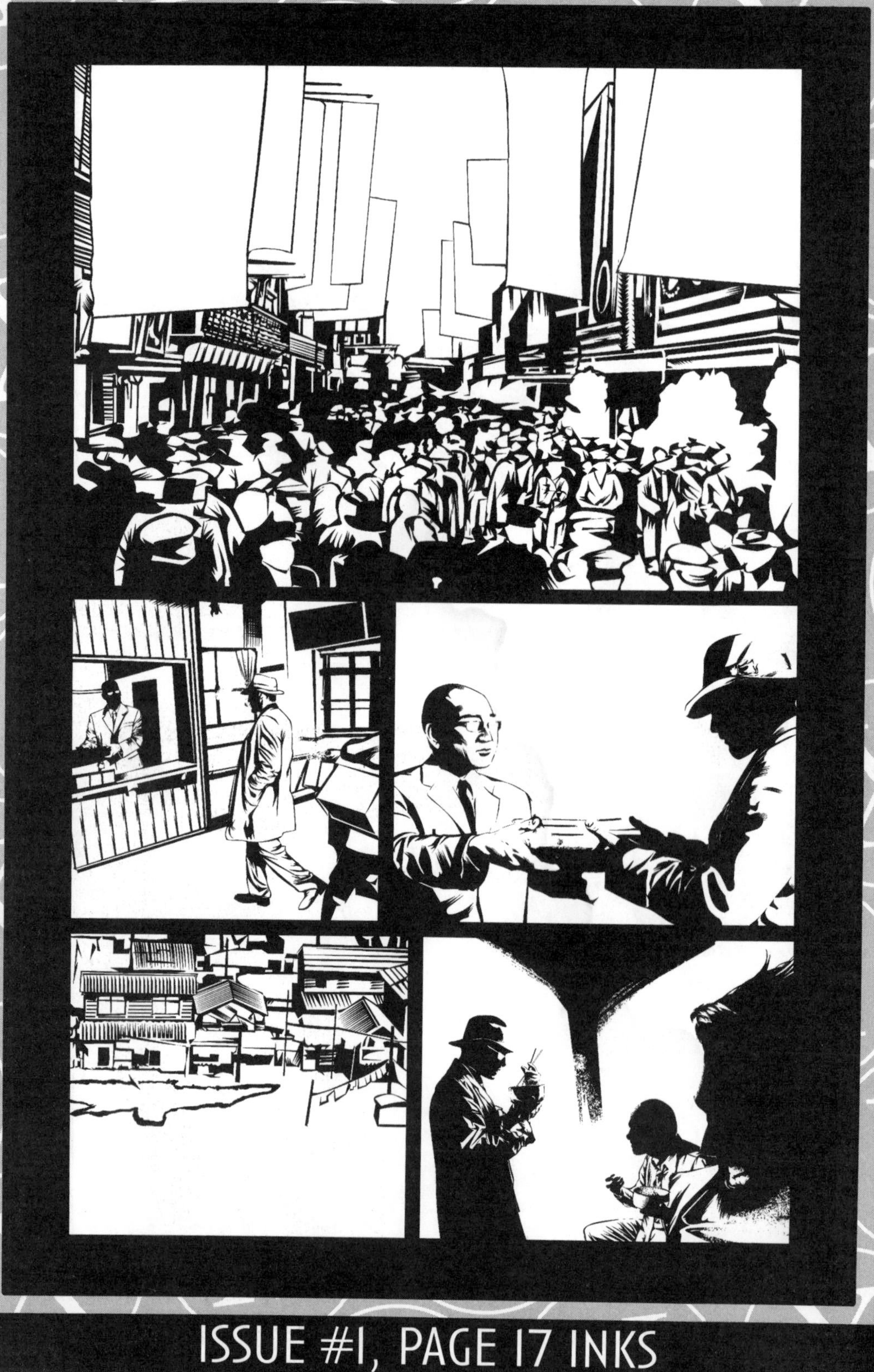

ISSUE #1, PAGE 17 INKS

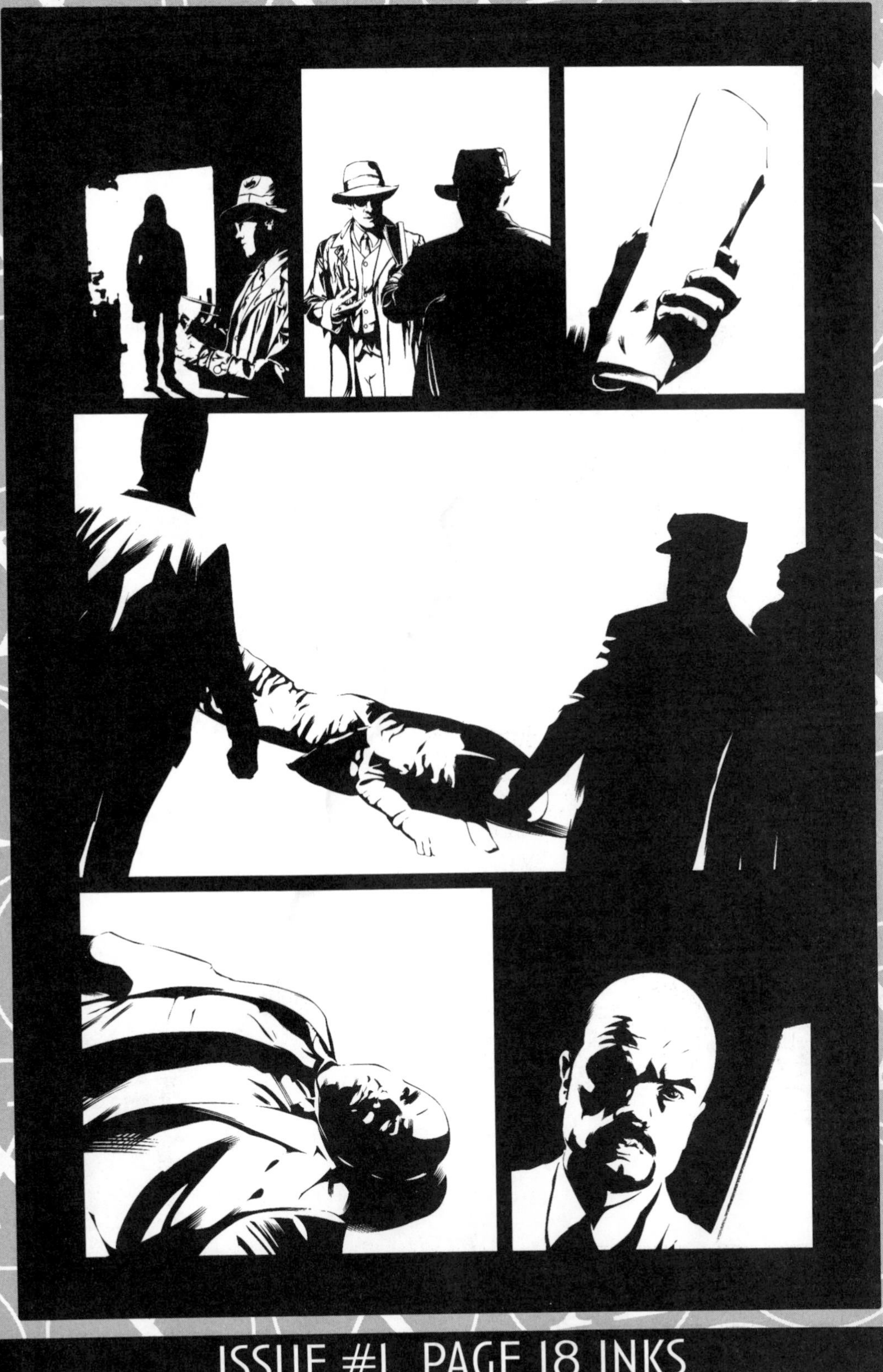

ISSUE #1, PAGE 18 INKS

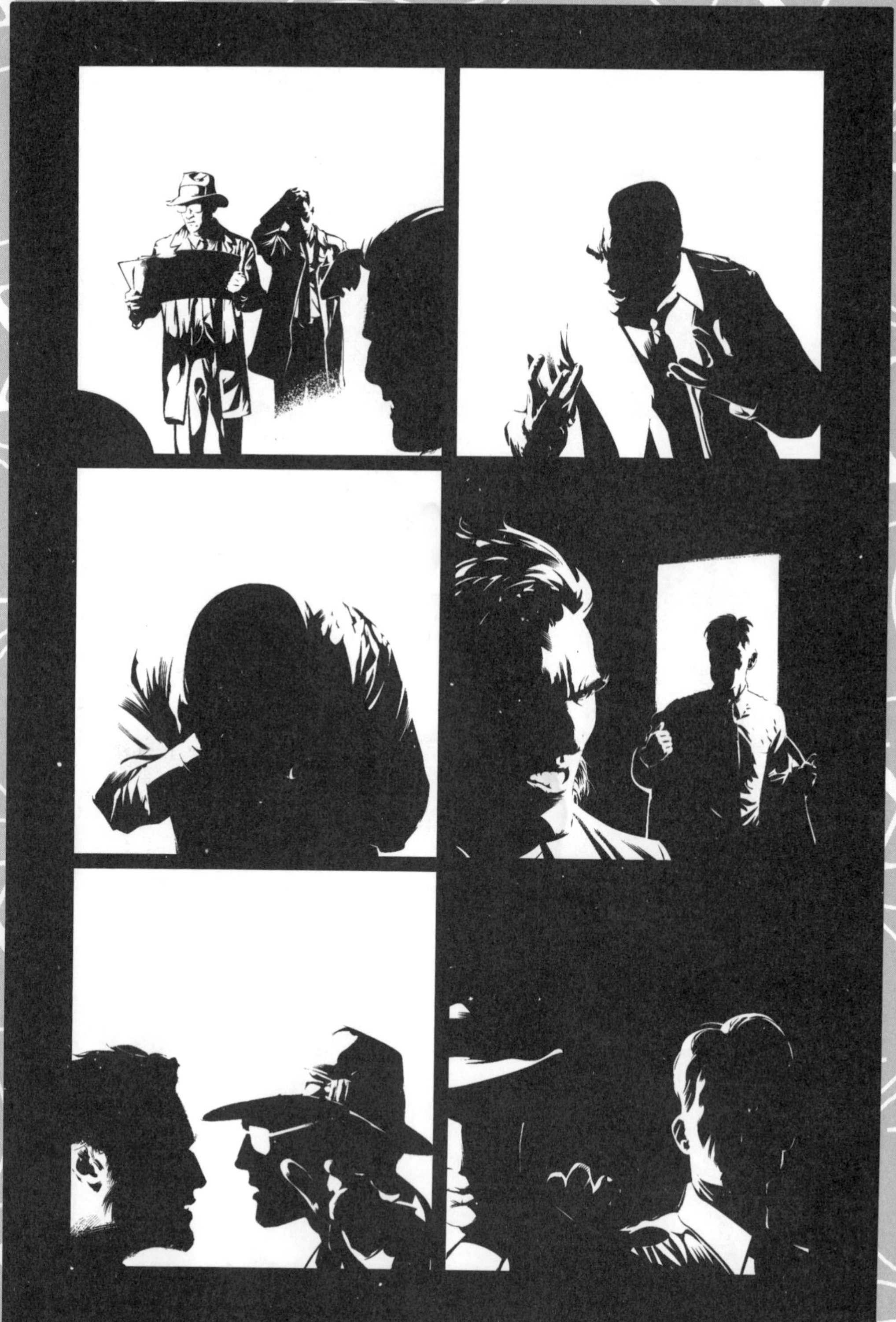

ISSUE #1, PAGE 19 INKS

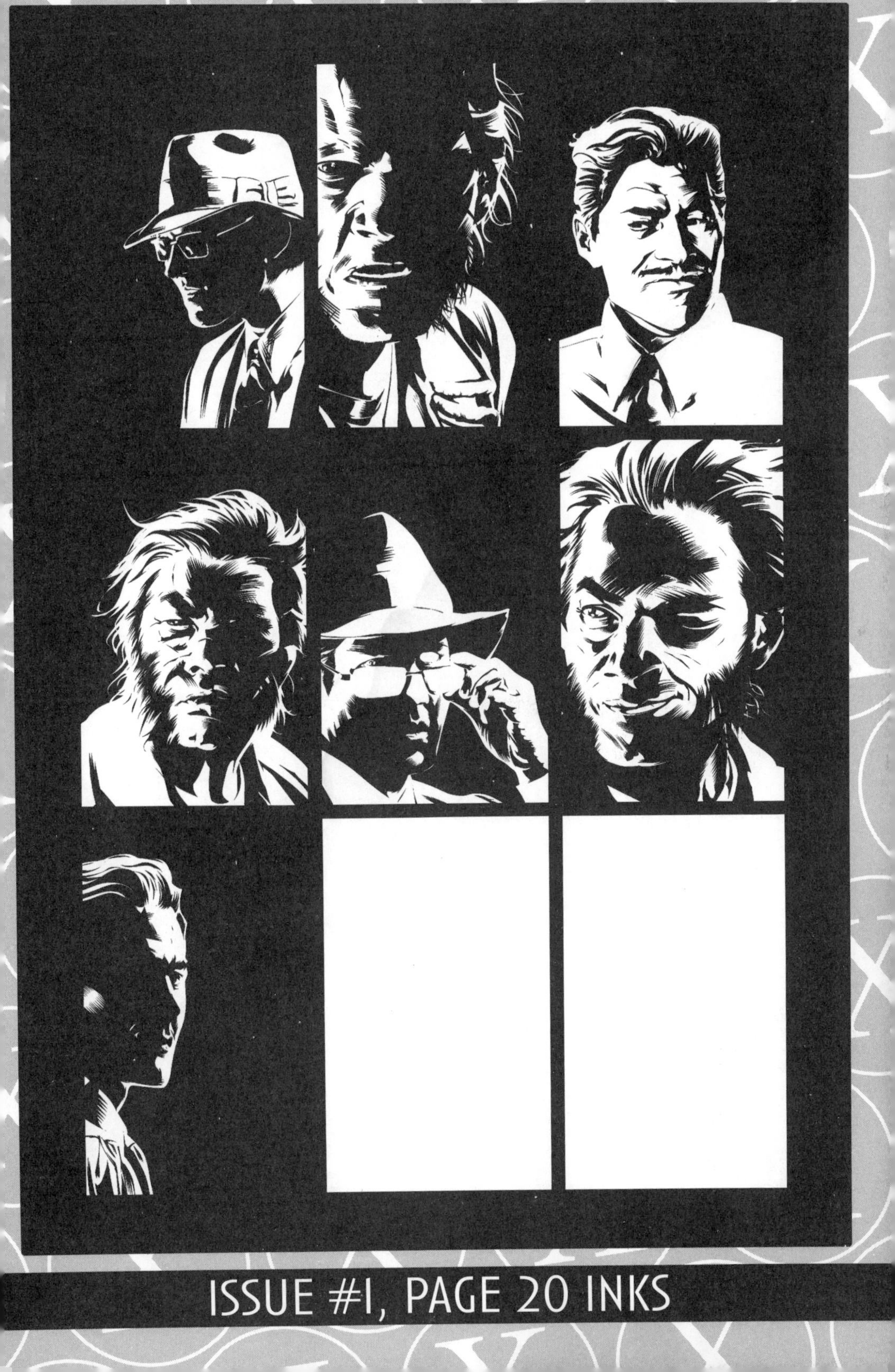

ISSUE #1, PAGE 20 INKS

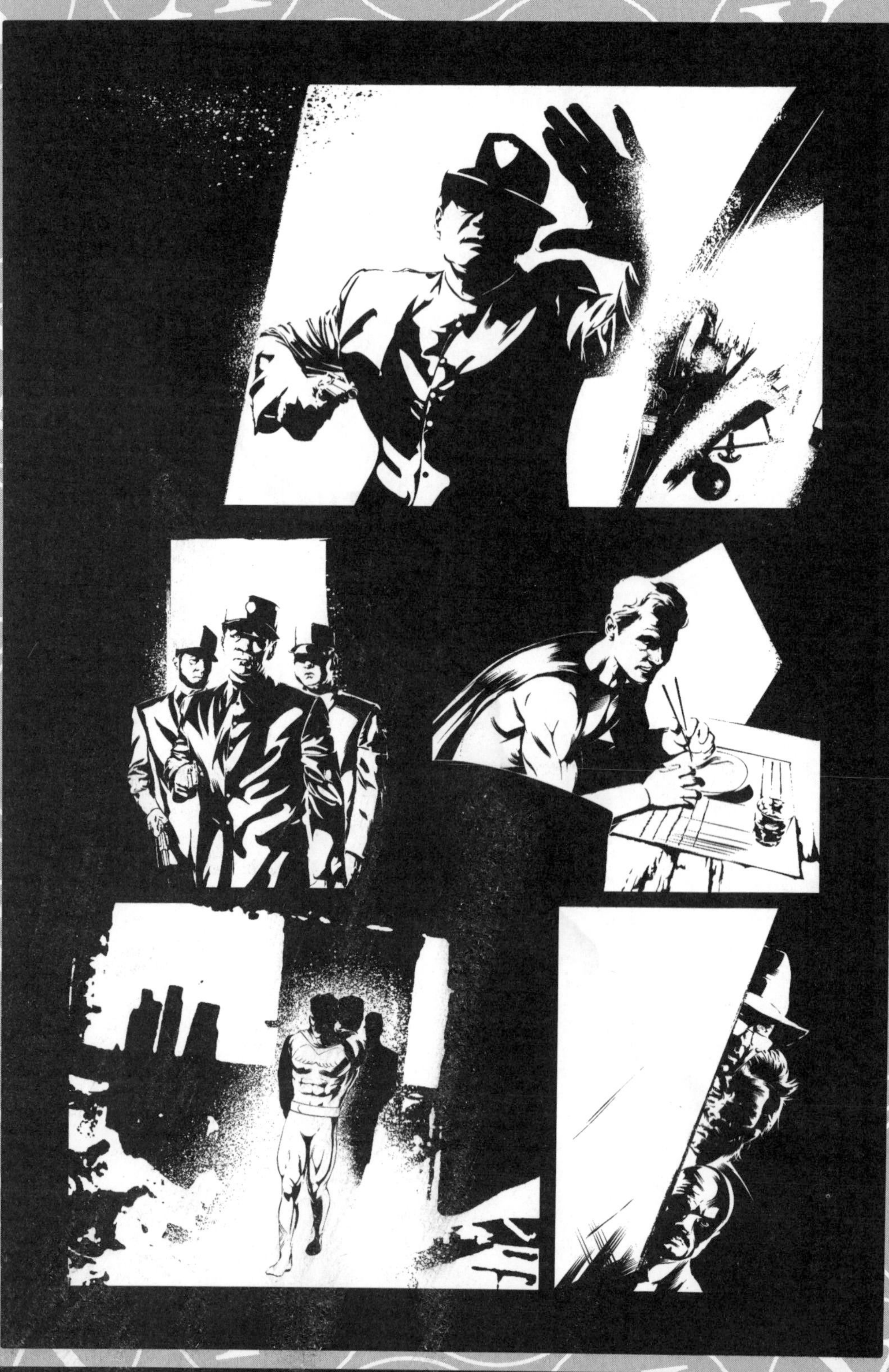

ISSUE #1, PAGE 21 INKS

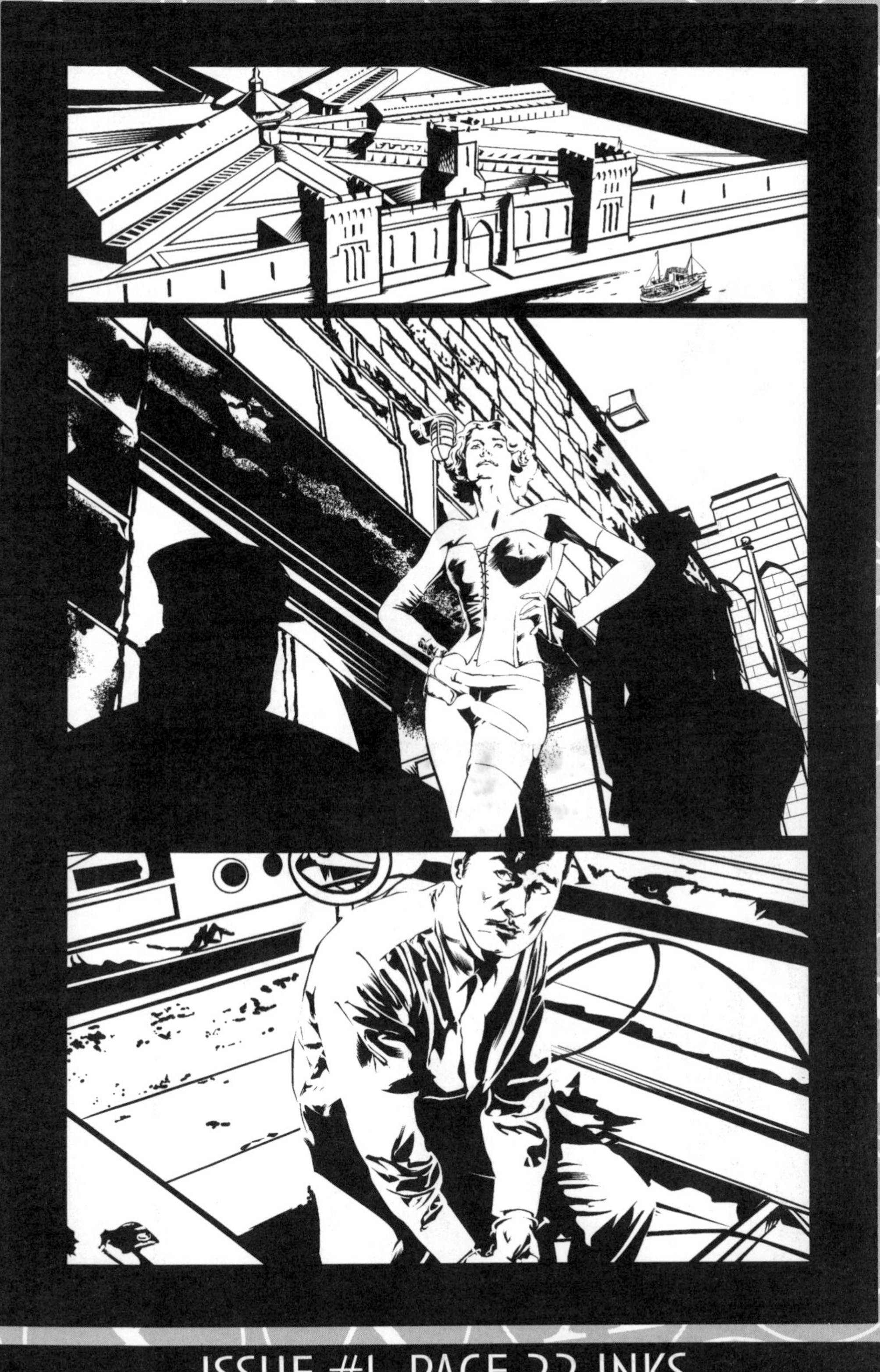

ISSUE #1, PAGE 22 INKS

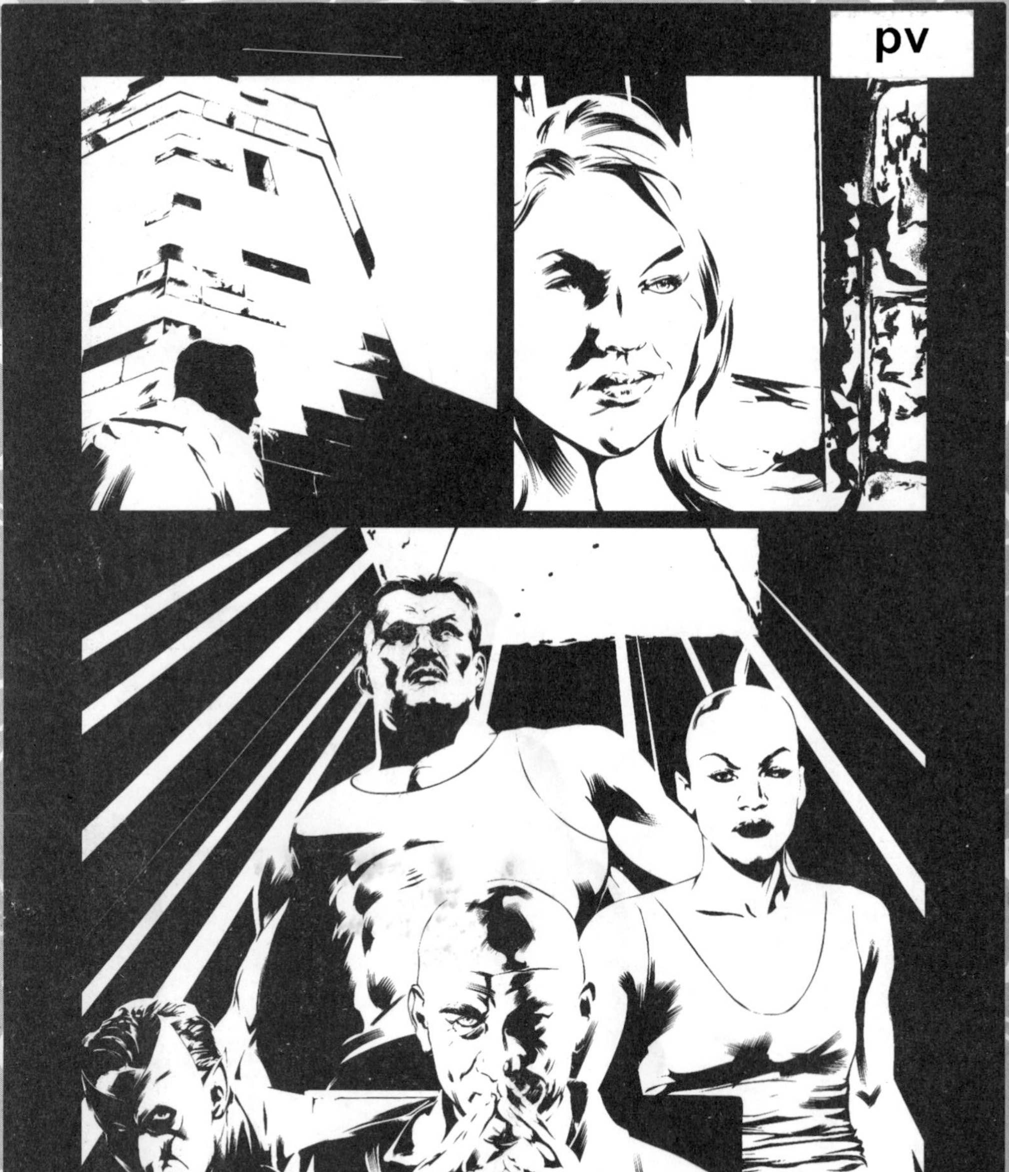
pv

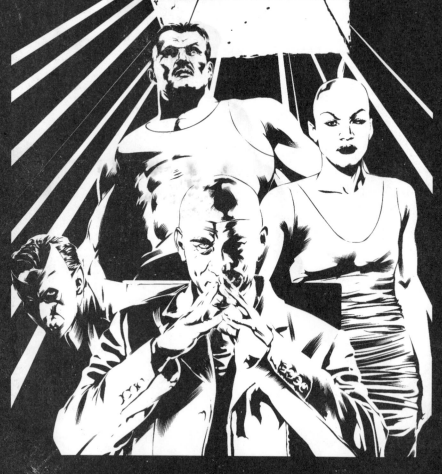

ISSUE #1, PAGE 23 INKS